The Michigan Historical Reprint Series

Reprints from the collection of the University of Michigan University Library

This volume is produced from digital images created through the University of Michigan University Library's preservation reformatting program. The Library seeks to preserve the intellectual content of items in a manner that facilitates and promotes a variety of uses. The digital reformatting process results in an electronic version of the text that can both be accessed online and used to create new print copies. This book and thousands of others can be found in the digital collections of the University of Michigan Library. The University Library also understands and values the utility of print, and makes reprints available through its Scholarly Publishing Office.

For access to the University of Michigan Library's digital collections, please see http://www.lib.umich.edu.

The Scholarly Publishing Office seeks to disseminate high-quality, cost-effective scholarly content through both print and electronic publishing. Information about the Scholarly Publishing Office can be found at http://spo.umdl.umich.edu.

The Scholarly Publishing Office
the University of Michigan
University Library

SHOEPAC RECOLLECTIONS:

A Way-side Glimpse of American Life.

BY

WALTER MARCH.

NEW YORK: .
BUNCE & BROTHER, PUBLISHERS,
No. 126 Nassau Street.
MDCCCLVI.

W. H. Tinson, Stereotyper. George Russell & Co., Printers.

These Recollections,

STRUNG TOGETHER, LIKE INDIAN BEADS,

INTO A

WAMPUM OF FRIENDSHIP,

ARE RESPECTFULLY DEDICATED

TO

COLONEL CHARLES G. GREENE,

Of the Boston Post,

BY HIS UNWORTHY FRIEND,

THE AUTHOR.

PREFACE.

A LETTER FROM THE AUTHOR TO THE PUBLISHER.

Mr. Publisher

I send you, by the hands of a mutual friend, a pair of *Shoepacs*, or, old-fashioned Canadian shoes.

Happening to sojourn a few days recently at the ancient City of Detroit, I crossed over the beautiful straits which separate it from Canada, and there, to my surprise and delight, I found the article for sale at a smart, modern, country shop. After I had bought them, a good-humored old Frenchman—or "Kennuck"—passed that way, who laughed heartily at my simplicity in making such a purchase. When I assured him earnestly that the celebrated La Salle, and the famous Hennepin and Marquette, nay, probably Montcalm himself, had worn Shoepacs, he only laughed the more; and that too in spite of my word and honor for it that these men were all highly distinguished in the history of Canada, his own land—for he had never heard of one of them. But when I told him that I had once worn them myself, and that, with them, I had trod the long and wintry road which led up to what little rank and fortune I had secured thus far in life, he grew serious at once, and was polite enough to believe me—his gay humor rose even to respect.

On being questioned, he told me that Shoepacs were yet in use among the old-fashioned, humble people of this part of Canada—those who still earn their living by working in the woods, killing ducks, and catching white fish. He remembered the very first Frenchman in all the region round about, who had the extravagance, or even courage, to put on a pair of modern shoes; and what a sensation he created as he drove up to church in a calash, alighted and helped out his wife, and strutted up the path leading to the church-door. The people were gathered in the yard, waiting for the bell to ring for service, laughing and talking, and some even wickedly cracking eggs: and when the new shoes appeared, they pointed them out to each other, exclaiming, *au large! au large!* room! room! and made way right and left, with mock bows and pretended ceremony, for the enviable possessor of such a treasure.

Ah, "room! room!" is the word that expresses the history of the Northwest. The moccasin must make room for the Shoepac, and the Shoepac, in its turn, for the iron heel of the British, and all together exclaim—

"Room! room! for the American!"

It was at the period when Indian, Frenchman, Briton, and American commingled harmoniously together, and there was room enough for all and to spare, that the story of my "Recollections" commences.

I remain, sir, with profound respect,

Your friend,

WALTER MARCH.

CONTENTS.

SHOEPAC RECOLLECTIONS.

CHAPTER I.

OUR CITY.

OURS was a little antiquated city. Its inhabitants were mostly French. At the time I came upon the stage of events, the transition to a modern American town had scarcely commenced. The body of the population was still of the *ancien régime*. The few Americans were officers, or ex-officers, of either the general or territorial government, and their families, relations, dependents, and friends, whom they had persuaded to venture beyond the "jumping-off place," as Buffalo was then termed. The spirit of emigration had not been fully aroused; and the spirit of speculation, if felt at all, was confined to the fur-traders, a class made up of all nations.

I cannot compare the society more nearly than to that of some principal East India Company station in a city of Hindostan. There were the governor of the territory and his family, the judicial, executive, and military functionaries, with their families and dependents; like subahdar, nabobs, begums, and the lesser lights—traders and natives, French, Indian, and half-breed. But one could not well imagine a pleasanter state of feeling than mutually existed, with sufficient distinction between the different castes or classes to prevent wrangling, and yet sufficient community of interest, prejudice, and pleasure to make everybody sociable. The French gave a tone of gaiety—the military, both elevation and hospitality. There were balls, where everybody danced with everybody's wife and daughter. There were theatricals, where the most dignified gentlemen took parts. It may be a mere whim, but I think I never have elsewhere met such easy polish and affability among gentlemen. There was no touchiness about position in the social scale, and consequently neither stiffness nor affectation; and to this day, the same easy grace of manner is notable among the sons and daughters of the good old city.

The traveller, journeying at that period from New York westward, after leaving Albany, penetrated into regions where civilization grew dimmer and dimmer as he advanced, until he became quite certain of having passed the *ultima thule*, when he would stumble with astonishment on our little community. There he would be welcomed with a courtesy no less gracious, and a hospitality much warmer than he would himself have extended to a stranger in the metropolis.

Yet there he would behold the Frenchman, riding in his two-wheeled cart to market with white fish and onions, and screaming a rascally *patois*. Or he might observe a wedding procession, of the same mercurial race, driving through the principal—or rather only—avenue, at full speed to church, two and two, in little antique *calèches;* the bride, of course, dressed in white, but wearing no bonnet, though rejoicing in a veil that sweeps the ground, and her bridesmaids driving after, as bonnetless as herself—a happy state of things to which the dear ladies of the present day are fast returning.

As he sauntered along up the street, he would see old-fashioned buildings, stores and dwellings forming a promiscuous row, with high gables and dormer-windows, roofs peaked like Vandyke hats, with their edges notched and painted red, and doors panelled into four parts, and opening by subdivisions, like modern window-shutters. Motley groups, consisting of French, Americans, and Indians, sit with their sociable pipes enjoying confabulations made up of words, nods, shrugs, and the impenetrable "ugh! ugh!" of the taciturn red man. Peeping into the halls and rooms as he passed, he might here and there discern a carpet, but generally the floors were covered with Indian mats. The shops would be filled with bales of furs, gaudy-colored calicoes —known as Indian calicoes—mococks of maple sugar, broidered with painted porcupine quills, deerskins, moccasins, and Indian trinkets; few such, however, as are now palmed off upon the curious and credulous stranger at Niagara.

Often he may meet on the sidewalk an Indian—some dark Potowattimie, or tall, painted Sac or Fox—one of Nature's own noblemen, erect and martial in his bearing, and with a single ridge of stiff, black hair, standing like the crest of a helmet on his head; or, peradventure, groups of Winnebagoes, with blue blankets on their handsome squaws, while their own arms, ears, and noses would jingle with silver ornaments; or, skulking along, some thievish craven of a Mennomonie, whose name was no less a term of reproach among the nobler tribes, than that of the Samaritan with the disdainful children of Judah. Passing above the town, he might find large, conical, birch-bark tents pitched on the long slope of the river bank, and graceful, light pirogues drawn up in regular rows on the shore; these belong to the Indians, whom he may, if it chance to be payment season, behold in hundreds, or even thousands. Succotash is boiling in huge iron or brass pots over the fires. A small army of famished, wolfish-looking dogs lie around, winking lazily in the sun; and no smaller army of naked children are running every where—some pitching bright coppers, others shooting with their bows and arrows, and others swimming and diving in the limpid water; while around on the trees or fence, or sides of the wigwams, he may behold many infant papooses sleeping in their hanging cradles of hide and birch; or with their heads strapped back, looking on the scene with wise, unwinking eyes. They seldom cry, and are no inapt representations of Patience on a monument.

He would meet pretty, fawn-faced young squaws who glance coquettishly at him, and no less so at themselves, or rather some ornament, or little rude mirror half-concealed on their persons. Now and then one peeps at him from behind the blanket at the tent-door. Respectable elderly women would be sitting around, at work on mococks, mats, or moccasins, or cooking game, or pilfered chickens in the sugar-boiler, or smoking fish, depending from a stick sustained over the fire by two forked uprights. Shame to the Pale Faces!—he might hear drunken noises issuing from a lodge here and there; or worse, see an Indian and his wife, or several squaws by themselves, alternately caressing each other and quarrelling, moved by the demon that lurks in fire-water.

There must be dark shadows in every picture, especially in a picture of human life.

Gratefully, now, let him turn, at the soft sound of an Indian flute, played with no great skill or variety of cadence, but plaintively, by some young dandy. It is a reed, into which holes are burned for the gamut of notes, and around it are wound deerskin thongs to prevent splitting. Possibly, your Indian Pan may be joined by a musical brother on the drum, which is naught else, after all, than a species of rude banjo—a skin drawn over a hoop, as everybody knows. Then fortunate the Gothamite might deem himself to witness an Indian dance at that comparatively primitive period.

As he strolls out further from the town, he is struck with a peculiarity in the divisions of the farms; for each one is but a narrow strip of land running back into the woods two or three miles, so that every farmer may have a front on the river. A hundred or so yards from the beach stands the farm-house, similar to those already described, with only more amplitude of dimensions, and a broad, indolent, sun-loving porch, on which sleeps an old dog—practised no less in raccoon lore than experienced in swimming after wild-ducks. In cozy familiarity, an old cat is blinking by his side, or purring as she rubs her electric coat against his shaggy hair; or perched upon his back, a piping chicken is with difficulty balancing itself, as it picks at the flies which buzz around his nose, or alight with a tickling mischief on his lazily-flapping ears.

In front of the house are the cherry-trees, and in rear the pear and apple-orchards; and the traveller is surprised to find the best of fruit thus far beyond the pale of civilization—fruits brought from sunny France, and planted by the skillful Jesuit; apples, red to the core, large and luscious; cherries that rival nectarines; and pears of every variety, and of every season, from July to November. Nor will the patch of onions escape his notice: it is a Frenchman's flower-garden—the invariable concomitant of every family who may claim a foot square of mother earth. The fish-net or *seine* is stretched on the fence. The long, flint-lock duck gun, with leathern pouch and powder-horn, is hung on wooden hooks in the hall. The canoe is drawn up on the beach.

But hark! you hear the sound of distant voices come stealing over the water. Turn towards the river. See a long pirogue, or more ample Mackinaw boat—perhaps a little fleet of them in a single line, manned by *voyajeurs*, or *courreurs de bois*, and loaded with packs of peltries. The oarsmen have fitted out at Mackinaw, to appear in style at Detroit—the greater station, and nearer civilization. Probably the present is the glad occasion to which they have looked forward, and they have talked over their plans concerning it for many, many months. Each *garçon* has a sash around his waist, and pulls a red oar. They keep perfect time—and it is joyous quick time—with the notes of a French song which was chanted in France a century ago:

> "*Malbrooks s'en va t'a guerrah!*"

Or perchance the air is one you may not recognize:

> "*A Lon-don day.*
> *S'en va coucher!*"

No music could be more lively or inspiring. It comes over the water—is accompanied by the plash of oars. It is roared out with the utmost spirit, too, by that most glorious of all instruments, the human voice. It has pealed through the woods, and over the rivers and lakes, for thousands of miles. It has animated those brave adventurers in camp, at *portage*, through summer and winter, rain and snow, sickness, peril, and death; and now, joy! joy! it greets the steeples of St. Ann! The children run out of the houses, down to the river shore, to hear it; the maiden turns pale, and blushes, and hurries to the door; the old man hobbles out and waves his hat. Troops of people rush down to the wharves to see them land; and such shouts of welcome and rejoicing never were known before.

CHAPTER II.

PLEASANTRIES.

Stilled is the hum that through the hamlet broke,
When round the ruins of their ancient oak
The peasants flocked to hear the minstrel play,
And games and carols closed the busy day.

ROGERS.

AH! that was a happy time for everybody. Our little community was not yet divided on the question of Bibles in schools, or wine on the side-boards. Slavery was little talked of, and as for disunion—the mere word was considered, by the veriest *Kenuck*, as a profanation of human language.

But as settlers from New England began to thicken among us—*Bostonians* they were indiscriminately denominated—it gradually came to light that our lively little community were scarce a grain better than the wicked, nay than the very heathen; witness the fiddling and dancing on Sunday evenings (and pleasant Sunday evenings they were deemed by us, in our dreadful ignorance), wherever there was any little neighborhood of French people—on the great wide porch, or beneath trees on the grass; or, if in the house, with the doors and windows thrown wide open. And there were the prettiest and most mischievous-eyed French girls, dancing away for dear life with the good-looking, frank-mannered *voyajeurs*, or *courreurs de bois*, in their red, yellow, or green sashes, long black hair, and blue calico shirts. Such abominations attracted the "growing attention" of the strict sober-sides from the land of Jonathan Edwards, as he passed these dens of Apollyon, on his way to the place where prayer was wont to be made. Then was there not racing to church the year round, and racing home again? And were there not regular trotting matches on the afternoons of the great days of the church, which brought the people in from the country, up and down the river? Especially, was there ever anything like it in the winter season, when the wicked river would even wink at these atrocities by freezing over, so that nothing was seen on Sunday afternoons but carioles turned up in front, in a curl like a skate, gliding, or rather flying, over the ice, two and two? The little Canadian ponies held their tails up in the air like banners, and their noses protruding into the clouds, or snorting between their legs—they trotting like mad, while the *garçons* whooped like Indians, shouting, *whey! avance! arriez!* ever and anon stealing a flashing kiss from the bright demoiselles at their sides.

Then on Easter morning, was not the church-yard of St. Ann's fairly riotous with boys cracking painted eggs? Nay, in the same precincts, were not idolatries frequently committed? Was not the Host carried in procession by chanting Jesuits and nuns, to a high mound called Mount Calvary, where there was a huge cross, and beneath which lay the tomb of our Saviour? Doubt not that these abominations smelt in the nostrils of the sons of the Puritans.

But, in the time of my boyhood, the feud had not taken any religious turn among the boys, who, I must confess, were very far behind the boys of the present day, and knew little of religious controversies, and talked not dogmatically of these, nor of the various ologies in which the present juvenile generation are so good and wise. There was, however, a feud; it was the boys of one schoolyard against the boys of another schoolyard, and easily waxed warm, in consequence of any collision, invasion, or interference. It might occur over a game of ball, or the schism might arise over a combat between individuals of the two opposing schools, which would always lead to a choice of champions, and wager by battle to settle the respective merits; but which generally raised new grounds of controversy, and involved greater numbers, till each and every member of one community stood ready to thrash each and every member of equal size on the other side.

But as I have already hinted, the quarrel was not bad enough to be stigmatized as a religious quarrel. In fact there were many Catholic boys in the Protestant school. And then they fought manfully against the Arabs, as the enemy was called. War was usually carried on by words, sometimes by fisticuffs, and occasionally stones flew. And it was a curious fact in boy phenomena, that those who had the longest tongues had the shortest fists, and flung the fewest stones in the enemy's face. I remember that once the windows of our school-house were all smashed, and those of the Arabs lying at a tempting distance began to suffer, although protected by the awe we felt for the church and its patron, St. Ann, in the holy precincts of whose skirts it lay. One after another, however, holes were visible in the windows of good St. Ann, till the swallows that flew in, and knew not how to fly out of her, disturbed the devotions of the congregation, particularly those of the wrathful priests, who taught the school below on week-days, and performed mass above on Sundays. Whereupon there were, on befitting occasions, watchings on the part of the brethren—nay, even at unusual hours—and when a slinger of stones was caught, woe be unto him! for the gates of mercy opened not beneath the folds of the black gown.

Things would sometimes go so far as get to the ears of the trustees and heads of the respective schools, which event would most likely be followed up by a conference between grave doctors, but which, unlike most scholastic conferences, would result in an amicable compromise between them. But the upshot of the whole matter for us would be a judicious resort to that rod, which Solomon so strongly recommended. I never, by the way, could be made to forgive Solomon for that unkind proverb; and I am sure that the "rod" was a medicine rarely administered to the young prince, at the hands of good old King David, otherwise he never would have become so "spoilt" in his latter days.

Be this as it may, it was a settled opinion among the boys, that more children are spoilt by the abuse of this antiquated instrument of torture, than by the sparing thereof. And it is with great joy I see, in the reforms of the present enlightenment, a disposition to do away with the rod; and consequently a more manly, independent, self-sufficient, progressive, unbroken set of young colts never have scampered over the world than the young prize specimens of the present day.

The Vicar of St. Ann's was the pious and polished old missionary, Father Robert. Where this son of the Scarlet Lady hid his cloven foot, I never knew; for of all men he was beloved in our community—even among the *unco good* Protestants. He was celebrated in the Catholic annals of the Northwest for his learning, self-devotion, and enthusiasm. He was the first to do honor to the neglected remains of Father Marquette, the explorer of the Mississippi. He established the first newspaper; though, whether this was an act of grace and Christian charity, some of the Berkeleys of the day may be disposed to doubt. He was likewise entrusted with our interests at the seat of the Federal Government, as our territorial deputy to Congress,* and was

* The real name of the gentleman above alluded to is Father Richard. The following is from Shea's History of the Catholic Missions:

acknowledged by everybody at home as the best-hearted and most agreeable of men. He did good Protestants the honor to respect their heretical prejudices, and was a frequent visitor at their houses.

"Ah! Mrs. March," he would sometimes say to my mother with great politeness, "if all Protestants were as good Catholics as you, there would be no trouble in the world."

Good old man! he died before the evil days drew nigh, or ere the men came who would have known him not.

There was yet wanting in our cup another element of

"Soon after the outbreak of that terrible war on religion (the French Revolution), the active and laborious Sulpitian Gabriel Richard, was stationed at Detroit. * * * * As early as 1799, he visited Arbre Croche, where the Ottowas of Mackinaw then were. The memory of the Jesuit missionaries was still fresh. Tradition had handed down the death of Marquette, invested with ornaments of romance; and many were yet alive who could point to the favorite walk trodden by Du Jaunay while reciting his breviary. * * * * Richard visited the shores of [Lake] Michigan in 1821, and was conducted by the Indians to the spot where Marquette had been first buried, and where, as Richard supposes, his remains still lay. To honor the founder of Mackinaw, he raised a wooden cross at the spot, in the presence of eight Ottawas and three Frenchmen, and with his penknife cut on the humble monument (the only one ever raised to the honor of the discoverer of the Mississippi),

'Fr. Ih. Marquet,
Died here, 9th May, 1675.'"

The fortunes of Marquette, Allonez, Brebeuf, Richard, and other northwestern missionaries and explorers, form not the least poetic part of our legendary lore. I am surprised that the field has been suffered to lie so completely neglected by our *littérateurs*.

happy discord considered now indispensable in every well-organized city—the foreigner question. We scarcely knew what foreigners were, except as brethren in pursuit of fortune and happiness. The Frenchman who left his cherries to the birds, his sheep to the dogs, and his fish-seine to *le diable*, for the purpose of shouldering his musket at the call of General Hull, would have been astonished to have been branded as a foreigner. And as for the English or Scotch fur trader, whose packs had been pillaged by the British at Mackinaw, whose money had flowed freely as his blood would have flowed in defence of the town, and who cursed "Old Hull" as a traitor, or pitied him as a coward—no one ever thought of him as a foreigner. In fact we all dwelt together harmoniously, to the best of my recollection, and knew no more distinction of blood or nationality than they are innocently supposed to know in heaven.

CHAPTER III.

OUR FAMILY.

Aye, sir: to be honest, as this world goes,
Is to be one pick'd out of ten thousand.

HAMLET.

SUCH then was my native town, or city, as its inhabitants have jealously called it from time immemorial; and such was the society in its primitive state.

My father was an Englishman. Being a younger son, his chances in merry old England seemed slim enough. With what little cash he could command, he had departed from the ancestral halls, in the north of England, near the little town of Keswick, for America. He was a mere youth when he landed at New York; but fortunately his letters secured the good will of Mr. John Jacob Astor, then an active fur trader, who at once appointed him an agent in the American Fur Company, and without any delay he set out for the little city of Detroit, the head-quarters of his future business operations.

The only relatives of my father, settled in America, were the family of an uncle, who was a professor in the University of Cambridge, Massachusetts. Thither it had been the original intention of Mr. March to proceed, especially as the worthy professor had boasted no little of the beauty of his two daughters; and my father, little dreaming of ever wooing among the native daughters of the land, thought possibly the time might arrive when a wife would be desirable. Besides, Mr. March supposed he should need the advice of his uncle, with reference to choosing himself an abiding-place in the country to which he had come for the achievement of home and fortune. But the friendly advice and substantial offer of Mr. Astor, were the means of changing this plan, as we have seen.

Mr. March had not been long settled at Detroit before his heart became conscious of the charms of my mother, then a very young girl, the daughter of an officer of the American army, stationed with his regiment at our city—Major Fanshawe, 3d infantry. Notwithstanding her youthfulness, such was the impetuosity with which Mr. March urged his tender suit, that my mother found herself married at seventeen, and my father's uncle, the professor, never wrote to him from that day.

All his life, hitherto, Mr. March had been an impulsive character. But from the day of his marriage, such was the curb he imposed upon this trait, that a radical change ensued, and from one of the rashest of men, he advanced to be one of the most gentle, patient, and deliberate. This change became of frequent service tc him, not only in his family government—for I take it, that a man entrusted by God with a family, should be patience and deliberation personified—but it was more extensively useful in his dealings with the wild sons of the forest. To any stranger, Mr. March would appear in the mild light of a gentle spirit whom nothing might ruffle. But on many occasions, Pigeon-hawk, the name by which he was known among the Indians, had displayed more of the fierceness of the hawk than of the meekness of the dove, particularly when his anger was aroused by treachery or oppression. In the main, the children of the woods respected my father for his virtues, and thought him very honest—for a white man.

The several children that clustered upon the parental boughs displayed, even at no late period of their child-history, greater or less evidence of their connection with the paternal trunk, not unmingled, however, with the tokens of my mother's excellence. In early life, she appeared little other than warm affection and easy good humor; but time and trial proved that there lay dormant energy itself.

There were four of us: John, the eldest, had inherited his father's quick boldness of spirit; my brother Guilford his more deliberate fire; Maud, our only sister, standing in age between John and Guilford, gave signs of patience, tethered with courage, yet both disguised under a self-distrust, often laughable to behold, so superfluous and surprising was it in its manifestations; as for me, I may in all modesty be allowed to show myself out in the course of this eventful history.

And here I may as well present my apologies to the courteous reader for the absence in these pages of the one thing needful in modern novels. It is beyond my power to produce a fashionable infant phenomenon. Low as it shall be our lot to descend into the pits of misery, we cannot descend far enough to fish one up. It would be rare delectation to happen upon a foundling, or still more abandoned yet beautiful imp, follow him in his career from his origin in some odoriferous back alley in the City of Destruction, through the Slough of Despond, led on by the magic of some Ariadne clew or moral perfection, on through the Augean Stables, the Dungeon of the Giant Despair, the nets and pitfalls of a shocking world, on to the foot of the scaffold, whence to rescue and reproduce the hero, striding through Fifth Avenue palaces, where he is astonished to find himself perfectly at home—becomes leader of the ton, president of a bank for the benefit of obscure paupers, marries the mayor's daughter, and dies on a bed with yellow satin coverings. No! I give thee fair warning, we have nothing to do with such fascinating fungi.

The family tree flourished in a healthy soil. And yet it is pleasant to know that such prodigies have blessed the world—whether German myths or genuine Greeks, or of no particular paternity save the city fathers—sleeping beneath porches or dry-goods' boxes, a little unwashed moral Athens, with a severely-just ostracism and a profound Areopagus, and like that renowned people, possessing all the virtues, save the unimportant ten virtues of the decalogue. Alas!—again I sigh alas!—that it was not our good fortune to be thrown so pitifully low, to rise again so transcendentally high. Yet bear with me, O lover of a less dazzling, a more simple nature! My road winds over an uneven country, such as many have travelled, and even now diverges off

> "To that mysterious realm, where each shall take
> His chamber in the silent halls."

CHAPTER IV.

SUMMONED FROM ON HIGH.

Beyond is all Abyss,
Eternity, whose end no eye can reach.
MILTON.

I REMEMBER a little of my father. A tall, not stout, mild-visaged man, with a grey hair here and there streaking his head.

One's attention was always attracted to his mouth, where there presided a not uncertain, though not quite apparent expression, not undecided, nor yet with the least strain of reserve, much less of closeness. But it was an exhibition of *power under power*. If mouth might say what the tongue would not, his mouth said, "*this* must be curbed, *this* is a folly." Hast thou ever seen such a mouth? In spite of what that "expression" might say, I think that thou, my friendly reader, wouldst call it no "folly" at all, but rather a strength; and a glance at my father's eyes would assure one that the strength was good.

Yet Mr. March, as well as Mr. March's mouth, thought best to hold a tight rein.

Why he took so special an interest in me, I never

could prevail on my mother to disclose. Such, however, was the fact. But I was the plainest, and, I rather suspect, the dullest of the family, and no favorite at first with even my excellent mother. And so it may have happened, after all, that I fell to my father for his sympathy and compassion. This gave me some pride, this apparent partiality over the other children, who I always fancied envying me. He always seated me next himself at table, and cut up my food very nicely; and they have all since declared that this early care he took is the reason why I am an inch the tallest of the three brothers.

I remember that there was a desk—is not that desk my own sacred property at this moment?—with very tall legs, I then thought, standing in one corner of the room Mr. March used as his library, but which was our favorite sitting-room. Whenever he came home from his business, and particularly after any long absence, he would go straight to the desk, and draw forth cakes and confections, or sometimes even a more valuable gift. It was always well known who for. At any rate, I knew better where they went than how they ever got there, which to this day remains as perfect a mystery as the means by which the stones were laid at Baalbec.

Then it was my peculiar destiny never to touch a dish of glass, or other breakable, without the ensuing of a crash; and furthermore, it never was my good fortune to escape therefrom without an energetic thump of the thimbled finger of my mother, or a sly pinch from my careful sister Maud. But my father would always say: "Never mind, my son, it's nothing."

And then would he rub the bruise softly with his delicate hand, and under his gentle protection and reassurance I would soon recover the self-respect I had lost—that lay on the floor beneath the mass of ruined crockery.

Only to rise, however, and sin just so again.

My dear, dear father! What though he stood well among his neighbors? What though he commanded the only uniform militia company our city then boasted—the French Hussars? What though a vestryman, and the chief pillar of St. Paul's? What though already nominated, and soon to be unanimously elected, the federal representative for the whole Northwest? Did not the messenger from a higher court stand knocking at the door?

I was only seven years old. We had just returned from a family visit to a gentleman's farm that lay ten miles or more down the river.

Those beautiful river banks! With what quiet pleasure he enjoyed their loveliness. I remember his looks as he pointed them out to us. The red tower windmills, with long arms and dragon teeth. The green and yellow slopes, dotted over with white sheep; the crimson orchards; the brown nut trees; the autumn-damasked drapery of the forest; the darting squirrel we saw, and so eagerly longed to catch, and which Mr. March so cruelly shot! I remember it all, as if a pageant of yesterday; and a sense of beauty entered my dreamy, listless soul, that seems now to have come from an angel. Shortly afterwards came sorrow; and Beauty and Sorrow have ever visited me together, like loving twin sisters.

Our visit lasted a week. We set out to return at sunset. It was a beautiful moonlight night. The canoe was loaded down with the good things we brought away. There were bushels of hickory nuts, and a basket of hens' eggs, with some great goose eggs that took my eye —I had found them, too, hid away somewhere under the barn; some white wool for Mrs. March to spin and weave into home-made woolen sheets, a bag of the reddest apples in the world, and a little box in which I brought home a pair of doves. But the air was laden with miasma. Mr. March, Maud, all of us except Mrs. March, were in a few days successively prostrated with the fever. My mother nursed us all. Nothing seemed to bewilder or confound her. Nothing was too arduous for her to do. She was everywhere at the same moment. When the house grew still at night, she would suffer the neighbors, who were ever ready, to relieve her. But not a voice of pain issued from a room but it reached her ear, and she stood over the bed with cooling drink or soothing balm. Her very hand was magical on my own heated temples.

After a while, one after another recovered, save one— the one, the all in all to my mother and to me. I remember some person taking me silently by the hand one Sabbath morning. Every night on retiring to our room, my father was accustomed to come in gently after Guilford and me, and kneel down on the floor at the bedside. This was likewise his custom on Sunday mornings. But during the last few weeks we had struggled through our prayers the best we could alone, and the burden of our petitions was for him. Our thoughts were full of this subject now, when one came to lead us into his apartment. As soon as we reached the bedside we knelt down and clasped our little hands, ready for him to begin the supplication; but with a quick sob, the female who had brought us caught me in her arms, turned down the sheet which covered his face, and—

Oh God! was I, was I fatherless? How came it so? The latest we had heard was, that he grew better.

It could not, should not be!

I threw my arms around his neck as well as I could. By this time, Guilford was there too. We kissed him long and convulsively. Oh! how cruelly cold he was. The cold entered my bosom and congealed the fountain of tears. They carried me away as one dumb, and for the first time I began now to know, even thus early, what solitude is.

But the sense of solitude is not always weakening. I felt strong, too, under the weight of a great, intense grief, and that is next in strength to intense passion. Child! there were no tears for me. To weep would have been sweet. Tears are a sort of company.

Soon the vacancy of my little chamber grew oppressive. The walls seemed never so wide apart—the ceiling never so high. Objects became suddenly and largely idealized. There seemed indeed a height—it was heaven. There, too, were depths—profound depths, down which, I remember I would awake, as if falling, in my half-conscious moments. In fact, there suddenly rose around me a world: I never had known it before —never thought of it; but here it was now, stretching on, and on, and around me, near me and afar off; and I alone! alone! alone!

I wandered about the house to escape the dreariness of this world, seeking companionship, but found none; there was nothing to be seen but tears, or, what was worse, the sudden stoppage of tears whenever they saw me coming, while they glanced stealthily at me and whispered to each other,

"Hush! there he is, poor child, poor boy, poor little Walter!"

As if I were walking on some terrible crag, away down below them—as if I were the only one of them all to be pitied.

Was I? We shall see.

CHAPTER V.

THE DEPARTURE.

Thou look'st a very statue of surprise,
As if a lightning blast had dried thee up,
And had not left thee moisture for a tear.
MARTYR'S TIMOLEON.

MANY neighbors, friends, and even strangers, came to attend the last sad offices. Father Robert was there, and wept like a child. Here was a sight the brave old Indian missionary could not brave. There were many half stifled sobs. I heard their steps as they carried my father along the hall—slow, shuffling, hollow, dragging steps, sounding more loudly, or at least more lingeringly *distinct*, than a firm loud tread. Those dead, dull steps, marching to their own muffled music, the mournful utterings of the Hall to the Master, who shall come there no more as of yore bringing joy. How mute, inanimate things do sometimes speak!

A sweet, kind little woman—I wonder who she may have been?—came to my chamber, desiring me to go with her to the churchyard. I had no such material curiosity. And she stood by my side there, as I watched with my white face at the window.

The procession formed and moved away.

Father Robert, with his face buried in his handkerchief, and Mr. Cradle, our own excellent clergyman of St. Paul's, Catholic and Protestant side by side, led the train. Clumsily mounted and clumsily dressed hussars, with drawn sabres, and a dreary band of music, preceded the hearse. It was followed by his own horse, with shabrack and equipments; a sabre dangled from the pommel, a blue cloak was thrown over the saddle, and boots were in the stirrups, reversed.

Alas! that mournful sight—the riderless horse.

Then came a little body of freemasons, and a mechanics' society, with regalia in weeds; the gentlemen of the government, those of the Indian agency, fur traders, with their *employés*, whose bronzed faces were moistened with tears, for such are the brave men that weep—for others—French people, and other citizens of the town. Countrymen followed; even stalwart Indians, in their plumes, loitered at the skirts of the procession, lending a dusky fringe to the dream-like pageant.

I would have given worlds for the muscular power to turn away from the scene, or my very life for a tear to blot it out from my mind for ever; yet by some irresistible force was I chained to the window, with my gaze fixed down upon them till they had all wound away out of sight.

For the first time since he died, I now asked to see my mother. My companion, the kind little weeping woman, led me by the hand to the apartment. I cannot, and would not describe the scene. In me she saw—I know not what, but she clasped me in her arms, and strained me to her heart, weeping as if it would break, and murmuring over and over again:

"His child! His darling Walter!"

Oh! how I now began to love my poor mother! The doctor came, and I was borne out. I did not then know, nor till long afterwards, of the extreme danger through which she passed. I lingered near her door till dark. Then Guilford came, and gently urged me with him to our own bedroom.

We knelt down together. Guilford began:

"Our Father, who art in heaven!"

Now the tears burst forth as a torrent. We fell upon each other's necks, or rather I upon Guilford's, for he was always much the more manly, and the first natural child-like grief I knew came welling up from the broken fountains of the great depths.

"Our Father, who art in heaven!" Gone! gone! "Oh! who," I exclaimed to Guilford, "will now teach me my prayers? who will ever take poor Walter's part? who will cut up my meat? who will love me?" My brother endeavored to comfort me, but I would not.

And from that sweet, bitter night, "Our Father, who art in heaven" never rises to my lips, without his image—that pale, gentle presence, those calm, loving eyes. Yes, in many a strait, in darkness and evil, in joy and thankfulness, he comes, a messenger from God, an angel friend of Christ.

Since that night I have never been alone.

CHAPTER VI.

THOSE LEFT.

The adventurous boy that asks his little share,
And hies from home with many a gossip's prayer,
Turns on the neighboring hill once more to see
The dear abode of peace and privacy.

ROGERS.

NATURE'S resources were almost exhausted in my poor mother by the fatigues of many days' watching, long-strained anxiety and much overwork. The sudden and complete departure of hope would have deprived her of the little remaining strength; but that terrible loss of blood which followed the shock prostrated her so completely, that her doleful wish to die were well-nigh accomplished. But all hope gone in one direction, leaves the mind to fix itself on new objects with new and better hope. And now to combat despairing Life came desperate Resolution—to live for her children; and new thoughts, sudden desires, new energy, even new ambition, began to prevail.

My mother did not shut herself in her bedroom with Mr. March's picture, and go slipshod for a year and a day, according to the approved custom of those who are married again before you know it. Her grief became a thing of life, and a matter of hope beyond the grave.

But what was the prospect immediately stretching on before us?

Mr. March had left his affairs in a poor way. Extensive as was his business, all his means were employed in schemes which next year he hoped to see produce the desired results: next year, the *ignis fatuus* of fortune-hunters, the maid of the mist that draws them into the vortex: next year! the rock on which so many stately ships have split. The mind to calculate, the hand to guide, were gone. Everything was found to be inextricably confused, overcharged, pledged, mortgaged, embarked—nothing brought to port, nothing matured to hand and ready for use. The very house in which we dwelt, a large English cottage built by himself, was ours now only by courtesy. True, the gentlemen whom my father had appointed as our guardians informed Mrs. March that much might yet be saved by means of suits at law, but she had inherited a repugnance for the perplexities of business, and had a holy horror of all chancery proceedings; in fact, the proposition was rejected as unworthy the memory of Mr. March, who never sued a man in his life.

"Here, too," said my mother, "in the very neighborhood where he has been so beloved! lawsuits! never! Maud, my darling, my brave lads, we must work!"

And so Mrs. March resolved to keep her family together by the sweat of her brow, and to buy back the homestead, if so be God would bless her labors. This, indeed, seemed a great undertaking. Kind neighbors offered to take different members of the family to their homes, and rear them up as their own children.

"Which of you, my dear ones, will go?" inquired Mrs. March. "Mr. Latrobe will adopt one of you, boys, and Colonel Sedgefield wants one as his private secretary."

M. Latrobe was Mr. March's most intimate friend in the fur company. Colonel Sedgefield was the superintendent of Indian affairs.

But neither Guilford nor myself answered the question; as for John, he was, according to the dying wish of Mr. March, to be sent as soon as might be to Cambridge, to be educated under the care of his cousins—two accomplished women—the daughters, in whose cause the professor had tacitly resented the marriage of his nephew to my mother. Mr. March never knew how destitute his widow was to become on his death. But his expressed wish had always been my mother's law, possible or impossible; and to college, by hook or by crook, go Master John must.

"What do *you* say, Guilford? you may be rich one of these days," my mother added with a faint smile.

Guilford hesitated a long time. At length, the deliberate boy arose from his seat near the window of the library—wherein we were all gathered for a family council—walked over to his mother, who was standing near the blue desk, where she had been engaged with some papers, and looked up with his fine full face—very solemnly he looked into the eyes of motherly love.

"Are you truly in earnest, mother?"

"Yes, my son, the welfare of my children is the one great wish of my heart. I can see nothing that promises so well for you in a worldly view, Guilford."

"Then, mother, who would be left to take care of you, and Maud, and little Walter here, after John goes?" He always looked a great way down upon me, although but three years my senior.

"God, my son," replied Mrs. March, with a little agitation.

This answer confounded Guilford a moment. Then he gathered strength.

"Well, if God intended that Mr. Latrobe or Colonel Sedgefield was to bring me up, he would have given me to them himself."

Saying which, the young ethical philosopher walked back to his seat at the window, with the air of the head of the family, and there entrenched himself.

John began to grow provoked at this tom-foolery, as he was pleased to style Master Guilford's refusal.

"Walter," he exclaimed, "come, be a man; you will have to go."

But my mother did not seem at all displeased with Guilford; in fact I thought I detected a look of lurking satisfaction. She now regarded me very fixedly.

I do not know what my face replied, but if ever heart thumped violent remonstrance, mine did at that awful moment. The sense of home, with its thousand associations, pervaded me; that terrific sense of loneliness in the world, which lately had nearly deprived me of reason, overwhelmed me. I stretched out my arms towards my mother—but paused irresolute.

"Unfeeling, unmanly boy!" cried John, in a passion. My mother held her hands towards me, and grew suddenly pale.

"Would you kill her?" continued John, as I stood hesitating. Indeed my heart smote me.

"To hold on at the apron-strings! to see your mother work with her own hands for your support!"

My heart nearly crushed me. I looked towards Guilford—he was gazing on the street; towards Maud—she shook her head imploringly; at my mother—alarm and unusual agitation were twitching at the corners of her pale mouth.

"If I must go, dear mother," I said, "I will for your sake; but——

Again she held out her arms. I understood it now, and leaped into those eager arms with a burst of joyful tears. She held me a moment, then put me on my feet, smiling through her emotion as she said:

"With the aid of that young gentleman," looking rather proudly at Guilford, "I think we shall get on very well at home." In vain John disputed the point. John felt uneasy concerning his own course. The noble-hearted fellow threw every possible objection in the way of his being so unceremoniously "billeted on the family," as he said. But Mrs. March was a firm little woman, though, I dare say, neither very brilliant, nor, as women go, would she be voted strong-minded. And John, seeing no hope for himself but to accept his fate, had strenuously urged the plans of the two friends of Mr. March to relieve our mother, and place Guilford or me, or both of us, in the way of assisting her.

He knew her too well to strive any longer now, and it was with a feeling of relief and satisfaction we sat around the little round table in the library on that evening.

The wood-fire had not burned so cheerily since his death. The library was one of those little snuggeries for which everybody is ready to desert all other rooms in the house. The moonlight broke in leafy patches through the branches of the lilac trees, now in full bloom. The glow of the fire on the hearth lit up smiles on the pictures of my father and M. Latrobe, facing each other on the opposite walls; that of Mr. March hung over the lounge on one side of the fire-place, and that of M. Latrobe on the other side, overlooking the great armed and cushioned rocking-chair where my father used to sit so habitually, with Maud or me on his lap; or, if at night, with his books, till the middle watch.

That wide, open, friendly fire-place, with its lively, crackling mirth, or its sweet twilight embers, always appears to me the meet emblem of a contented, great heart, answering back to your own joy, and lighting up your shadows. And sometimes, surrounded by strangers, the object of dull remark or cold criticism, or ignorant condemnation, how have I pictured to myself a world of warmth like unto the great fire-place at home, where every man should be greeted with, "Welcome! welcome, brother!" and a comfortable, snug corner of his own; and where all answer to each other with the sympathy and cheer of shining faces over the glowing hearth. Look kindly on the stranger, gentle friend, thy looks are either so many sweet sunny beams that betoken the common fellowship of true humanity, or so many icy rays that chill him to the heart—that freeze little by little the fountains of love—that fill him with distrust of the world and hatred of his species. No man knows for how much of others' wickedness and wretchedness he may be held accountable. A look of thine may breed sorrow in thy brother, though a stranger. A look of thine may do a good deed, may shine from thy face to his face, and be reflected, like a ray of the sun, over half the globe.

Live, ye gentle scenes of home! Light up, ye bright fires of the domestic hearth! Glow, ye pleasant fancies of the wood-fire! Smile ever, ye dimpled portraits on the walls of childhood! Come in, ye sweet lilac breezes that rustle through the cozy curtains, the blossoms of youth and the airy old cobwebs of memory are shimmering in your light! Place may change, friends come and go, hearts grow cold or wear away beneath the drops of care till they crumble and moulder beneath the clod of the valley, but a pleasant home, where childhood lived and loved, never dies. The memory thereof is a fortune, an indestructible faculty of self-renewing joy.

What is Heaven itself but the renewal of the fresh hearts and delightful pleasures of childhood's home? A happy child looks forward to a happy home above. The hireling initiated but too early in guilt and misery, or in misery without guilt, he seldom hopes for better accommodation at the journey's end; and the shadow of his childhood descends before him to the grave.

Man is like the adventurer who treads the dangerous mountain rocks and thorny defiles of the isthmus between the two western oceans; and blessed is he who judgeth not the Pacific of Life to come by the Atlantic of Life begun—but rather looks back to the Pacific of a happy childhood, and onward to the still more glorious Pacific of Heaven.

Ye who have little ones playing around your knees, parent or faithful friend of the fatherless, fill their silver cups with peace and joy; for the true elixir of Life is the memory of a Happy Home.

CHAPTER VII.

THE MAGROYS.

There is a love which, born
In early days, lives on through silent years.

FANNY KEMBLE.

M. LATROBE secured a passage for John March as far as New York with the servants of the fur company, and that young gentleman was soon made ready to start. His wardrobe was small, plain, neat, and prepared by my mother and Maud. The latter added a little pincushion and needle-book, the handicraft of her own fingers, and the admiration of all. In the little silk bag attached, John found a world of buttons; and at the bottom, as if the last thing to be used, was a purse containing his pocket money. John took it out in his chamber before Guilford and me, and there was little besides the curious rare pieces of coin which Maud had a fondness for gathering, and had kept for years.

"What would you do, boys," said John.

"Give them back," said I.

"Keep them," said Guilford; "you might possibly need them, and Maud would never forgive you if you did not take them with you."

John determined to preserve them as relics.

"I shall need no pin-money," he said, with a sigh, thinking of his mother and Maud.

Professor March had died. His death was announced to my father by Virginia, his eldest daughter, between whom and Mr. March a warm correspondence had since been kept up, till the day of his illness. He had often visited the ladies; for on going to New York on yearly business, he never was so engrossed as to lose sight of the claims of friendship and kindred. He always returned home with so much to tell us: what great men he had seen—Lafayette, or the eloquent Mr. Clay, whom he admired to the skies. In fact, he frequently went to Washington for the sole purpose of seeing the world, which he thought less provincial at the political capitol than at the greater metropolis of commerce. How he, a business man, could devote so much time to his family, to his friends, and to the improvement of his noble nature, I cannot understand, since the spirit of present progress has seized me.

"He had better have stuck to his business," snarls out Adolphus Fitz-Mammon of Pearl street.

Perhaps he had.

At any rate, confess we must, that there were we, his wedded wife, now a poor widow, and his lawful children, now penniless, at the foot of the ladder, about to start away on the ocean of life, and forced from the start to paddle our own canoe.

I have a tender regret, O! gentlemanly reader—not

for our family pride, but for thy sake—that the backward state of those times would not furnish Mrs. March with genteel labor—embroidery, wax-work, writing for newspapers or magazines, lecturing on the rights of the softer sex, God bless them. Indeed there seemed to have been no machinery set in motion, by upheavings of the social world, for raising the wind wherewithal to bear up conscious dignity, suffering under a cloud. These days of such blessed short-cuts to fortune and fame are paradisaical, when compared with those long, old-fashioned, rugged roads up the hill. With due shamefacedness, I confess that Mrs. March, my mother, and the widow of a rather distinguished man, took in washing. Though she rarely bent over the tub herself, yet many a night have I laid snug under her ironing-table, pretending to sleep, so that she might feel free to sigh aloud in the midnight hours, as she wearily and heavily leant on the smoothing-iron.

It was six months after the great catastrophe before Mrs. March could, earning the family subsistence the while, do anything beyond getting John to Cambridge, with the fee necessary to enter the preparatory school. During the remainder of this year, sufficient money must be scraped together for the first payment due on the cottage which was once our own. The good people of the town called it Lilac Cottage; it stood on the edge of the city, at the extremity of a little green lawn, shaded on the two sides by elms and locusts.

Great as was the need of economy, as well as the

labor of each tiny hand, yet no sooner had the blue-bird began to pipe for spring than my mother said we must make ready for school. Accordingly, as soon as the weather settled a little, and the damp earth began to grow dry, we started on a bright, breezy Monday morning for our schools—Maud one way, and Guilford and I another. The lilac bushes nodded us a morning farewell as we set out.

I do not remember that the boys, our schoolfellows, treated us any the worse after our misfortune. Boys are nobler little fellows than they are generally written —noisy, mischievous rascals as they are. But Maud, on the other hand, did mention, in a quiet, uncomplaining way, some notable instance of insolence on the part of her school companions.

"I am not surprised, my dear," said Mrs. March; "we are very poor, and must not expect to escape the load of obloquy which poverty is liable to carry. Let your manners be simple, and your behavior as prudent as I hope it may be innocent, and you will soon begin to see rise up around you a respect more valuable than that paid to mere wealth."

We all looked on and listened, with a sort of growing solemnity, till my mother closed this, the longest harangue of her life.

It must be acknowledged, in extenuation of the conduct of the young girls, whose rudeness had wounded our little self-deprecating bird, they were daughters of some honest people who fancied my mother proud because she persevered, even now in the hour of her desolation, the even tenor of her laborious days and nights, without accepting either the proffered assistance of the good and great around her, or the society of the vulgar, who were as far beneath her as ever.

Our fall in the social scale was not very far. Such was the esteem felt for the character of Mrs. March, likewise for the memory of her husband, that strange as it may appear, we were now almost as respectable as ever. I say very honestly this was strange, for I defy any man to look narrowly into his own heart and say, that he regards the person of his fallen brother, with precisely that amount of respect he entertained before his fortunes were clouded.

In spite of your honest protestations, the difference is just equal to the cash lost.

The gap may be filled with pity or interest, or even with admiration, but it is quite another thing.

It may be a nobler, for the savor of Monsieur Mammon's presence is gone.

Yet those times were not blessed, as these are, with so many charming refinements, and necessary extravagances, in the manner of living. Between the citizens of our little city there was no great disparity of dress, nor of style in anything outward.

The Governor's household often rode to church in a French cart, all sitting on the clean straw laid on the bottom, or at most a buffalo robe. Now, had they ridden in a chariot, who so unreasonable as demand them to nod their heads so familiarly as they did to John Baptiste with his check-apron family driving by, jerking the reins of that wicked little trotter? No, my simple, yet honest friend; our smiles of recognition vary with the difference of altitude between our relative seats. It should be that such divine things as smiles should bless the more, the further they descend; but alack! alas!

But there was one important member of the good old society that did not think it worth his while to disguise the difference in his favor towards us: no less a worthy than Mr. Archibald Magroy, LL.D. Mr. Magroy was a rich retired fur-trader. A tall figure, a heavy, shaggy forehead, a lumbering gait, a totally disagreeable manner of address, so pedantic, withal, that you must fain believe the whole world had gone mad, and he had lost all patience with it.

In the early days of his career, when he was struggling to obtain what the world owes every man, however contemptible the creditor—a living—he had married a thriving Yankee woman. It was the common belief that Mrs. Magroy was born with a duster in her hand and a turban on her head. She certainly was never seen without them. That parlor of hers was irreproachable. Once on each day she opened the back door of the same, flew in, flourished her duster, bastinadoed any unlucky little spider that astonished itself at being found there, scampered off the flies, and herself flew out again—breathless. But she breathed more freely the rest of the day, and dusted all over the house more leisurely. The front parlor-door was always locked, the curtains always precisely fixed for company—that never saw them; the blinds down, as if the light of Heaven were impure in her sight. In truth, no human being, except the neat matron Magroy, knew what treasures of immaculate furniture that precious parlor contained. Her visitors were always shown into the dining-room at the extremity of the hall.

Mr. Magroy delighted in the glum solitude of an office in the wing. Over Mr. Magroy's door there figured his name with the Archibald of his fathers prefixed, and the title of some petty office he held under government turned up at the end of it, like the tail of a mastiff. " Old Growl," as the boys resentfully nicknamed him, kept constant watch and ward in this kennel of his, ready to bark at mankind as a whole and boyhood in units. For, in the angle between the wing and the main body of the building, there were flourishing a few choice fruit trees, some of whose luxurious branches extended over the fence, and therefore in pursuance to well known boy-laws, belonging to the passers by. Against this principle Mr. Magroy protested, and the contested point rendered him a miserable, suspicious, wrathful man for life, according to the boys. For the fruit was too tempting a prize for juvenile forbearance; it hung over the road, the corner was but a rod further on, and escape always easy. Still the depredator, though then and there escaping, was not beyond the reach of Archibald Magroy, LL.D. Woe to the boy, woe to his school, woe to his teacher, woe to the very parents whose pride was bound up in him. Old Growl was a constant school visitor, a self appointed trustee for the education of the poor ignorant world's children. Show me a Scot that hath ever taught school, and I will show thee a pedagogue egregious and eternal. And Mr. Magroy was a Scot and had taught school. With his Greek and his Latin, his latitudes and longitudes, Old Growl bestrode the world of classics and sciences, as he domineered over mankind's children. Who that went to school at that memorable time, but remembers the terrible visitor? And who that ever struck a plum from the bending boughs of his plum trees, that doth not repent in Greek and Latin to this day?

Mr. Magroy was a father.

The best natured, the most careless, idle, truant blade of a boy in the whole city, was Allen Magroy, only child of Old Growl. Allen had been the devoted admirer and sworn cavalier of our Maud, ever since the world began. Old Growl, before the death of Mr. March, seemed not at all loth to see this intimacy. He even smiled, or rather chuckled a canine approval—in his way. But when our catastrophe happened, and the poverty in which we were left became known, Mr. Magroy turned his back upon poor innocent Maud. And now, instead of greeting her as of yore, with a grim friendly nod and a handful of delicious fruit, whenever she passed that way, he shut-to the gate, and strode with his hands behind him through the little orchard into the kennel, his cane tail-like dragging behind.

Then Allen began to wear a long face, and for the first time in his life looked serious. And poor Maud began to think she must not as much as look on an LL.D.'s son, now that she was the daughter of a working woman; and so treated Allen with quite chilling reserve, and avoided him on all possible occasions. Allen would throw himself in her path between home and school, and on Sunday afternoons as she came back from church. She never so much as referred to Mr. Magroy, but she protested against Allen's desperate behavior. In fact Maud was a great deal prouder than ever she knew of.

Allen clung to her with Scotch pertinacity. He was now eighteen, a manly looking fellow with dark hair and mahogany colored eyes; he had a lithe figure, and there was that grand air about him in all his indolence, that we sometimes see with so much pleasure in the strut of a gallant soldier, as if he knew he had a perfect right to it. Yet as we have said, Allen was a careless, unstudious fellow, which was but too perceptible in the devil-may-care manner he carried about with him, except when in the presence of our sweet Maud. He was bound to her by no slender tie, viz., gratitude, a cable on the heart of a boy, though soon reduced to a cobweb in the grown up man of the world.

A few years earlier than the date of our story—I was a mere child—we were all playing in the yard, in the middle of which stood a well of wonderful depth. We certainly thought, at least I did, that it extended to the centre of the earth. Maud had her playthings under an elm near by, and Allen had teased her all day. At length for the boyish fun of frightening her, he climbed part-way up the side of the well-house. Maud grew frightened in a moment.

"Allen! Allen! come down, do!"

The young gentleman was delighted too much with his easy success. He went laughing at her fears, climbed to the top of the open side, and was walking on the edge of the board, keeping his balance, however, with much effort.

Maud held her breath, and soon became so pale that Allen fairly shouted. Suddenly he lost his balance, caught at the chain as he fell, and went thumping and tumbling down the walls of the well. He succeeded in catching the chain before he had fallen many feet, and the roller began to revolve furiously. Guilford and myself were paralyzed by fright; but Maud darted to the crank, which, too, was flying around at a speed terrible to behold. She caught it with sufficient force to check the roller, and impede the descent of the boy, who was now clinging to the bucket. In another moment she had seized the crank firmly. Her loud screams soon brought a troop of neighbors to the rescue, and Allen was drawn out. He had fallen a perilous distance; but though covered with bruises from head to foot, not a bone was broken. The heroine of the catastrophe fainted when the excitement was gone, and the fear alone was left. They carried Maud into the house, without her knowing whether Allen was dead or alive. Her wrist was dislocated.

"What of that?" said she afterwards; "possibly Allen might have been killed."

Her courage and presence of mind had indeed saved the life of the ever-grateful boy—the ever-after true and loving Allen.

When, therefore, his father commanded him to break with Maud, the reader may fancy his sorrow and discomfiture.

"That good-for-nothing little March girl! the little white-headed limmer! let me never see ye with her more, do you hear that, sir?" quoth Mr. Magroy, drowning the cry of gratitude and honor in loud words.

Allen was shocked, mortified, indignant. He began to reason; he grew casuistical. The path of disobedience began to show itself, winding amid his perplexities.

Mrs. March rarely bothered that little busy brain of hers on matters beyond the object immediately before her. Yet now, no sooner did she hear of the unbecoming behavior of her neighbor, and see in the face of Maud how it affected her daughter, than, with a touch of motherly compassion, she drew the child to her bosom, and encouraged her to pour forth the griefs that oppressed her. Previously Maud had kept her own counsel. Now, my mother and Maud became friends and allies—more like two loving sisters than parent and child.

Ah! sympathy! sympathy! enricher of poverty! balm of breaking hearts!

Draw thy child closer to thee, good mother—closer though she sinneth. The more need—the more need.

Our Maud suddenly seemed to unfold into a young woman. Hitherto she had been a mere child. The bud was quickened, and even in a night bloomed into a hundred-leaved rose.

Her pretensions to beauty were of no inferior order. Fair hair clung around her shoulders in wavy ringlets, beautiful to behold. Her eyes looked out as blue doves from their habitations—all peace and love within, all gentleness without. She had not yet reached the perfect stature of a woman, yet it was evident she never would rise beyond the medium height.

Little lady as she was, she carried a winning spirit and a brave, towards all beside herself—a subtle mastery that brought Power into the retinue of her attendant charms. Even her weakness, self-distrust, took the form of Grace. Poor girl, to have a history! Blessed is the woman that hath none.

Maud went meekly on her way—school and household cares dividing her hours. She looked an angelic creature, involved in a cloud—an illusion which those long, shining, blonde ringlets, fleecy as a summer cloud, and the color of her eye, changeable as the colors of the cushat's neck, with their moistened fringes, did not serve to dispel.

CHAPTER VIII.

SHOEPAC AND MOCCASIN.

My father's friend, M. Latrobe, was a French gentleman; he rejoiced in it. He was born in Paris. He remembered Napoleon—had seen him, spoken with him. Napoleon was his idol, of all hero divinities in clay. Every new day he told a new anecdote concerning the emperor.

M. Latrobe was not tall—rather short and roundish. His years numbered fifty, and yet spring sat upon his face, laughing at winter on his head. He was a gentleman of the old school, and handed you his snuff-box with a polished air. His eyes were piercing black; his mouth, a sharp, judicious little mouth, yet almost girl-like in expression.

M. Latrobe was really a great man; and such a friend!

The first yearly payment on Lilac Cottage has fallen due. I need not set forth, one by one, the trials and tribulations that fell to our family lot during that sad year. Nor need I dwell upon the anguish with which now my mother beheld the death's head, Despair, at the family board. I prefer without delay to usher in

M. Latrobe; he has just returned from a long tour up the Lakes; he had visited the far northern stations belonging to the company.

My mother was delighted to see him again; and there they sat in the little library, so often the scene of pleasantries between him and my father, where so many adventures in boats, on snowshoes, and in shoepacs,* had been told, and where Napoleon never had been forgotten.

"How are all our friends at Mackinac?" asked my mother.

"Ah! madam," he replied in a softer tone, "you will pardon my friendship in expressing myself before you, but the people up there loved your husband, my friend, my friend; I think I see him here again."

M. Latrobe raised his eyes to the picture of my father with such affection, such sadness, depicted on his countenance.

"I am ready to weep for you, madam—and for myself, too," he added, handing his snuff-box to my mother, with a tear on the lid.

The drops trickled down my mother's pale face in silence. Hers had long been the midnight agony; but her daily effort was to banish the past, for the sake of the cares of the present, and God had helped her on to fortitude. The present occasion was one of those rare

* The shoepac was a covering for the feet—half shoe, half moccasin—worn by the early French on the frontier.

instances when my mother's grief broke forth from her eyes.

The two gentle spirits, knit together by love for a common object, buried their faces in their handkerchiefs, and wept.

M. Latrobe was the first to speak. He told her of the interest manifested at Mackinaw in the fortunes of my mother, and of their grief over what was felt as a loss common to all. He spoke of a trunk-full of presents they had sent her and Maud. The Indians had a superstitious reverence for Maud, on account of her hair. The Dove of Pigeon-Hawk was invested with unearthly attributes, and strings of wampum attested their homage.

But M. Latrobe had a great favor to ask.

"I have long desired, madam, to place in your hands the keeping of my little daughter, Ma Belle."

Mrs. March looked surprised.

"Do not refuse me at once, wife of my old friend," he said, with the voice of one who most required sympathy, in attempting to bestow it. "Since the death of my excellent wife, I take little satisfaction at home, and am absent so many months at once, I fear Ma Belle will grow up in the streets.

"My dear M. Latrobe," said my mother, "is there anything I may do for your child?"

"Ah! yes, madam, I desire her to be a lady, and that she must become by no more than living in the same house with you."

M. Latrobe extended his snuff-box.

"I fear you are too polite," replied Mrs. March with a smile, declining the good gentleman's snuff.

"And I desire her to be educated," continued he. "Now, madam, if you would only take her *en famille*, and send her to school under the kind protection of Miss Maud, you would become my benefactress for my life.

Who could refuse such an appeal?

Then the good man became gay, talked of a laughable upset from a canoe into the rapids of Sault Ste. Marie, and spoke of a queer, whimsical old officer, stationed at Mackinaw, so as to slily draw in an apropos allusion or two to Napoleon.

I am not sure that Father Robert would have enjoyed M. Latrobe's success that day—the lively, agreeable talker.

As he rose to depart, he drew from his breast pocket a package, and laid it on the desk.

"Compliment is compliment; business is business," said M. Latrobe, laconically. "You will find Ma Belle's business in ze paper, Madam March." He pronounced *th* with difficulty under certain circumstances.

Mrs. March was not quite prepared for pecuniary considerations, poor as she was, and much as she needed the wherewithal; and a tear of gratitude stood in her eye.

"I thought, monsieur, your daughter was to come *en famille?*"

"*Oui, oui, en famille, en famille*, zat is it; zat will be ze happiness of Ma Belle and myself."

The polite gentleman had hastily gathered up his hat and gloves, and was bowing himself out, when my mother's remark, and the manner, caused M. Latrobe to stop. He returned hastily towards my mother, and took her gently by the hand.

"You would not force me to place my child in ze keeping of strangers?"

"No, M. Latrobe, your child shall be my child; I will love her for your sake, and," she added, in a stifled voice, "for the sake of one we both loved."

M. Latrobe began to feel for his snuff box. Suddenly he raised my mother's hand to his lips, and in another moment was gone.

That afternoon the first payment was made on the cottage.

Mabel Latrobe!

Our pet Mabel, how shall I describe her? No one can imagine, no one will believe how she looked; no one can see her as we saw her. A little thing, with clear amber complexion—those piercing black eyes of her father's, with a shade of soft Indian melancholy—his child-like lips, only what was purely suggestive in the father was growing here in the fullness of nature. Lithe and soft-footed as a mountain kitten, and gentle mannered and soft-hearted as a shepherd's lamb, and yet withal as wild as a fawn, when she first came to us, was Mabel Latrobe.

Her mother was a beautiful half-breed, who had been finely educated at Montreal, where M. Latrobe married her. The half-breeds were not a long-lived race, and Madam Latrobe had died young, leaving her husband this their only child—born late in their connubial happiness.

The little one had been named *Mabelle*—my beautiful—by her mother, but we Anglicized it into Mabel.

She seemed very glad to come among us, for her life had been lonely of late. Parting from her French nurse was a trial. M. Latrobe, however, insisted so strongly, out of regard to my mother, whose family was already sufficiently large, that Mabel became reconciled to it, and in order that the attachment should be completely sundered, the good woman was permitted to return to Montreal, whence she had come, and whither her sighs had long been directed. There she was living comfortably on the allowance M. Latrobe settled upon her, when last I saw the fat old dame, and doubtless she is living still—those Canadian people live green for ever.

Mabel became as one of the family in a very few months. She was but eighteen months younger than myself, and we were playmates and called each other brother and sister, though as for that she was child and sister to us all. Guilford she greatly respected, but his deliberate movements accorded not as well with her liveliness as my own character. As I said, we were playmates. I was her champion, the father, or husband, or brother, or even son, of her different dolls; whose several cradles, bedsteads, kitchens, carriages, horses, umbrellas, knives, forks, boats, etc., it was my good fortune to be able to construct. Yet sometimes I grew jealous of Guilford, whom I thought she respected above my important self—is not jealousy an instinct?

Mabel was mostly consigned to the care of the prudent Maud. However, it was sometimes necessary for my mother to interfere, very much as great nations do between small, in order to preserve the general peace of society. On the whole, the two girls did very well together, and Maud certainly discharged the sacred trust entirely to the satisfaction of M. Latrobe. The school to which they went was kept by a Madam Laon, near the Catholic church. Madam Laon was assisted by several nuns, who taught sweet music and pretty embroidery, and were very nice people—that is, for nuns; for I have so deferential a regard for commonly received notions, that I suppose I must qualify my words for people's sakes. Indeed, these nuns, and their mode of life, together, were so very fascinating, that the girls had not studied with Madam Laon more than two years before Maud gave tokens of desire, if not determination, to lead a cloistered life. As soon as discovery of this was made to my mother by the honest Madam Laon, the former took the children from the school, and placed them under charge of a New England lady, Mrs. Fanner, who gave great satisfaction. M. Latrobe never interfered with my mother's action in such cases, for the regulation of his daughter's education. And in the present instance he was so frightened at the idea his darling might catch the "contamination," as he called it, that he openly requested my mother to bring up Mabel in the Protestant religion. I fear he was a poor sort of religionist, to lose sight thus of his daughter's eternal interests; but he had a strange opinion that there was but one God and one Saviour for both churches; a belief which all sects would doubtless unite so far as to condemn.

How much the disappointment and sorrow Maud felt on Allen's account may have tended to turn her thoughts towards a convent, we cannot say. She persisted conscientiously, however, in no intercourse with the mournful object of her deepest regard. It was working sadly on the boy's appearance. He would throw himself occasionally in her way, and entreat her in such sad, tender terms to hear him, and not mind his father, whom he tried to pretend she had mistaken, that she must needs often drop her veil quickly to conceal her tears, and hurry on incontinent of his grief.

The poor lad was losing much of his buoyancy, though not becoming any more careful than ever in his behavior, which was only too frank and devil-may-care.

When Maud was about seventeen years of age, an incident happened which occasioned no little merriment in the family ever after, though the girl herself never joined in it. Among the Indian friends of my father was a fine old Potawatomie chief—Italisse—who always brought his family to our house at the times of the annual Indian payments. Well, it seems that his son had conceived a great liking for Maud, and after the death of my father began to manifest his passion. No one thought anything of it, however, until now. He came to the house every day after dinner, and after school in the evening, and would follow Maud around like any faithful spaniel; but he had not the courage to say a word.

One day the taciturn young lover brought his mistress a string of wampum, which she accepted innocently enough. This seemed to afford him peculiar satisfaction.

On the next day he gave her a little box of Indian paints, and on her accepting it, manifested the same significant joy. On the third day, he produced a pair of scarlet leggings, beautifully wrought. Maud hesitated, and consulted Mrs. March on the point of taking these, but the latter only smiled at the grave Italisse's earnest demeanor, and told her not to give him offence; so Maud accepted the leggings. No sooner had she expressed her thanks, which she did in the Indian tongue, and as it happened with unusual warmth, by way of atonement for her previous hesitation, than the young chief leaped into the air with joy, bounded away out of the garden, and down the avenue, striking his hand on his mouth and yelling as he went, in the peculiar manner of his tribe.

On the following morning, who should appear but the old chief and his squaw, in company with the young lover, now radiant with joy and certainty. The chief followed my mother into the library, and seated himself, as in grand pow-wow. His wife with becoming modesty of demeanor dropt on a chair near the door, and the son, still more respectfully, stood entirely outside the room in the hall. Old Italisse was allowed to light his pipe—a primitive tomahawk pipe. He took an initiatory puff or two, and then handed it to my mother, who gravely applied it to her mouth a moment, and passed it with becoming gravity and ceremonious inaction to the squaw, who was fully equal to the emergency.

The council was thus fully inaugurated.

The chief opened the confab, standing not ungracefully opposite my mother, and facing both her and the rest of his auditory. He said:

"He had known Pigeon Hawk many moons. The leaves had fallen on his grave three times, yet he remembered him as well as if the picture he saw on the wall were painted on his heart. The Dove of the Pigeon Hawk was dear for her father's sake. He would give her, and the children she might have by his son, all his land, his boats, his blankets, his mococks, spears, and tomahawks."

My mother now began to grow alarmed, she saw the whole thing in its most serious and embarrassing aspect. It seems that the three presents had been respectively a declaration of love, a request for love in return, and finally an offer of marriage, and all having been accepted, especially the last, under due consultation, Italisse imagined his fate decided and his happiness begun. It was with difficulty that Mrs. March could make the old chieftain comprehend the mistake. White Pigeon he knew to have been versed in all the customs of his tribe; Maud and my mother both talked Potawatomie, and blind to the light of all elucidation, he grunted "ugh! ugh!" and finally stalked off with his family, in high dudgeon. He never visited our house again.

My grieved and half terrified mother sent the presents to M. Latrobe, who returned them to young Italisse, and endeavored to soothe the disappointed lover and mollify the old chieftain, with what success I am unable to say. The circumstance occurred so long ago that no one in the family remembers more than I have narrated, and possibly it may be that the three presents were not all precisely what I have represented, yet the substance and manner of the courtship are true, "as set forth in the brief."

CHAPTER IX.

JOHN MARCH WRITES HOME.

Read over this;
And after, this, and then to breakfast, with
What appetite you have.

HENRY VIII.

By the magical influence of an author's wand, we must turn the reader back again in this history, to about two months after the departure of John March for Cambridge.

CAMBRIDGE, June 30th, 182—

"MY DEAR MOTHER:

"I arrived here this morning, and have retired early to the room Aunt Virginia has kindly fitted up for me, to write to you. Dear mother, it was too bad to leave you all; I might have been of considerable use to you, had you let me remain, but here am I now playing gentleman while you are working with your hands. I hope the time may come when I can requite it all by other means than mere words.

"We were three weeks reaching New York. The roads are bad between Buffalo and Albany, and the stage travelled slowly. The Fur Company gentlemen were very kind all the way. * At Albany we took one of the new fashioned boats of which we have heard so much at Detroit, called steamboats. They are very swift, making six miles an hour against the wind. Whether they will ever dare to try them on the lakes I don't know, but they begin to talk of it. Think of that! But I would not like to cross Lake Erie in one of them, for fear of a storm.

* A slight anachronism.

"When I got to New York all I could do was to exclaim New York! New York! such great three story buildings, such a great post-office, such banks, and so many people hurrying along. The shipping reminds me of a forest of pine trees; yes, a perfect forest of them.

"Aunt Virginia was very glad to see me, I think. I am glad you have sent her money enough for my board, schooling and everything for the year, as she is very poor. As you have not heard anything about her except what she used to write herself, I will tell you what Aunt Carrie says. She says 'That V— was a great belle, and was quite celebrated at Washington, Philadelphia, New York, even way down to New Orleans, and that she had many offers'—which I can readily believe, as she is so good and lady-like in her manners, and so beautiful, too, even now in her 40th year. I will tell you and Maud just how she looks. Tall and straight, fine neck, and person, large black eyes, slightly aquiline nose, black ringlets, and such a musical ringing voice I never heard. But she would accept nobody, rich men, learned professors, statesmen, nobody, so Aunt C. says. And what do you think is the reason? Why, Aunt Carrie is blind, and has three little fatherless children, and Aunt V. has devoted herself to them all for life. Don't that sound like a romance.? It's almost like you, mother. Well, Aunt C's. husband left little or nothing, so Aunt V. who was unmarried when her father died, and left her everything, turned it all into enough money to purchase this little place of a house and six acres only, and here they live by raising vegetables which they send to Boston market to sell. Aunt V. did not know anything about it, but she got books, and read everything on such subjects, and now does very well indeed.

"She teaches two of the children, the little girls, herself, and sends the boy to school. She says I must commence right off to go to school and prepare for college by next year. My candle is most burnt down, so good night—love to Gilly and Walter—kiss Maud.

"Thine,

"JOHN MARCH."

This letter was brought by the postman, who is a little Frenchman, mounted on a strong but rough Canadian pony, with burs in his mane, tail, and all over. He goes round with a long tin horn, which he blows in front of every house where there is a letter to be delivered, till they come out. Then he takes his letter out of his saddle-bag and gets twenty-five cents, or more, if it be a double letter.

It was a great shame when the town got so great as to abolish good Antoine, and establish a post-office. In the first place he was thrown out of employment, as well as his horse. In the next place, instead of having your letters —as the newspapers are now-a-days—brought to your door, you must go after them. And in the last place, and worst of all, if you are a poor old man, or any kind of a poor man, or poor woman, or servant—which you cannot help and which God made you—the upstart clerks are sure to insult you. And ten to one they don't turn you off without looking over the bundle of letters to see if you have got one. The first time I arrived at Washington, I found a letter after a week's daily inquiring, which must have arrived the day after I did. I remember it because it was from Mabel herself. Now little Antoine knew you had a letter before you knew it yourself, and great was his hilarity on giving it to you.

"He! my friend!" he would call out, "what you will give for one *lettar*, one fine fat lettar? from Philadelphia. Ah! you no care eh! By gar I will keep him myself," and he would pretend to rein off his steed. Then he would turn back and say sharply,

"Quick! non, allons! I have not time for de trifle," and you would pay the postage and read your letter.

I am such a stickler for primitive times, that, though I may be mistaken, I think the letters of those days were worth the postage you paid. The topics of a letter were infinitely various, from the last murder to the last marriage, and there was nothing mercenary about it. Theology, politics, and all the interesting affairs of the world, were touched upon at greater length. Now, the newspapers pretend to do all that, but not half so well. You never see a letter now-a-days but you fear to open it, lest it should turn out a notice of assessment due on paltry stock, or a protest, or note due, or pew tax. There was little of that sort of thing then.

SECOND LETTER.

"*July 1st (2 years later).*

"MY DEAR MOTHER,

"I have received your affectionate epistle with great satisfaction. It rejoices my nerves—the illiterate would say heart—to hear you are all well. It would be quite to my taste to extend to Miss Mabel Latrobe an elder brother's greeting. Please convey the message to her, with a labial accompaniment from me.

"That vulgar affair of Johnson's was execrably shocking. To think of his suing you at law! Would that I had my ten digits in his hair and eyes. Of course Judge McD—— decided in your favor, and no wonder the people carried Guilford home on their shoulders when the decision was announced. I submitted the case to our law lecturer, and knew how the case would terminate long beforehand; only I was afraid it might not, or that you might consider me vain and presumptuous. But the more I learn, the less I think I know: like Newton, I only seem to myself to be on the shore of the great Ocean of Knowledge.

"Think of Aunt V—— taking up German; yet she actually has—partly for the pleasure of reading Goethe, and partly in order to teach the children. As for me, I don't think much of modern languages; give me the language of immortal Homer, or that of the Bard of Mantua—which I hope to know something of next year.

"I have passed a good examination—25th in my class. Hurrah! one year of college through with. How the boys will stare at me when I go home in three years from now with my diploma. I will shake it in the face of old Magroy himself; the old dog! does he frighten all the little cowardly boys yet! I wish I could get hold of him. And don't he speak to Maud yet? Who is *he*, to put on such airs? the old Scotch herdsman! I half believe his father tends his flocks now on the Grampian hills. I hope you will send me all the money you can. I am running in debt here and in Boston. With much love to all the children, I remain,

"Thine,

"JOHN MARCH."

My mother read this letter aloud with a troubled visage. The tone of it was ill suited to our circumstances, to John's prospects in life, to good taste, to good manners, or to Christian charity. The pedantry, my mother told me afterwards, she could overlook. All college youths, she said, seemed to regard the world outside their narrow circle as woefully ignorant. But the evidence it afforded of an uncurbed spirit, little in keeping with his early religious feelings, and expensive habits, as little in keeping with his means, made a deeply unfavorable impression on her. She said nothing, however, but laid down the letter, and silently went about her household duties. Guilford took it up, and mounting a chair, read the letter aloud in an affected high tone.

"Children!" said he, coming to the end; "who does he call children, I'd like to know?"

"Don't Guilford," said Maud, in evident pain, for John was very dear to her, as well as Allen's great friend.

"I cannot help it," said Guilford, unusually excited. "John is a fool."

"A fool," repeated Maud in astonishment. "Why, Gilly, don't you remember what the Bible says, 'He that calleth his brother a fool'——besides, John hasn't said anything against us."

"But it's the way he writes," said Guilford, recovering himself. "He talks as though *we* were all heathens, and *he* the King of the Tongo Islands, at least. He forgets that here we are all working for him to be there—mother almost killing herself, and everybody so kind to her, and to all of us."

"Well, well! Gilly," said Maud, soothingly, "perhaps he'll come home and give you your turn next."

"I won't take it," said the boy, stepping down from the chair.

"It is not his fault," continued Maud gently. "You know father wished it."

"Yes," murmured Guilford, "I know that—I forgot that; but he mustn't, no, he must not, write so. I'll tell him myself;" so saying, he thrust his hands into his pockets, and went into the yard to see what might require his attention in that quarter.

CHAPTER X.

GHOST STORIES.

> But soft! behold! lo, where it comes again!
> I'll cross it, though it blast me.—Stay, illusion!
>
> HAMLET.

GUILFORD MARCH and his brother Walter, were as man and boy the first few years of their half-orphanage. The distinguished young head of the family was skillful and strong in hewing wood and drawing water, while the young male branch trudged along in the subordinate sphere of chore-doer general—in a light way.

And it is high time the dainty reader should know that the mother of the two young gentlemen changed her occupation on coming into the second year of widowhood, and for a while we may now contemplate her in the employ of sundry tailors and shoemakers. For the former she stitched on shirts, underclothing and pantaloons; and for the latter she bound shoes—herself employing, to aid in these useful purposes, a small number of respectable young females, of whose history we knew nothing, beyond their fingers' ends.

Not the least dignified among the small pursuits of Walter March, was to fetch and carry bundles to and from the shops of the above-mentioned tailors and shoemakers; and as seamstresses and shoe-binders never since the world began were known to finish their work before night, it fell out that my journeyings to the shops of our patrons commonly took place at night.

Now, by chance, there was on the street along which I travelled, a vacant house—a dreary, clapboard-rattling, shutter-flapping, haunted house, which nightly gave forth sounds, not unmusical, but unearthly. Opposite the corner of this building there stood a white post, marking a boundary of the lots, and rejoicing near the top in the two letters, O. Q., the initials of the owner of the property. It is needless to hint to the imaginative reader, that those black letters shone forth from the white post like two spectral eyes—dim, hollow, far.

The supernatural sounds issuing from the haunted house, together with the appearance of the white figure —demon-eyed—sometimes, in fact frequently, constrained Walter March to quicken his footsteps as he approached the fearful neighborhood, or to take the middle or opposite side of the street—to whistle with apparent unconcern—to start with affright at the least unusual object, man or beast, suddenly coming in sight, and in short, to clear the infernal region at a goodly run.

It is equally needless to go into less important particulars, such as the tenor of Walter March's dreams— the nightmares that were bestrode by a familiar post-goblin, whose ears were posts, whose legs and tail were posts, whose head was full of O's and Q's, whose snort was like the earthquake of falling houses; of a vampire that sucked the dream-blood of Walter March, planted in the victim's breast, like a post driven through him, and holding on to that young gentleman's eye-brows by his vampire eyes, O. Q. Further particulars were superfluous.

For many and many a month Walter March was an unhappy little haunted lad, ridiculed by the head of the family, and laughed at by everybody. The serving-woman, Bowes, was the only friend who condoled with me in my misfortunes, the only person who had faith in the delusion—in short, the only being who believed in ghosts. On one or two occasions the good soul accompanied me through the dismal region, and helped the matter no little by scampering off at the first sound. My manly brother, Master Guilford, condescended so far to notice my fears as to propose a visit to the haunted quarter by day, and a thorough exploration of the premises. We accordingly climbed in at a window, and perambulated over the rooms, and spied into the closets and corners, from base to garret of the mansion, without finding any satisfactory clue to the mystery, or key to the supernatural music. I began to believe myself the victim of mere groundless fear, when, as we were about departing—Guilford had already descended to the ground from the window—a sweet, unearthly, moaning sound echoed through the deserted apartments, and lent wings to the speed with which I bounded out after my brother.

"What is the matter?" he asked, astonished at the sudden quickness of my movements.

"Did you not hear it?" I asked, breathlessly.

"Hear what?"

"That noise! those sounds! that piteous complaint in music!"

"My dear brother, I fear you are losing your senses; you will soon be demented. I will go up again and listen, just to convince you."

He climbed to the window, and sat on the sill, listening attentively. Of course he heard nothing, or, at least nothing unusual, and soon jumped down again. He walked away from the place in silence; but there was an expression, half-sneering and half-pitying, on his countenance, which cut me to the quick.

I now vowed to myself that I would solve the difficulty in the most direct manner. I would go to the spot by night, alone, for nobody should laugh at me more. How whist was I all that day! how preöccupied with anticipated conflicts with goblins, witches, dwarfs, dragons—what not!

At the accustomed hour of my errands to the shop at night, a little before nine, I proceeded resolutely to the enchanted ground. I saw the white post.

"'Tis nothing but a white post," I said to myself, cheerily.

I saw the two eyes.

"They are nothing but two letters, O. Q.," and I said O. Q. aloud; I even heard an echo O. Q.!

"That's but an echo," said I, falteringly.

I had gained nearly the front of the house. The wind came and shook the building with a noise that before would have frightened me.

"Ha, ha!" I laughed, "that's nothing but the wind!"

The next moment I heard another sort of sound—the noise of a chain! I paused—listened eagerly, distrustfully, unbelievingly.

There! I hear it again. Yes, it is distinct, the clank! clank! clank! of a chain. My teeth began to chatter—my knees to tremble. I was not prepared for this. My legs refused to do their office. The noise ceased, but I turned away with a faint, sickening sensation, with difficulty reached home, and tottered up to bed.

"What is the matter with Walter?" was asked several times next day, both at home and at school. I was pale and dumb. My mother managed to draw out my secret. She was indignant at Bowes for encouraging ghost-notions in me, and took Guilford to task for his ridicule and want of sympathy.

Blessed mother!

I had more faith in her than in Bowes and all the world, upper and lower, put together.

"My son," said she, "there is no such thing as ghosts."

I was foolish enough to believe her. What would the spirit-rappers say to that? Bowes! Bowes! time has proved you right, and my matter-of-fact mother wrong. How glad Bowes must be to have her ghost-stories confirmed—lit up with science and philosophy! proved mathematically! judicially! politically! by scholars, judges, statesmen!

I now resolved to encounter the monster, since there was no monster, or if one, as my mother said with one of her humorous smiles, "he must be fettered, and can do you no harm." The night was cloudy moonlight—"Such as spectres love," whispered Fear; "So much the better," whispered Courage.

The white post appeared and disappeared almost momentarily. I came to within a rood and listened: no sound whatever. I moved forward a step or two, and heard the dismal clank. My heart began at once to throb. The moon, too, conspired against me. She flared out of a cloud with sudden brilliancy, and in her light the post gleamed whitely, and the two eyes—impossible to mistake two eyes—glared upon me. I remembered, though indistinctly, my mother's words. No ghosts, no ghosts, I whispered to myself. But as I advanced, the chain was again heard, with a quick, loud rattle, over the boards which composed the side-walk, and the post became converted into a skeleton figure, which appeared to retreat before me with a grin of vast satisfaction at the sport this adventure seemed to afford him, but terrible to behold on my part. My courage sank; my knees felt as if doubling beneath the weight they bore; my teeth—I would not let them chatter, but with a last desperate flash of resolution, I leaped forward to grapple with the enemy.

"It is, it must be, a chimera!" I cried, with tears in my eyes.

Reader, the moral courage inspired by the last spark of faith, is often the fire of the Body Guard—that which decides the battle and gains the victory.

The insignificance of the cause of my alarm, compared with the magnitude of the alarm itself, may excite a smile.

My hobgoblin turned out to be a setter dog belonging in the neighborhood. Insecurely fastened, he had escaped, dragging his chain along with him. The haunted dwelling was one of his places of resort; for persecuted dogs, in common with lonely lovers, ever seem to seek solitary places, where they may pour out their complaints to the moon; besides, dog-rendezvous are notoriously ghost-haunted. My terror had transfigured innocent Tray into a manacled skeleton.

That was the occasion, sir, on which I won my spurs. I became Mabel's true Knight of Romance, and my courage was respected alike by Guilford and Bowes, and by all the Shoepacs and Arabs of the city.

Yet I stood in awe of Stebbins. Stebbins kept a shop—a merchant tailor's shop. It was to return bundles to Stebbins that I was forced to pass by the haunted house. I entertained great fear, or at least extraordinary respect for Mr. Stebbins, perhaps more than for Mr. Magroy, with better liking. He patronized my mother; and all my mother's patrons were angels, or saints, or good genii with golden wands. Stebbins paid promptly; but I stood in great awe of him, because he insisted, with the grandeur becoming a patron, that the "work" should be promptly done; and oh! how sharply he did inspect the aforesaid "work." I remember how I trembled, and how relieved I felt afterwards, as I shrank out of his presence, gained the open street, and capered along homewards.

Stebbins was a tyrant, but he didn't mean to be. His position as patron of poor women, frightened girls, and trembling boys, made him a tyrant in spite of himself. His frown was awful. Why need good men, who give poor people work to do, frown? God loveth a cheerful giver of work to the poor.

Stebbins, then, was a giant—a good giant—but nevertheless a giant; and I have always associated him with the haunted house and the terrible-eyed spectre. Poor Stebbins! when I grew up to be a man, I found him in reality a little dapper-whiskered fellow, not the ninth part of a giant. In fact, he turned out to be the little-dog reality, to the giant apparition of my fears.

Far be it from me, friendly reader, to disparage an old patron. I think well of him, and would have your honor think well, not only of him, but of every acquaintance of mine who shall be introduced to your honor.

Mr. ——, no, Colonel, Stebbins was indeed an important personage in our city. He drilled the Shoepacs long and well. Afterwards he was promoted to the Colonelcy of the 1st Regt., 1st Brig., 1st Dist. Mich. Militia, and rode a great cream-colored horse that jumped wide ditches, kicked his heels in the air, and ran away on field-days, occasionally. Such was the Colonel's popularity that he became Justice of the Peace. This dignity abroad, and a sharp wife at home, promoted Stebbins to an idler—a gentleman-loafer, too proud to work. He began to frequent the tavern, and lounged on the corners of streets.

Now Stebbins has no work to give the poor.

Guilford March was tormented by delusions of another sort.

Owing to his steadiness of character and deliberation of manner, my brother was patronized by lads older, and necessarily wiser, than he.

"Do you chop wood, Guilford? asked one of his young gentlemen acquaintances.

"Of course I do."

"What for?"

"Why my mother works for a living, and I need not be ashamed of it."

"Oh, she's a woman!" replied the rising Solomon.

"Is not your mother a woman too?" demanded Guilford.

"Yes, and she works"—the lady kept a genteel boarding house—"but my father was a gentleman, and I play gentleman too."

"According to my idea, old fellow," said Guilford familiarly, "in this country the gentleman is the man who works—works for himself, his family and others. It was so in ancient times. The real gentlemen of Greece and Rome were those who by their own labors laid the foundation of states. So in the days of chivalry. The great knights worked their way up as pages, squires; could cook a dinner, chop a tree, turn a horseshoe, mend a saddle, knew what hunger was, and with their own hands and strength achieved greatness."

"Why, Guilford, you're a book!"

"No I am a boy," said Guilford, after the fifth vain blow upon a knotty piece of wood which he was essaying to split. The sixth blow was successful.

"Yes, old fellow," continued the lad, as he leant upon his axe and wiped his brow. "I like playing gentleman, its pleasant to stroll and hunt ducks and pigeons; but there's little satisfaction in thinking that it all comes to nothing in the end. I'd like a career."

Accordingly Guilford tried a career. It was three years after our father died. He had been a fond frequenter of the docks, and fallen in love with ships and sailors. My brother Guilford was not immaculate—not infallible, like most young heroes of romance, Guilford ran away, hid himself on board a brig bound for the upper country, and after the vessel had cleared the straits he showed himself to the captain, who pleased with the lad's spirit and engaging frankness and judgment, readily undertook to make a tar of him.

Nobody at home knew what had become of Guilford March during several weeks. Then he wrote to his mother, who never scolded, but replied to his letter in endearing terms, entered with him into the spirit of his undertaking, told him to visit home on next passing Detroit, and promised the usual care of his wardrobe, a kit of which should be ready, nicely washed, mended, and done up, with a little Bible to read.

Guilford called, in a tarpaulin hat with an unfathomable length of black ribbon—which the mischievous Mabel cut off unknown to Jack Tar—white pants with a belt, blue shirt with the collar on the shoulders, and a small quid of tobacco—which seemed to make him sick.

Guilford took but one more trip. His wages were next to nothing, he dreamed of his pale mother. The coarseness of his associates disgusted him.

His return among his old associates and to the little duties about the yard, renewed the irksomeness of a vacuous life.

School did not seem to occupy his mind. Guilford had no very great taste for school books. He learned easily and forgot quickly. His pleasure-grounds lay in histories, and books, where facts of real life, and solid information were spread around him. Yet even these did not fill the void within, or occupy the desert before him.

One day my brother made his appearance before us with his clothes tied up in an Indian shawl. With straight forwardness, he announced to his mother that he was going to seek his fortune.

"What do you propose to do first, my son?" she asked with a smile of good humor peculiar to her.

"Be a farmer, mother."

"Where will you go?"

"Mr. Jumps will take me, I will work my way up till I become the owner of a farm, and then you shall all come and dwell with me."

"Why should you go away from home?"

"This for ever doing servant's work is beneath me, and offers nothing for the future."

"It is not beneath me," mildly remonstrated Mrs. March.

Guilford hesitated; then with a blush he said, "You are not a March, mother, that blood you know comes to me through father.

"How do you do, Lord Guilford?" curtsied Mabel.

But Lord Guilford was not easily abashed; he held on bravely and sturdily to his project—declared that Cincinnatus and Washington were farmers; that his mother could never give both him and John a profession; as for learning any trade, or turning "counter-jumper," he never would; farming was the only work to content him, and—"

"Very well, my son, you shall go," said Mrs. March, and there was a peculiar expression, not entirely free from pain or displeasure on her face, as she said it. She put on her shawl and bonnet and said—

"Come, Guilford, let's go."

My brother turned pale. Mabel ran out of the room. Maud kissed him with a pinch. Our old servant, Bowes, came in, wiping her hands, and told him she'd never forgive him, but she stuffed a plate of dough-nuts into his bundle. As for the chicken-hearted writer of these pages, he blubbered louder than was necessary or usual on parting solemnities. Guilford thrust a stick under the knot of the bundle, threw it over his shoulder, and took up his new line of march.

They found Farmer Jumps just yoking in his oxen near the market.

Mrs. March took him aside and spoke earnestly with him for some time. He listened very attentively; but, whereas my mother talked and looked never more seriously in her life, her auditor seemed on the eve of a momentary explosion from laughter. I do not know what Mrs. March said, although novelists are supposed to hear everything; but Mr. Jumps seemed to concur with the little woman in black very heartily, and said aloud,

"I'll adopt a course with him."

Then my mother took her leave of the good farmer, kissed Guilford tenderly and long, and silently passed away from them. In a few minutes the team was ready. Jumps gave Guilford a lift by the arm, which tossed him easily into the wagon, cracked his long whip, shouting,

"Go 'long! Gee, Bright!"

Guilford March was once more adrift on the wide, wide world.

The absence of my brother was felt at once by all the family. Maud thought she had neglected him. Engrossed as she was with her own secret sorrow, she had not entered into the courts of her brother's troubled heart, and now, with her accustomed self-condemnation, she stood convicted in her own eyes of unsisterly carelessness.

Bowes declared we couldn't keep house without him.

"Law me, suz!" Bowes more than once exclaimed, "if my little man was only at home!"

She always called Guilford her little man. "If my little man was only at home, things wouldn't go on so at sixes and sevens. Why, Miss Maud, he's worth more than all of 'em put together."

"All of 'em," meant myself and a negro man who came over every night to do anything too heavy for me.

Even old Brindle, our whimsical cow, appeared to know the difference. She now came home later in the evening, and presumed occasionally to stay out all night. Finally, her ladyship must be put at pasture. It was with difficulty that I could let down and set up the bars that allowed ingress and egress for old Brindle to and from the pasture-field.

I always felt friendly towards cattle; their breath was so sweet and their ways so odd. It was my delight to drive a long line of them home as the sun was setting, or in the mellow twilight. Brindle always placed herself, methought, at the head of them, as they moved along, swinging and switching their tails and chewing their cuds—increasing in number as they came, and lowing musically in different keys. I had accompanied Guilford sometimes in his wanderings in the woods after the cows, and these wanderings together began to make companions of us again. It led to many long talks, world-wide musings, and extensive foundations for air-castles. After he went, having no one to talk with except an occasional French boy, I went dreaming and talking to myself, thought of my "father in heaven" and my poor mother on earth, and had many a little story to tell Mabel at night, sitting in front of the kitchen fire by ourselves.

But what more of old Brindle?

Ah! she was an eccentric genius. I have already mentioned one peculiarity. Another of her favorite customs was, to kick; she did kick outrageously. She broke her foot once, kicking; though that made no difference, except that one part of the hoof turned over, and rested partly on the other. This made her limp sometimes, but everybody knew it was sheer female affectation; for, let a cow attempt to pass her limping ladyship in the procession home, and see with what a firm, fast, quick tramp she recovered her position at the head of the line. And, as I have already intimated, the broken foot caused no diminution in her kicking propensity. Indeed Bowes always tied her hind legs. When Guilford stood by, however, it was only necessary to lay the rope across her feet, so that she might feel its pressure. It was fly-time now, and Guilford was gone, to boot, and so poor Bowes and Brindle had no peace.

"She kicks dreadfully. I don't know what ails the crittur," quoth Bowes.

CHAPTER XI.

THE SCHOOLMASTER OUT WEST.

On yon gray stone that fronts the chancel door,
Worn smooth by busy feet now seen no more,
Each eve we shot the marble through the ring,
When the heart danced, and life was in its spring.

ROGERS.

SCHOOLBOYS have always their leaders. It is not scholarship that is required so much as courage, audacity, tact. The best scholar may be a Tom Tit, the idlest truant, king.

Our champions were Abe and Dick.

Abraham was a strapping young fellow, no one ever knew where from. He "hired out around town" as the phrase was, and did service, now as ostler and out of doors servant for a gentleman whom every body loved—consequently was universally popular. He was our recognised leader.

Equal to him in all but color was Dick, a clever mulatto boy. His master was a merchant, and his own servant, companion, right arm, everything, was a beautiful dog, a Newfoundland—widely known as "Cap" among friends, and "Captain" among strangers.

Now it is notorious, that the celebrated little city of

Detroit is intersected at right angles through what was formerly the centre of the city—in fact it was thought by many generations that it always would continue to be the centre, notwithstanding the prognostication of the little crazy engineer who, being employed to lay out the streets, threw the centre a mile back from the river. This proceeding only shows how one crazy man may be wiser than a whole city, for time has proved the wisdom of the thing.

If my reader will pardon the digression, I will also relate how the little crack-brained engineer outdid the city wag, even into the putting of money into the good little gentleman's purse.

Few soberminded men foresaw the rapid settlement of the great West at the early time of the *petit maître d'école*, and civil engineer, Monsieur Adolph Theodolite. This prophetic genius, however, did foresee, and made arrangements to enrich himself thereby. He made a map. The emigrant needed a map, inquired for Theodolite's map, bought the little French mathematician's map, and for the first period of his life Adolph owned two good coats. Then the shrewd Yankee auctioneer and city wag, Mr. Jephunneh Nutmeg, with the charitable view of enriching himself even at Adolph's expense —for who would mind taking profitable advantage of a little crazy Frenchman?—entered into negociations for Adolph's map. To Mr. Nutmeg's astonishment Adolph was too prudent to part with his treasure, without a fair compensation. Nutmeg offered fifty *piastres*.

"By gar! Monsieur Nutmeg, you tink me fool, heigh? you shall not have de leetle map for less dan one tousand dollar!"

In vain Nutmeg assured Adolph that the emigration fever would soon subside, and pointed back by way of confirmation to the decades of years already elapsed during which no such thing had ever been known.

Adolph's reply was, "Then what for you want him?"

In vain Nutmeg raised his offer to one hundred, two, five, seven, eight hundred dollars. Monsieur Adolph Theodolite had his legs planted in immovable rock.

Finally Nutmeg paid the price, and issued numerous flaming advertisements which he sent East and West, North and South, far and near.

Meanwhile the witless Adolph was not idle. He took his thousand dollars, went to New York, where he got out an essentially new map covering the same country but embracing new surveys, new towns, new counties, up to the last hour.

What was the surprise of Jephunneh, the shrewd Yankee? His visions of riches gone! Outwitted by a Frenchman, little better than a fool! How the towns-people laughed in their sleeve as they passed the auctioneer! How they stopped at the street-corners and joked about it!

It was good to the *ancien régime* thus in the midst of the conflict raging between their easy old customs, and the sharp, eager, pushing innovations of the Yankees, to see one of their little ones gain the advantage.

Monsieur Adolph Theodolite gave up school teaching and surveying for the nonce, and took to selling his new map, which brought him a fortune. Would we might leave him here. The restless little man plunged into new schemes, dived with excitement into the sea of speculation, and came out the same as a poor man. .

Alas! poor Adolph Theodolite!

And yet the wisdom of his enterprises is now admitted. Steepled ports and towns are towering where he predicted they would stand. Like most men in advance of his age he was stigmatized, in a laughing way, as insane.

But to our story.

At the intersection of the two main avenues of the city stood the market-house, where the butchers from time immemorial had honored Saint Patrick by hanging his saintship in effigy. This, or rather the open square in front, was the common rendezvous for the clients of Abe and Dick.

Soon after dusk on any moonlight night, in pleasant seasons of the year, you might hear the loud whistle and cheery voice of Abe, as he came capering down the street. Then followed the banging of doors, as the lads rushed out after him, having incontinently thrown down their books.

From the opposite part of the town came Dick, trolling one of the early negro melodies, "Zip Coon," or "Ole Virginny neber tire," with the loud accompaniment of rattling and banging doors, as the boys from his end of the city flew after Dick.

When gathered at the market-square, what sports! what merry games of red lion, crack the whip, or leap-frog!

Sometimes we would consort together at the school-yard—that green spot in every man's memory. Our school-yard was covered with grass. The basement of the school-house made us a capital jail. Abe was the jailor, Dick the sheriff, with Cap for deputy. We hid ourselves anywhere within certain limits in the vicinity of the school-house; and when buried far in the depths of a hay-loft, or among the dark places of some ruined building, or in a wood-pile, I used to enjoy such excitement—listening for the dreaded, yet half-wished-for steps of the stealthy Dick, and the searching Cap, with his eager bark or disappointed snuffle.

Cap was trained to the highest point. He was as accomplished a man or boy catcher as a bloodhound, and as expert a thief as any London pickpocket. Seldom known to bite, he would hold you gently by the collar till his master came up, and then pick your pocket with a grace. Dick was such a good-hearted fellow, he never abused the power this dog gave him over the boys. Little did I know then how much influence the acquaintance with this mulatto was one day to exert over my earthly career. Lucky, happy days of boyhood's democratic equality! I love you more and more as I look back.

Behold us again, seated or lying on the grass in the bright moonshine, or along the fence, perched like so many sociable birds, telling stories or singing songs. Those were times when the wisest of us all more than half-believed the tales of fairy land, the Arabian Nights' Entertainments, and Pilgrim's Progress—an astounding favorite with me. And who now so rash as gainsay the truth of the good old stories? Happy he who partakes largely of these Eden trees, eating the fruits in childhood, and digesting the truth of them further on in his pilgrimage!

Then the music of childhood, boyhood, youth! What opera airs, trilled by *maestro* or *prima donna*, so sweet as the good old simple songs, in the long ago of tender years and tender hearts?

Dick's negro melodies, with our rude choruses, were miracles of harmony. But "Blue-eyed Stranger," that was one of Dick's better songs, our greatest favorite. Then there was a little lisping urchin, a tavern-keeper's son, whose singing was popular, from his lisp, and from the quaintness and rustic simplicity of the words. I remember but one verse:

"Oh! can she knit,
And can she sew,
And can she make
The shuttle go,
Jimmy, Jimmy, boy?
Yes, she can knit,
And she can sew,
And she can make
The shuttle go,
Mammy, mammy, dear."

Whereupon, in the succeeding verses, the mother grants consent, and Jimmy marries the accomplished damsel he loves and praises.

But independent of Dick's dog and his Blue-eyed Stranger, there was an additional interest excited by Dick in the hearts of small boys at that time. The Morgan excitement was running high, and Dick the sheriff, on catching an urchin, always inquired—

"Mason or Anti-mason?"

and let the prisoner go free, or *toted* him off to the jail, according to his reply. We youngsters long thought Dick must be initiated in all the dreadful mysteries of the secret order. And to this day, I remove my hat reverently whenever I meet a man known to be a Mason (or even Know Nothing), for Dick's sake. That both Abe and Dick were Shoepacs I never had the least doubt, and I respect them accordingly.

A distinguished occasion once served to test the ability and courage of our champions. After having managed the schoolmasters since the beginning of time, as proved by all accounts, both traditional and historical, the boys of our quaint little antique city had imposed upon them, at the hands of Archibald Magroy, LL.D. and other trustees, a master who dared to assume the reins of government himself. During the golden age when Allen and John were little lads, the numbers of ferules and birchen rods destroyed must have been great. An occasional punishment by violence was tolerated, but every abuse of the penal power was resented, either secretly or openly, by the good fellows of the school; and schoolmasters were taught, by wholesome experience, what those limits were, beyond which they passed at their peril.

The present worshipful chancellor of the rod, Mr. Merciful Thrasher, chose, presumingly, to mark the jurisdiction of his own court of equity; and such an infraction of popular sovereignty was not to be tolerated. Mr. Thrasher was a gentleman of medium height, slender figure, a decided expression and manner, and much pride of character. His first step was to take the bull by the horns, and thrash the largest youths. His boldness overawed the little Athens, and they forthwith began to conspire together to undermine his throne; but by virtue of his spies, he outwitted them here. As a measure of last resort, the aid of Abe and Dick, their allies, was demanded.

An innocent little fight between two lads—bullies among their fellows—had been arranged and went off nicely. The principals, accessories—before and after—witnesses—in short all parties to this case, were brought to light, and on the following day were to be brought to punishment. Now the time-honored right to put boy against boy and raise a fight at a moment's notice had, to say the least, been winked at by all persons in authority—and here the oppressed parties determined to make a stand for their ancient privileges.

A meeting was held by night in the school yard.

The case is stated.

"Well," said Abe, "what is he going to do?"

"I shouldn't wonder," replied one, "if he flogged us to-morrow from a to izzard."

"With what?"

"He sent out this afternoon to the bush, and had a dozen birch sticks cut and brought in.

"I'm of the opinion," quoth Dick, "that you'd better all cut stick yourselves—that is, come up missing to-morrow morning."

"That will only defer the matter till another day. All Merciful takes his time. I never knew him to whip a chap on the spur of the moment. He's as cool as a cucumber."

"Then," said Dick, "suppose you all quit school?"

"Folks at home won't stand that."

"Then I gives it up."

Abe, however, was not of Dick's despairing humor.

"Where are those rods?" he asked.

"In the desk."

"Can you unlock it?"

"No, we've tried all the keys in the town I believe, every one of us brought all we could from home."

"Is the school-house door locked?"

"Yes."

"Are the windows fastened?"

"No."

"Abe, and Dick, and several of the larger boys now drew off a one side for consultation. On their return they announced nothing to be done that night, and the little fellows were told they might as well go home—which the most of us, myself among the number, innocently did. It came to light afterwards that there was a lurking suspicion in the breast of one of our urchins, who ran straight to Mr. Thrasher's lodgings, and made known to the master everything that had been so far said or done.

Shortly afterwards Abe and Dick, who had pretended to go home, returned to the school-yard in company with the boys, and proceeded to fulfill their intention. The rods must be destroyed that night by some means or other. At last it was thought best, for fear of detection, that the two champions only should have a hand in it, for there was as great a desire to outwit their master as to escape the threatened flogging.

Accordingly the two worthies advanced to a window and raised it. Abe climbed in. Dick remained outside standing guard. The first thing heard from Abe was an exclamation of pain as his leg came in sharp contact with a bench.

Dick laughed, "Hope it wasn't you shin, old boy, he! he!"

Abe was next heard to utter something about the darkness of the room, and all was again silent.

"Can't you find the desk?" whispered Dick.

"No! I don't believe there ever was one here."

"Be quick!" said Dick; "I hear a step.

"Quick! quick! golly, somebody's coming—Massa Thrasher himself!"

"I've found 'em!" cried Abe.

"So have I, you rascals!" pealed forth the voice of All Merciful, as he pushed his way through the dark to where Dick stood, whom not minding, he sprang for the open window to catch the ringleader himself.

"Don't let him in!" cried Abe.

Cap had already seized the schoolmaster by the seat of his pantaloons.

"Down! down, Cap!" cried Dick, as he took hold himself. The obedient Cap let go, and Dick drew down the enemy, who turned upon him fiercely; and while the two were struggling, Abe shouted—

"Hold him! hold him!" until he had destroyed the rods, regained the window, and leaped over their heads to the ground.

According to the plan previously concerted, the two champions were to escape detection, if possible. By a violent jerk, Dick succeeded in extricating himself from the clutch of Mr. Thrasher, and took to his heels. But ere Abe, who stood by, waiting to see his companion free, could follow his example, All Merciful grasped him, evidently bent on distinguishing who it might be that had so boldly invaded his dominions and destroyed his magazines. But Abe was favored by the darkness.

"Let go! Let go! I give you fair warning," said Abe, averting his face.

"Who are you, sir? I believe you are a thief, sir!" cried Mr. Merciful Thrasher.

This enraged the honest Abraham, and twining one of his long arms around the schoolmaster, he grasped the slender man as if in a vice, and lifting him from the ground, attempted to overthrow him by an effort of main strength. But it seemed that Merciful was no poor wrestler, and his agility put him on a level with Abe, and a regular wrestling match ensued. Dick would fain have aided his friend, but the latter ordered him off.

"Keep off, Dick, just see fair play!"

By this time a few of the boys had gathered around the wrestlers. Great was their mingled awe, astonishment, joy, and semi-regret, to behold the only master they had ever feared or respected wrestling on the grass with Abe the ostler. At last Abe got his adversary under, so as to hold him.

"Promise to do nothing about it, Mr. Thrasher," said the boys' champion.

"Never!" gasped forth the schoolmaster from between his teeth.

Two of the boys came forward and interceded for their vanquished enemy. But Abe vowed he would hold him down until morning, unless he promised what was required. Attempting at this moment to change his hold, his adversary seized the instant, and nearly succeeded in turning Abe. The latter now called for Dick, and by means of a combined effort they dragged the discomfited knight of the birch to the door of the basement story of the schoolhouse—their jail—and were about to make him prisoner, long enough, at least, for them to secure their own escape, when Mr. Thrasher rendered the promise.

"Neither to say anything about this night, nor punish any of the boys to-morrow?"

"Neither!"

"Never flog any of them again?"

"Never!"

"Keep your word like a man?"

"Yes!"

Abe and Dick let go.

"Gentlemen," said Merciful Thrasher, to those of his scholars who were standing near, "I have taught school in many places. This is my first defeat. I shall take a steamboat to-morrow morning for the West."

The boys handed him his cap in silence. He drew it over his brows, and strode homewards—the boys making way for him respectfully.

Before he reached his quarters, however, he was overtaken by a committee of the lads, who attempted to apologize through their spokesman.

"No sir! no sir! No apologies."

They offered, in the name of the school, to make any amends in their power.

"No sir. You were obliged to call in foreign aid. I will not trust any of you again. No atonement possible—no atonement."

His feelings, however, were touched by their kindness and regret. He shook hands with them gratefully, yet proudly, requesting them to prevent the lads of the school from going to the boat the next morning to see him off. This was readily promised.

On the following morning the school met as usual. Nothing was said of the incidents of the previous night until the hour of the steamer's departure had gone by. When the fact of the vacancy of the throne was announced, three cheers were given for the dethroned monarch, three times three for Abe and Dick. The boys dispersed for their homes with the news, too good, almost, to be true,—"No school! no school!"

The question of school discipline now became one of grave importance with the city patriarchs and squires. The interregnum lasted many months, no one being forthcoming of sufficient self-confidence to assume the pedagogic reins.

After great pains, and extensive inquiries over the Eastern States, the place of Merciful Thrasher was filled.

The name of this hardy adventurer was Oliphant, and he was an M.D. The boys called him Dr. Oily Fat. Boys are ingenious at nicknames; they frequently express contraries. So it was in this case, for Oily Fat was as lean as Cassius, and never had known the luxury of fat in his life. But he was an athletic, sinewy man, and combined knowledge with power beyond precedent or rivalry.

What his true history was, no one ever knew; for he told such extraordinary things of himself, that no one but the youngest pretended to believe anything he said —at least concerning himself. And yet it *might be* true, for he appeared equal to any emergency. The doctor was a remarkable man every way. His look was ludicrously frightful; he had straight standing black hair, black eyes that "never fell before mortal or immortal," so Oily Fat often declared emphatically, and immense whiskers. Those whiskers! I never shall forget them. One was black, the other a fiery red! This is no fiction. Did he not dye the red one every month or two, and did he not, while the process of coloring was going on, wear a white kerchief around his face, and say he had the tooth-ache, when any little innocent kindly inquired of the doctor what was the matter?

Doctor Oliphant's appearance went a long way in his favor from the threshold. Then his course of proceedings was no less inspiring. God forgive him the false words he spake, though doubtless for our good, and in order to obtain that influence necessary over young minds, and the use of that ferule necessary to young shoulders.

He had taught school in no less than fifteen States This was not the first occasion he had been summoned to break in refractory schools. He had been sent for frequently from one end of the Union to the other for precisely this purpose. He never had any trouble but twice. In Georgia, he was obliged to knock down ever so many tall fellows. He had marvellous stories of handcuffs and fetters. And in Tennessee he did not succeed in curbing the spirit of insubordination until he introduced coffins, and laid pistols on the table, coolly remarking, that the first mutineer should fill one of those coffins.

His pathway to our hearts was no less bold and admirable, though not so horribly picturesque. He permitted little manifestations of insubordination on the part of small boys to pass. The first victim was the largest boy in school, and son of the greatest man in the city, no less a dignitary than our newly-arrived Governor. This youth was a wild, good fellow, the ringleader in all mischief. On this occasion he declared the master should not thrash a certain one of the little fellows, as the doctor was proceeding to administer one or two light blows of his ferule on the hand of a wincing, whimpering urchin.

I shall not attempt to describe the scene which was enacted before our eyes. Suffice to say, the doctor conquered, and flogged the rebel intermeddler soundly. He seemed never to have done. He ordered him to stand on the benches, on the desks, on the very stove, and at each hesitation on the part of the victim, he administered a "dose," as we always called his thwacks.

That bold punishment put an end to school-boy reign in our city. Many fine points there were, too, about our terrible master. His absolute sway was never abused but in the one instance recorded. A poor boy, or one of tender years, he scarcely punished. He was an eloquent lecturer, and introduced an entire change in studying, for although it had traditionally been voted a bore to study—now it became a pleasure. He lectured enthusiastically on arithmetic, the driest of subjects, and performed beautiful experiments in chemistry—then a new science among us. So great was the interest in this study, that many scapegraces sat up all the night, voluntarily, and laboriously burnished plates of the now old-fashioned galvanic battery, with which he performed such wonders!

Yes, I believe, after all, that our good friend, Dr. Oliphant was a gentleman and a scholar; And if God forgave, or he himself believed, the ingenious fictions which he palmed off upon our credulous young minds, I have no doubt he died as a Christian. God may forgive a falsehood told a child, but the child never does. No matter what apparent necessity, or how good soever the motive, when you come to detect the deceit, and see that those who had the care of you imposed upon you, trifled with your understanding, cheated, deluded you, it lessens your confidence in the integrity of man, and violates the majesty of truth eternal in your breast.

CHAPTER XII.

A GLIMPSE OF SQUATTER LIFE.

None can describe the sweets of country life,
But those blessed men, that do enjoy and taste them.
MAY'S *Agrippina*.

"WHEN will Guilford come home, mamma?" said Mabel, one evening as we were all sitting around the sewing-table.

"I wish, Mabel might tell me," replied my mother. "He grew weary of the apron-strings, I suppose; and became too much of a man for 'chores.'"

"Too much of a man!" exclaimed Mabel, "why, he is only twelve years of age—not much older than Walter, and he never will grow tired of us, I know."

"Twelve years!" said Maud, "he is twelve centuries! Has he not running in his veins all the blood of all the Howards?"

We were laughing at this when the door opened and there appeared an unknown character in a strange costume for our town—not yet opulent enough for beggars. A little old stunted giant in rags, at least out at the elbows and out at the knees, his hat torn on the crown, and slouched over his dirty face. No one recognised this unique personage.

"Friends," came a low voice, "can you give me something to eat and a"——

Here the low voice broke down completely.

"Take off your hat, young sir," said Mrs. March, not knowing what else to say.

The hat was removed.

"Guilford! Guilford!" shouted Mabel, and she ran up to the ragged urchin and threw her arms about his neck.

Mrs. March, too, caught him in her arms and strained him hysterically to her breast. "My boy! my Guilford! my son! what in the world has happened thee? Where have you been? How comes this so?"

"Farming," answered Guilford.

Then he came and sat down between Maud and me in front of the bright fire-place, while Mabel ran out to tell the news to Bowes.

"I have had enough of farming," said Guilford.

"Good! good!" laughed and cried Mabel, who reappeared with Bowes, wiping her hands on her apron again and again. She always did this when excited.

Bowes ran up wildly to her "little man," kissed him and rushed out nearly tearing her apron to pieces. Then Bowes flew away to the cow-yard, shouting

"The little man's come! Brindle, the little man's come!"

And she patted Brindle on the shoulder. But that dignified quadruped vouchsafed no reply. She gave one or two uneasy switches with her tail, and finally tossed her horns wickedly around towards the little crazy woman. And Bowes called her an old thing, or hussy, or something severe, and hurried back to the kitchen, where she found Mabel zealously hunting after some potatoes to put on to roast for the hungry returned prodigal. Then Bowes and Mabel had a very satisfactory talk on the exciting cause of so much stir about the house, and in a little while they came in with cold meat, hot baked Mackinaw potatoes, Bowes's bread, and Brindle's butter.

As soon as he had finished his supper everybody drew near the fire, Bowes and all, to hear Guilford's story. But as he was frequently interrupted, and he himself frequently strayed off in his narration, we shall convey it to the reader in a more straight-forward manner of our own, though the story may suffer by the telling.

Farmer Jumps and Guilford reached the farm-house at about nightfall. The sweet smell of the woods pleased Guilford now in a new sense, he began to feel a sort of proprietorship in it, it was to be his atmosphere.

Great was the manifest surprise of Dame Jumps on beholding our little hero. How a well-dressed city boy should ask her old man Jumps to come out and live on the farm, was a nine days' wonder: she continued all the evening to gaze at him with astonishment.

"Why Jumps, what on airth are you going to do with him?"

"Make a farmer of him."

"Wall, I do declare! Wall, did you ever? Wall, I never!" was all that she could add.

There were three little Jumpses, though one, the eldest, was a pretty long leap, a tall stem of a youth, that looked as if he had sprouted forth in a night. This was Joram Jumps. He was about fourteen years of age. Then came a boy of twelve, and a flaxen-haired limp of a girl of ten. The children seemed to regard Guilford with the wonder of their mother, added to a little awe of their own, and they moved about like mutes, treating their city guest with an occasional stare.

The interior of our beautiful peninsula was but thinly settled, and the country around Farmer Jumps's was almost a wilderness. His house was a mere cabin of logs, chinked with a clayey mud, composed of one story, and that contained but the common room in which the family ate, sat, slept, shook with fever and ague, and held periodical prayer meetings for the pioneers of the neighborhood.

Some short cakes were baking in a spider over the coals as Guilford entered. An iron tea-kettle was singing a cheerful welcome and waving its little fleecy banners of steam, and by the time Jumps had turned off the cattle and re-entered, the cabin, was filled with the rich odor of frying pork and potatoes, and Dame Jumps, assisted by her daughter, whose name was Susannah, was setting the table for supper.

The crockery-ware, said Guilford, consisted of the odds and ends of many different old sets, of as many different colors, originally brown, blue, white—even yellow was not wanting. These relics of antiquity were ostentatiously set up, each piece separately, on its edge, on the shelves of a red cupboard. It seems that above everything in the house, except her feather bed, Mrs. Jumps valued her "*cheena*," as she denominated this rubbish of broken wares; and it is a curious fact, that people always bother themselves and fret away their lives on what they foolishly fancy gives them the most happiness. So it was with the dame, as, with a trembling care, Suz handed down the plates, cups, and saucers for the table, her mother fumed and scolded at her, at every turn, lest she should break the cheena.

Before the table was set, Suz had quite fully enlisted, though unknowingly, the sympathy of Guilford. This sympathy was still further excited when all drew up to the table; for when Mrs. Jumps came to pour tea from a black tea-pot with a cover that would be ever coming off, and when Mrs. Jumps deposited sugar in the cups, she put the least in Susannah's—poor Suz was the only one at the table who cared for sugar at all. But Guilford managed so as to give the little pouting girl his own cup. This won her over to him; so that after supper, and she had helped her mother to clear away the dishes, and received the same amount of abuse as before supper, on account of the cheena, she got the two brothers together, and all three of the farmer's children settled around Guilford very sociably for the evening, in the light of the fire, candles being reckoned an extravagance. It may be needless to say what everybody knows—that all town boys are regarded by their country cousins as a sort of superior race. This inly acknowledged superiority, however, the country lads are ever ready to dispute. To Guilford's knowledge, on the occasion before us, these farmer lads were soon ready to defer, for the purpose of more fully extracting information on sundry matters in which they stood in ignorance.

Accordingly Guilford interested them deeply in his accounts of caravans, circuses, militia-trainings, fire engines, skates, schools, kites, tops, jewsharps, and marbles. They were disappointed, however, to find he knew so little about ginger-bread, a goodly array of which, in bird-like, beast-like, man-like, and woman-like forms, they had once seen in a shop window. There had been a lurking disposition at first, on the part of the young Jumpses, to humble my brother next day—so Susannah afterwards revealed;—but his frankness, and the satisfactory information he gave, on the whole, changed their intentions; and far from desiring now to expose his ignorance of the various secrets of woodcraft, they resolved to aid him all in their power to learn farming. As for Suz, she was perfectly charmed, as she told me long afterwards, with his gentleness and superior understanding. To her, Guilford was of a new order of being, and at once she began to "slick up," as she said.

Then bed-time came. Guilford had observed but one

bed, and wondered whether Jumps and his wife and family and he were all to sleep in it. But Mrs. Jumps soon solved that problem, by drawing from beneath the bedstead a truckle bed large enough to hold the three boys; and a couch was made for Susannah on a long blue chest—which, by the way, had probably held their worldly goods and chattels when they emigrated from Vermont.

Mr. Jumps being the last to retire, blew out the light, that is to say, covered up the fire, leaving the hearth in sole possession of a speckled cat, and a pan of buckwheat batter, placed there to "rise" for breakfast. But no sooner did silence prevail in the loghouse, than Guilford heard a long dismal howl, that arose from the woods in the midst of which they lay. Soon came another, longer, and mingled with fellow-howls, each one seeming to draw nigher and nigher to the door, till at length it seemed to be besieged with a roar of dismal howlings.

Guilford drew the coverlid over his head; but his bed-fellows only laughed at his fears. Ashamed of betraying himself in such wise to these country bumpkins, he uncovered his head. A perfect blast of roars and threats, mingled with whines and screeches of disappointed yet greedy rage saluted his ears.

"What is it?" demanded he in a whisper.

"Nothing but wolves. Go to sleep."

"How do you like country music, boy?" asked Mrs. Jumps, with a coarse laugh.

Mr. Jumps interposed now, and soothed the alarm of Guilford by telling him that the animals were of a small, harmless sort, and though they had howled, apparently, at the door every night since he had squatted there, yet on getting up to drive them away he never found them anywhere near, so that now the family took no notice of them.

At daybreak the household was astir. Guilford arose with his bedfellows, and Mr. Jumps set him at once to work. He was dispatched with Tobias, or Toby, as they called the younger lad, after the cows. They were soon found, and easily driven home; but Guilford returned with his feet and legs wet to the knees in the heavy dew. Then he assisted Joram at chopping wood for the house, so that breakfast-time found him already fatigued. Even Susannah laughed a little at his pale looks, but soon checked herself, for fear of breaking a piece of the yellow cheena she was taking from its throne on the red cupboard. My brother was not at all discouraged; he had a stout heart, and breakfast refreshed him. After the morning meal, all went to a small clearing not far from the house—not more than forty acres of the Jumps estate was as yet under cultivation. The work before them now was *follering*, as the squatters called it, or clearing the land of felled trees or brushwood. Serviceable logs were drawn off, and that which was left they gathered into great heaps, and set on fire. Jumps and Joram busied themselves with the logs, and made the woods ring again with the blows of their axes, and the sound of their voices as they shouted over the oxen.

When dinner-time came, Dame Jumps appeared in the angel avocation of blowing a trumpet—that is to say sounding a long tin horn. She showed herself at the corner of the cabin, and with the instrument applied to her mouth with one hand, while the other arm she held akimbo at her side to assist in the mighty effort, she brayed forth a Jericho-shaking blast. There was no resisting this call, it said in Mrs. Jumps's most decided manner:

"Dinner's ready, and waits for no man."

Guilford was hungry and ate heartily. He deserved some reward for his plight. His hands were scratched, his face blackened, and his eyes filled up with cinders. Suz expressed her sympathy by bringing a tin wash-basin, and water—none of the cleanest—from a spring near by the house, distilling through the black vegetable mould into a barrel which was half alive with insects, while occasionally, a lingering frog who had come up to sun his body out of the torpor of an October day, plumped himself down with a splash as you approached.

After dinner the party betook themselves to the clearing again, where they worked away till near nightfall, when Toby and Guilford were again dispatched for the cows; no trifling errand, as the animals wandered far during the day—water in the woods being plenty—and the boys were both fatigued.

And the evenings, how different they at Green Run

from our sweet, quiet, yet lively evenings in the library at home! The good humor and refinement of my mother, the high-toned, soft spoken morality of Maud, the incessant raillery of Mabel; these were exchanged for the blunt good sense of Mr. Jumps, the trumpet clangor of Mrs. Jumps, and the vacant wonderment of the young Jumpses.

A fortnight or more the male inhabitants of the cabin were engaged in the clearing, during which time the fatigues were too great to admit of much conversation at night. On some very pleasant evenings, however, the fascinating Indian summer atmosphere would tempt them to sit out in front of the door, one on a bench, another on the stump of a log, and while the evening came on, soothed into quiet by the chirrup of the cricket, and the monotonous drone of the tree toad, and lit up by the fire-flies in the bush, Jumps would hush the ever prevailing complaints of his wife, and the stupid questionings of his sons, and moralize learnedly over his pipe to the more intelligent Guilford.

"If I weren't a farmer, I never would be one; no, its the last calling on airth for a man in this country. Now here's my boys and that gal, what do they know? hardly enough to come in when it rains. Now, let me advise you to adopt a course."

"Yes sir," said Guilford, "what course would you adopt, Mr. Jumps?"

"Wall, every man that gits tired doin anything else, or breaks down in life, always thinks he can make a farmer of himself, just as easy as rollin off a log, but it ain't so tarnal easy. A man ought to have a turn for it, with a constitution like a horse. He must work like a dog, and be weather-wise as the Prophet Elijah. And that ain't all nuther—he must adopt a course."

"Yes sir," said Guilford—who knew already that "to adopt a course," was the Jumps philosophy—his panacea for every ill. Jumps rarely condescends to explain himself after uttering this indisputable dogma. And so now, he arose, entered the house to rekindle his pipe, and reappeared with a live coal, which he shifted rapidly from his right hand to his left, and as swiftly from his left hand to his right, vainly endeavoring to plant it in the bowl. The refractory coal dropped on the floor. Jumps took the tongs to it.

"Yes!" resumed the smoking philosopher, "a man may think he knows all about farming and get his fingers burnt after all. Now if it weren't for fear of going through the woods like an over particular gal, and taking up with a crooked stick after all, I'd change my"—

At this moment Joram broke in.

"Dad, don't you think I'd make a smart minister of the gospel?"

Mr. Jumps, senior, did not reply. He rose up hastily, knocked the ashes from the bowl of his pipe on the nail of his thumb, went in the cabin, covered up the fire, and —went to bed.

"Every fool thinks he can be a preacher, too," quoth Guilford to himself.

Guilford was not too young to perceive some of the hopeful peculiarities of thought and feeling among the squatters.

First, they were of the opinion that their lot in life was a little the hardest on the face of the earth.

Second, to vex the patient souls of this primitive people, there must always needs be something wrong in the daily course of events—peculiarly theirs to suffer—the world around them of course exempt, as everybody else's world always is, and always was, of a *couleur de rose*.

The cow was always dry; the ox always wanted shoeing; an utensil was always broke, or a neighbor had borrowed it just when it was wanted; the weather never suited the crops, and the crops neither suited the weather nor came up to their expectations; there never was time to do what was required to be done *now;* Mrs. Jumps thought she worked herself to death, and had no comforts; Susannah was always out of shoes, and yet *would* wear them, though they cost a fortune; the boys wanted jack-knives, jewsharps, new caps, and school-books—they never could be prevailed upon to study when they got them. In short, Mr. and Mrs. Jumps had left the pleasantest home, the dearest friends, the most lucrative business, the best schools, the grayest parson, and the greenest hills, at home in good old *Vairmount*, to come to Michi*gan*, where they had no neighbors, no parson, no hills, and the children were growing up without education, they were all working themselves *to* death, and, after all, didn't seem to get on. With reference to the last complaint, we may as well anticipate a few years, and state, that notwithstanding this melancholy list of grievances, the Jumpses continued to exist, nay, to thrive, from year to year, till, as we shall see, in due time, they had the best farm in the county, and the Jumpses became one of the "first families."

Guilford observed this very satisfactory account, which it gave them such evident delight to draw, and thought that as it is only necessary to see an evil in order to avoid falling into it ourselves, he himself would do better; therefore, he continued to hold on steadily to his course.

But Mr. Jumps seemed to take a peculiar pleasure in making Guilford March work.

"You have adopted a course, my little fellow," he would say, "and you must stick to it through thick and thin."

Accordingly, there was little peace or rest for the poor boy, until night came. He began to fancy himself growing dull, like Joram and Toby. The thought horrified him; yet all the boys he saw were of the same species. "All work and no play makes Jack a dull boy," sure enough, thought he.

There were a hundred people in the vicinity—two-thirds of them were down with ague or bilious fever.

The nearest neighbors to Farmer Jumps were the O'Gradys. They lived a mile down the creek or run, whose greenish, vegetable color, gave name to this neighborhood. They were Irish; had been in better circumstances, they said, as all old country people, I believe, do say. Whether they descended from the King O'Grady I never have learned, but I dare say they did.

At any rate, their descent was very great, as both husband and wife got drunk, and frightened Guilford more than once with their dreadful oaths and beastly conduct.

It was some time in December that an incident happened in the O'Grady family, which, added to what had already been preying upon the sensitive youth's feelings, was the means of his leaving the detestable precincts of Green Run.*

* The incident alluded to is a fact that came to the personal knowledge of the writer, on the occasion of a visit he made, in his boyhood, to the farm of an uncle in a new country.

An Irishwoman being taken with the pains of childbirth, this writer was mounted on the only horse in the neighborhood, and dispatched to the nearest village, seven miles distant, after a doctor. On my return, the affair was over, and I overheard my uncle and aunt talking about it in the night after all the house had gone to rest.

It seems that the child survived its birth but a few moments. The husband arose from the bed, where he had been lying in a maudlin state, seized the infant from one of the good squatter women attending, and in the midst of profane execrations flung at the head of his wife, he took water, baptized the child with his sacrilegious hand, and tossed it over the back log into the burning fire.

Of course the author does not pretend to infer, that such evil practices are common among the pioneers of the West. Yet it were vain to deny, that brute force, and independence from the restraints of civilization, develop themselves under revolting forms here and there—especially among the semi-barbarous elements introduced from foreign shores.

The terrible event haunted his imagination day and night, and gave a horrible significance to the howling of the wolves.

He took sudden flight one morning when he had been sent after the cows, without Tobias, who had cut his foot. He left his best suit of clothes behind him, with the secret of his flight, in Susannah's keeping, and appeared before us in the manner already related.

My mother's plan for curing Guilford of a desire for farm-life had succeeded—aided as it was by fortuitous circumstances, of which the good lady never had dreamed.

"My son, you will go to school to-morrow."

"Yes, my dear mother, as soon as I have wood enough chopped to last Bowes all day."

CHAPTER XIII.

THE RIVALS.

It is a fearful thing
To love as I love thee, to feel the world—
The bright, the beautiful, joy-giving world—
A blank without thee.

L. E. L.

MRS. MARCH was an ambitious little woman—at least for her children. To educate them for the well-doing of their parts in life, to fit them likewise for a better world, and to render them not only useful but agreeable members of society, were grand objects ever before her. No straight-lace philosopher was she. The tree of life was not to be trimmed into an Egyptian pyramid at her hands, but its boughs were to be adorned with things pleasant to behold and sweet to the taste. In a word, Mrs. March's maxims of morality constantly relaxed into the means of present and prospective happiness. In another word, with all her notions of right and wrong, sense and nonsense, she was—or rather wished to be—as sociable a little lady as the most sociable town the northwest boasted, might be able to produce.

There were many fine old-fashioned parties at Lilac Cottage, which, by the by, was not ill qualified for such gatherings. A long, wide hall, two large parlors, and the library, furnished room enough for the guests to dance to their hearts' content.

It may not be generally known how the houses were furnished in those part French, part Indian, and part American times.

Behold a pair of huge elk antlers bristling at one end of the hall, and stag antlers at the other. See a long birch bark canoe stretched along the sidewalk—possibly effigies of Indians sit there in full trappings, with red paddles in their hands. Be this last as it may, walk into the parlor and view the portrait of a noble red man—who unlike most of us white men had a name of his own, won by manly deeds. The other ornaments of the room may be quivers of arrows, light and graceful snowshoes, marvellous moccasins, painted feather headdresses, and porcupine work.

The cost of an entertainment in those unfashionable days did not compose, as now, the chief item of boast. A couple of Frenchmen and a negro for fiddlers, set the affair agoing, and people made themselves merry with each other. A haunch of venison, a couple of wild turkeys, Colville apples, sandwiches, and hickory nuts, cake, wine and brandy, formed the simple refreshments. And such smacking of honest lips, and such brimming bumpers to the toast, and such polite toasts with graceful allusions to the next wedding, and such gems of anecdotes and witty sallies, and pealing laughter, in a word such merry men and pretty women never got together and made themselves and each other happy elsewhere in the world. But then, such a total absence of stiff bows and grand funeral procession entrées, tipping of white-gloved fingers, conceited artists, frothy authors, Munchausen travellers, after-dinner speech-making parsons, painted belles, eye-glass beaux, honiton frippery and foreign air foppery—the absence of these *things* so essential to a present time *soirée*, or *reception*, or *at home* refined assemblage, causes me to draw back lest I lose caste in describing my dear old friends' parties.

There were no pianos in our city at that time. It was not until several years subsequently that my ears were stunned with the Battle of Prague, or my sensibility blunted by school-girl thumpings of Days of Absence. The first piano created a sensation; people listened with a mixture of curiosity, wonder, awe, and pleasure; you might have heard a pin drop. How happy are we now that those fine instruments are best appreciated when silent. That is to say, the crack performer, some corner-loving governess, or professional player, or bashful school-damsel, is requested to play by all the assembly, urged forward, pushed through, and when once seated to her melodious task, everybody sets up a tempest-roar of talking, which drowns the voice of your obliging performer.

Behold one of our pretty lasses in the antique city called upon for Sweet Home, or other English ballad; or a twinkling eyed French girl for a merry song of sunny France; or a bluff Scot for John Anderson my Joe; or an Irish gentleman for a humorous catch, and everybody for a chorus—that was a thing got up to be enjoyed.

But of all things a French wedding was the most celebrated for downright enjoyment. My eyes fill with swimming scenes of mirth as memory recalls one of those joyous occasions. The real fountain of rejuvenation was a French wedding. Here old people bathed and came out young again. The oldest danced for dear life, and the gayest and lightest dancer was sure to be some fat and heavy old gentleman, with a no less elderly and sizable partner. They bowed and courtesied with a grace and a joy, they tip-toed it up and down, round and about, pirouetted and coquetted, balanced and swung, cheated and chased, with a vivacity that brought hoary old Time himself into the set as youthful and happy as the rest of them. Such innocent, hearty, and delightful frolics give your bridal couple a fair start in life, though I have little doubt they might startle the soft and gentle votaries of fashion from many an accustomed nap through a cotillion. But we have no fault to find. Let each enjoy himself in his own way, the hearty heartily—the feeble feebly.

Those were dangerous times for old bachelors, though the less said of such unhappy souls the better. Nevertheless at the period to which in the course of our history we last arrived, a new admirer of Miss Maud's appeared on the field, a veritable, ancient bachelor, one of the most glorious specimens of that worthy class.

Major Fontenoy was an officer of our army in the late war. He had been stationed in different parts of the country, but having seen Detroit—he was serving in the unfortunate Hull expedition—had fallen in love with her. Ten years after the war closed he resigned his commission and came to be one of her children. The major was fond of young people. He had long known Miss Maud, but as she always avoided notice, he never found it worth his while to be struck with her charms until now. On this occasion he attended one of our little evening parties, and as he entered the room, Maud sat at a species of dulcimer, singing some sweet ballad of olden time. Her long blonde ringlets waved down her shoulders in cloud-like drapery. But when she turned, on the conclusion of the music, the major never saw such eyes before—in fact

"Then was Juno herself disguised as Diana, hey?" he said.

You already perceive that the major was a man of sentiment. The major was enchanted with the gentle Maud.

Bear with me, fond hearted reader: for I have not only lovers on my hands—behold here a rival to the forlorn Allen Magroy. And such a rival! Our progress grows more perplexing. How may I please the eye of beauty beaming down upon this page? Picture to thyself an Adonis worthy to compete with Allen, an Achilles entering the lists against the youthful Paris. Tall, straight, with flowing locks, smooth face—the moustache movement not yet announced—eyes of majesty, lips of burning coal.

Is that the model lover?

Or shall we shadow forth a reserved gracious soul of

goodness who never does or says anything inconsistent with classic repose, or at any other time than the right moment—no impulse, no carelessness like Allen's—all strength under reason, and all passion under ice.

Is that thy *beau ideal*, beauteous Clarissa?

Alas! the major was gallantry itself. He had fought the British to the cannon's mouth at Chippewa, where he lost a hand; and in various hotly contested Indian battles Major Fontenoy was seen holding his snuff-box in the crook of the handless arm, and taking snuff coolly while he issued his orders. Yet is he no such Adonis, Achilles, or John Humphreys as thou hast fancied.

The major, as we see, was decrepit by the loss of his hand, and moreover, the major was slightly bent at the shoulders. Yet though no model, the best of men in many respects was he, as we shall prove in the course of this story. He took great notice of Maud that night. Thank the stars! Allen was not there, for the artless Maud received everybody graciously, especially at home, nor dreamed of coqueting. The major was odd and amusing, and like many fine gentlemen of that day, he was a very agreeable talker, and had something to say other than investments, road stocks, and opera tragedies—performed behind the scenes—patent leather boots, curling-tongs, and cosmetics. He could turn a compliment so you never knew it was a compliment, till you went to bed. He could tell an anecdote without boring you: he could hand you a glass of water without spilling it on your dress, and I defy a Fifth Avenue beau to do either. The poor major was innocent of small canes, banditti hats, tight breeches, the Jenny Lind *entrée*, an article in anybody's magazine, or a mysterious intrigue *d'amour;* and yet he was the most perfect gentleman I ever saw. So I fancy he will not be a favorite with the one or two of my city friends, but for the life of me I cannot help it—such was the backward state of those times. With the dear sex, as God, nature and their excellent mothers have made them, I feel sanguine that the major will not be very despicable, whatever may be his fortunes with the fair Maud.

On the following morning, and on every Sunday morning thereafter, Maud received the most exquisite of *bouquets.* That was no indelicate reminder of the existence of Major Fontenoy. Moreover, there could be no fine cameo, or other beautiful article of art-jewelry heard of, but what it must be sent to Maud—name of the giver unknown, and no excuse to return it: besides really the major had known us all for years, was considered as an oddity above and beyond design, who lived but for his fancies, in short, a rich old bachelor, with no wish but to be on polite terms with everybody, who would have his little humors gratified, but was considered too old, too lame, too much of a general favorite, to marry. And so there was no such thing ever thought of as making war upon him by the unnecessary display of squeamishness, as returning gifts "from an unknown" giver would appear to be.

That the giver was known, and that after the beam of joy on the sight of his beautiful presents, came a shade of perplexity and doubt on the brow of Maud, is not to be denied. Place yourself in her shoes, prudish one, and reflect well ere you condemn her. The major had the touch of Midas. He never made a purchase of lands on military or Indian reserves when the same came into market, but that it was sure to be the site of some future Troy.

With M. Latrobe and the major for frequent guests, our evenings stole pleasantly away. My dear mother, however, began to find that her severe labors were undermining her health. She was advised to abandon sewing, and take boarders. The town was growing rapidly, and alas! changing its features. The steam-boat experiment on the lakes had proved successful, and emigrants were rushing into the State, some settling down among us. Tall brick stores began to rise, and tower over their humble, droll, decaying neighbors with old fashioned Vandyke hats. Merchants with dandified clerks, lawyers with their sharp practices, landlords with their new devices, such as chamber-bells, dinner gongs, and boat-runners, were growing rich in our midst. Out of so many new comers it was easy to fill the cottage with pleasant—sometimes unpleasant—people. The library, however, continued to be the same sweet spot as before, sacred from lodgers' intrusion. M. Latrobe himself sat at the head of the table. The major, out of motives of sentiment, did not like to become a boarder with Maud's mother.

Meantime let us not forget Allen. After dangling around home listlessly a year or so after the change came between his father and Maud, he determined to study law. This he commenced doing in his indolent manner, with his heels perched upon the stove in winter, and on the window-sill in summer, and his thoughts wandering—no matter where.

After a year had elapsed, an event happened which set his blood in motion. His mother had died. Yes, she, the dust hater, who had been born with a duster in her hand, actually turned to dust herself. Old Mr. Magroy became gruffer than ever, growled to the slip-shod servants, snapped at the one-eyed housekeeper on all occasions, and so opposed was his idle son to all his mathematical, classical, and geographical ideas, that he lost all manner of patience with him.

The scholarly old gentleman himself fished in the mazy streams of the law, in order to test the advance of his son in those studies. Of course Allen was deficient. His father's wrath doubtless became great in proportion to the trouble self-imposed; but he kept it smothered until an event happened in another quarter.

Sitting in the doorway of the kennel, with his nose alert, he smelt out mischief. Notwithstanding his very reasonable order to Allen with reference to Maud, he saw that young lounger one day crossing over the avenue to accost the lady of his love. He saw him speak to her, join her, walk by her side towards home. He saw that Maud hurried her footsteps—that she seemed to wish to be left to pursue her pathway alone, that she dropped her veil, and said little.

"The crafty little cheat!" Mr. Magroy exclaimed. "She thinks to impose on Archibald Magroy, does she? I'll dissemble her!"

Allen was soon seen returning pensively towards home. As he re-crossed the avenue, and drew near the little plum orchard, a rap was heard on the floor of his father's office. The angry voice of Mr. Magroy called out:

"Allen! come hither, sir!"

The door closed upon the two. Mr. Magroy was too deeply agitated for many words. He raised his cane, and poised it over the shoulder of the sad delinquent.

"Father, you must not—will not, strike me?" His last words were soft and imploring.

"You have disobeyed orders sir!" shouted the enraged government officer. "Is this the first time I have seen thee with that flaxen-haired wench? Nay, I'll have no more of it. The little pox of deception she is!"—continued the Greek exegist.

"Stay father! Listen to reason," said Allen.

Mr. Magroy paused, and brought the cane down upon the floor.

"That girl is goodness, purity, truthfulness itself"—

The cane rose again.

"I'll send ye adrift o'er the four corners of the globe, an' ye dare dispute with me!" shouted the geographer.

Allen was strong, and a lad of twenty. He caught the blow ere it reached its destination.

"Father, will you force me to leave your roof?"

Again the rod rose high in air. The blow descended. And the boy went forth a man; even as the boy David was driven from the presence of Saul—a king! a king!

Now it was that Allen took up Blackstone with earnest purpose. The prospect of a wealthy inheritance fell from his shoulders as a camel's load. The desert before him, and he free! It was necessary, however, to earn his way. He hung out a modest little sign, with his name in white letters, and "copyist" below—for there was not sufficient writing of the legal sort to pay for his office hire, wood, lights, and daily maintenance. He advertised that he would write letters for the unlearned. Many a letter he wrote for nothing. Yet few went by his door bearing fruit, that he did not reap a gleaning—joyfully given by the happy poor; for the poor are grateful. Their confidence in Allen was unbounded. His popularity came on in its own good time; for the fruit of earnest endeavors and good deeds is general good-will. Allen could turn a ready hand to anything. Gladly would he take the place of sick or absent tradesman's clerk, an event profitable to the good shopman, as it was always marked by notable accessions of customers. Was there a prompt hand, a sagacious mind, an honest heart needed in an emergency, too difficult for clerk, and not great enough for Lawyer Floury or Counsellor O'Mar——, Allen was your man.

In short, the young scrivener was ready to do anything, at a moment's warning, even down to driving a French cart, or writing a negro love-letter. Thus brought in contact with the actualities of life, thus kept on the alert, his intellect sharpened, and his moral sensibilities were quickened. His sympathies every day found new channels. His successes buoyed him above the frequent pinchings of want, and gave him occasional glimpses of the better land which lies beyond the desert and the river. He saw life in new aspects. He regarded himself, his father, Maud, and the world, in a changed position.

Poor Maud! what was she to do? Her lover was his own master. With zeal he re-plead his cause, and pointed confidently to the future. Maud listened with a beating heart. Hope, long a stranger, or, with the young outcast a pilgrim, threw away his staff, joyfully plunged into the glowing bath-chambers of green Damascus, and came out full of aerial visions.

Yet the father's stern forbidding hung over the transported lovers like a cloud, and, in Maud's tender soul, grew from a speck to the size of a man's hand, and from that, covered the sky. She sought counsel from her mother.

Mrs. March spake little, though kindly, to her.

"I would not influence you, my daughter, in so delicate, yet important a conjuncture. I would rather leave you free to the guidance of your own conscience and good sense."

The word "conscience" pointed Maud to the difficult, narrow way, the straight road. She went forth from her morning prayers, next day, sadder, yet calmer.

Allen Magroy met her as usual on the path to school.

The accustomed greetings were exchanged—perhaps, on the side of Maud, with even more than the accustomed warmth. There was a sorrowful ardor in her looks, whenever she turned them upon the proud-bearing young gallant at her side. Even suffering had not deprived Allen of his dashing ease of manner; and fine address is not lost on woman—'tis no little of the divinity she attributes to her hero. Allen wore his hair long, as was the manner of the day; his black locks were worthy a knight of romance; he had, moreover, made a vow—silly fellow!—on leaving the paternal mansion, with the world before him, not to shear his hair until his father, proud of his success, should forgive him. That was a rash, boyish vow; and in the clearer light of a better reason, his long hair hung around him, a real covering of humility. As the two walked over the green grass now, a stranger might point to them and exclaim—

"There go the pride and beauty of the village?"

Strangers *would* call our little city a village.

Yet Maud, in her untrained ringlets, simple French straw hat, and plain attire, and Allen, in his poor apparel, might almost pass for rustics, were it not for their graceful, elastic movements. My pen! what hast thou done? Thy hero and heroine are atrociously, unpardonably stainless!

'Tis time, at length, for Maud to speak, for the quick eye of love has detected strangeness in her look and manner, and argued ill—as love always does, when not inflated by vanity.

"Allen, had I any lot or portion in the anger of your father?"

"Why, Maud! you have asked me almost as much, many times."

"Now I must know, Allen."

The truthful fellow could not—though how fain he would!—deny it.

"So I feared, so I thought. You will understand me, dear Allen; but I owe you something, and myself something—painful, oh! how painful; yet it must be heeded."

"My timid bird," replied Allen, "I know what you would say; yet listen: I feel myself my own master. I am my own master!" he added with energy, "in sight of heaven and earth! and if with you, my old, my only appreciating heart, I choose to go, it is my right."

"But what is my duty?" asked Maud.

"You are not responsible—it is my own act," he quickly rejoined.

"Yet, have I my duty to perform," said she, "to myself, to my mother, to you, dear Allen?" and she laid her hand upon his arm, but for a moment;

"nay, even to your father, however violent and unreasonable he may be? I must not keep enmity between him and you."

Allen's impatience was irrepressible.

Maud continued, with calmness, not unbroken by tearful emotion.

"You have been rudely thrown upon yourself. It will, it must be, the making of you. Your talents, and all your natural goodness of heart, must soon appear. To continue your intimacy with me, under the ban of your father's displeasure, will lower you in your own respect, and impede your progress upward all through life.

"You see, Allen," she said, with a sweet, soft, half-sad, smile, "what great things I hope for my dearest friend."

"Just as you deliberately abandon him," said he, with bitterness.

Maud trembled at all she had said; and perhaps, too, the idea of actually giving him up, or rather thus suddenly crushing the idol which had lain on her heart's altar so long, and now lay at her feet, did not diminish her self-distrust. Yet her sense of duty was not unshaken, and her resolution only in danger for a moment. She knew not what more to say.

"Well," said Allen, "I will not persecute you. I will—go."

Maud looked up at him half-reproachfully, half-surprised.

A gleam of honest pride, a whole beam of new light broke from his face.

"I think I begin to see both you and myself in a new sense, dear Maud; indeed, I have thought of it before."

The tears began to glisten through his troubled countenance, even as the stars break through the dark clouds.

"But you must not cast me from you at once. Help me to become the—the—angel that you are—no, I mean help me to see things more clearly, as you do, and"—

"You must look to God for guidance," said she, in a tremulous voice. "There is sufficient spirit of right in every heart, I believe Allen, to guide us, if we will only place it in His hands."

This was a subject a little beyond Allen Magroy. For a moment his brow grew dark again. He reviewed his career hastily, though religiously, and even the light of an honest, noble nature did not serve to cleave through its gloom. Then he looked forward, hope, love, duty, even prospective greatness, dawned upon him as through a glass darkly.

Maud watched his fine features, and with pleasure saw the cloud clear away.

"I will leave you Maud, now, my, my"—

"Sister," whispered Maud.

"Sister," echoed the young man. "Only let there be no quarrel between thee and me."

"Oh no! never," ejaculated Maud, "you know me to well for that."

"Good-bye, Maud!"

"Good-bye, Allen!"

He was gone!

The girl dropped her veil over her troubled face to hide the tears that she did not care to restrain. To go into the school-room that morning was impossible. She turned her steps homeward. And soon the mother, whose teachings and whose prayers had been the divine medium of illuminating the arches of that little temple of the living God, thanked Him that her daughter had withstood in the hour of temptation.

CHAPTER XIV.

FATHER AND SON.

Rightly to be great
Is not to stir without great argument;
But greatly to find quarrel in a straw,
When honor's at the stake.

HAMLET.

GREAT and manifest was the tribulation and wrath of Mr. Archibald Magroy on the departure of his son and heir from the family mansion. His first measure was to change his will. That Allen was cut off with a shilling no one doubted. But to whom Mr. Magroy's large estates were to fall, no one besides himself and his lawyer, Counsellor O'Mar, was presumed to know. The sagacious housekeeper, Mrs. Polyphemia Fidgets was not without her shrewd conjectures, and the note-worthy change in the domestic administration of the establishment, as well as in the personal attire of the tall, prim dame, gave rise to gossip—but what right have people to their gossip?

Old Growl grew more sullen, more watchful, more wrathful. His descent on schools became, though few and far between, as unlike angels' visits as possible to conceive. He did not hesitate to propose to the trustees that Greek should be taught by means of grammars written in Latin, and *vice versa*. The boys were amazed and frightened. Dr. Oliphant had too much good sense.

"For," quoth he, "learning language is like visiting a foreign country. Wherefore, most learned doctor of the laws—of whom by the way, Dr. Olihpant strangely stood in no manner of fear—it is my humble opinion that to think in one language, and to translate your thoughts into a second, in order to learn the mysteries of a third, would be like travelling over Europe with the map of Africa in your hand, to make you acquainted with the peculiarities of Asia!"

Whereupon Mr. Magroy retired to the shades of the kennel, and the same day appeared a placard at the gate of the plum orchard.

ARCHIBALD MAGROY, L. L. D.

WILL TAKE A FEW WELL BEHAVED YOUTHS TO INSTRUCT IN GREEK AND LATIN.

TERMS GRATIS.

Benevolent gentleman! a philanthropic hobby to ride! Dash the rowels of thy spurs deep into the flanks of thy Pegasus, or the world will escape thee—with all its woeful ignorance!

Strange ingratitude! no aspiring youths were known to present themselves at this free and newly opened fountain of classic literature. Lads preferred the odd whiskered Dr. Oliphant.

Astonished at the blindness and folly of the juvenile world, the bread which Mr. Magroy had cast upon the waters returned to his own heart. His eyes beamed once more upon his son.

Allen had at length entered the office of Attorney Floury, who furnished him sufficient writing for daily necessities, and the student was giving now his whole time and energies to the Law.

One day, while his senior was at court, Allen sat leaning over the desk—his mind lost in the perplexing, and useless, intricacies of the famous Chitty—how happy would he have been to make the better acquaintance of the clear, concise, and common-sense, Stephens!

Startled by a loud, sharp rap at the door, he turned and beheld his father—with his cane.

"Allen Magroy!"

"My dear father!"

"Are you doing well, sir?"

"Yes, sir, I shall soon be ready for examination. Be seated, father."

The face of Allen Magroy was suffused with pleasure. The old man took the proffered chair, and planted his cane with his two hands before him.

"Have you repented, sir?"

"Repented of what, father?"

"Repented of what? you rebellious young run-a-gate! Of leaving the roof where you were cradled"—possibly, the old gentleman referred to the "tree tops," famous in nursery song—"of following after that pest of a Maud March; of— of— of— bringing your father's grey hairs in sorrow to the grave, sir!"

Each sentence of this affectionate address was emphasized by Mr. Magroy's cane-ferule on the floor.

For such an outbreak the young man was not prepared. A hope had suddenly, violently, been crushed. It was with difficulty he could speak.

"Father, I would not reproach you; but what ever can account for this misunderstanding?"

"Misunderstanding!" echoed the old gentleman, savagely.

"What can account for it?" continued Allen, "but a want of knowledge, an absence of sympathy between your heart and mine? Could I but hope to clear up this cloud, could I but dare to unfold my views, my heart, my wishes, my whole being, changed, though trampled upon as I have been, I would thank, oh! how I would thank, the great, good God!"

Allen's hands were clasped together; his look was agony.

"God knows! God knows," he cried tenderly, "I would not embitter your earthly days."

"Then, sir," spoke Mr. Magroy, softly, "you have repented your rashness, you will obey me?"

"Dear father," replied Allen, "you see things in so different a light. The young lady whom you despise is my benefactress, you yourself once smiled upon. Why, sir, she is as much superior to Allen Magroy as an angel of light to mortal man may be. Look, father! I seem to myself to live and move in a new world, since, driven from your roof, I took refuge near her. She repelled me; she would not, angel as she is, stand between your heart and mine. And, sir, if I ever become a man," continued Allen, rising proudly from his chair, "if I ever become a man, whom you and the world may deign to notice *as a man*, it will be owing to that girl!"

"'Will be,' Allen; beware, my lad."

"Yes, sir!" repeated the excited soul, bursting nobly from his lips. "Yes, sir! 'will be!' for no power on earth can destroy immortal seed once planted. And, sir! whatever may betide—come sorrow, come wrath, come destruction itself—I feel my soul wedded to that of Maud March."

"The shaggy forehead of Mr. Magroy grew black as the pine forest beneath a thunder-cloud. For a moment his mind seemed wandering. His vision had a far-off, far-down look, as if dreaming over the lost and scattered Past. His frame shook convulsively. But, as if by a mighty effort, he regained his accustomed look, and Purpose resumed its sway.

"I tell thee, lad, thou'rt crazy; the daughter of a seamstress, a washerwoman;" again that lost look and convulsive manner.

"Father, are there such cobweb figments here as castes in society? No, sir! Where lies respectability? in blood, property, position? No, sir! Is it in rich apparel, luxurious living, coats of arms? No, sir! The pride of life consists not in ancient heritage, but in virtue and success. Any pure and refined maiden is the equal of the noblest born heir in the land. Is it not so, father?"

"Go on, sir! go on," was muttered from some unknown thunder region.

"Why do old men forget the past?" exclaimed Allen, "as if they never struggled—never knew the consoling sweets of precious truth, of hope shining from hill-tops, of pure natures exalting them to the skies."

"To debase them down to hell!" now burst from the lips of Mr. Magroy, with a gleam of lightning from the dark pine forest about his eyes.

Allen started back, lost in amazement. There seemed to be some hidden mystery, some mighty secret, on the eve of explosion. He waited with awe for his father to go on. Mr. Magroy was silent.

Allen, after waiting a while, patiently and respectfully resumed:

"I did not dare hope to convert you, father, to my views."

Call it prejudice, or the power of experience, but one might as well attempt to turn back the current of the long and deep-rolling Mississippi as the channel of an old man's thoughts. But this was not in Allen's mind; he *did* hope that his father would view life as he would have him; he *did* dare try to convert him. Soon his hope went out; his boldness forsook him. Mr. Magroy suddenly stamped with foot and cane impatiently, and cried—

"Moonshine! stuff! Will you come back, Allen? Do you repent the wrongs you have heaped upon your father, sir?"

"If," answered Allen, thoughtfully and earnestly, "if to repent, means contrition for provoking your anger, I do sincerely repent; if it means regret for what has passed between me and Miss March, I can, I do, pray your forgiveness, while yet I bless the hours spent with that superior soul."

Mr. Magroy chose to contain himself no longer. Springing from the chair, on which he had been sitting uneasily during the harangue of his enthusiastic son, and shaking his cane in the face of Allen, he exclaimed—

"I will make you repent it, sir—yes sir, in dust and ashes. I will humble you to the earth! you perverse, unworthy descendant of an honorable family! I have already cut you off from my will, sir. I will do more; you shall find me an enemy wherever you are, when you rise up or sit down, go or come, my curse shall follow you, and after I die my ghost shall haunt you."

Mr. Magroy turned to go. Then suddenly coming back, he cried:

"Those Marches, whom you have chosen for your gods, let them reign over you; but they are not beyond my reach, mark that, Allen, mark that!"

He left the office, punching each step of the stairway as he descended, and muttering to himself threats of vengeance on the Marches.

Poor Allen! How he paced the floor! The words his father had just uttered sank deeply in his heart. His mind reverted to the past. It was with bitterness that he felt the truth, that parents bring children into the world, and owe them *something* for the very act. Not neglect, not tyranny, persecution, destruction; but care, sympathy, a gentle hand to guide, a soft voice to counsel, and—not till these fail—the rod. But his father had forced him into rebellion, and but this moment had come, gone, and left a curse behind him.

To Maud, to whom he owed everything worth prizing, he could no longer look for consolation. Even she seemed to turn from him. There the curse of his father had already commenced. Then he thought of his father's threat towards the March family. This urged his feelings into a new channel, and called for action. What his father meant was beyond his knowledge. He sat down, and addressed a note to Maud. It did not suit. He tore it to pieces, and wrote a second, which he flung into the fire. A third was not without exceptions—so captious are lovers, even in the plainest matters—yet he thought well enough of it to put it in his hat, to leave at the door of Lilac Cottage.

CHAPTER XV.

CLOUDS.

They did not know how hate can burn
In hearts once changed from soft to stern.
BYRON.

It was a night of more than ordinary cheerfulness. The return of Guilford on the previous evening lent an additional brightness to the ruddy glow of the library fire. A knock was heard at the front door. Bowes came in with a letter, which she said, looking away, was for Maud. Allen Magroy had left it, without any message. Maud blushed and turned quite pale, as Mrs. March handed the letter to her daughter.

"Perhaps you would like to read it alone, my child?"

Maud retired, taking a light.

She was not gone a moment, but returned, and handed the opened letter to her mother. It was as follows:

"DEAR MAUD,

"You must, you will pardon me for writing, when you learn what I have to communicate. My father visited me this afternoon. I will not particularize what took place; but in going away he used threatening language concerning your mother's family. He never threatens in vain. But I don't know what it can be. My heart is wrung at the thought that I am so completely in the dark and powerless to befriend. But you must tell your mother to be on her guard.

"ALLEN MAGROY."

This epistle of course threw us into some consternation. Mrs. March alone maintained her calmness. Mabel declared that Mr. Magroy meant to burn the house down, and loud were her lamentations that her father was not at home to rescue us from destruction. M. Latrobe had gone to New York, with the expectation of sailing for London on business for the company, and probably had left ere this. Maud was silent and pale. Guilford said he saw no way in which Mr. Magroy could injure us.

"We are in a free country, and the law will protect us, mother."

Guilford thought highly of the power and justice of the law, on account of the experience he had enjoyed in witnessing a case in court, already hinted at in John March's letter. Mrs. March thought some terrible calamity might be impending over the head of her daughter, the innocent cause of the unfortunate quarrel between father and son; but she wisely kept her own counsel. At this conjuncture in our affairs how tearfully the widow thought of her husband, their natural protector. But was he not watching, and was there not a yet more powerful friend, even the widow's God? At last Mrs. March spoke.

"Whatever this danger may be, my children, I feel

assured in my own heart that God will provide a way of escape."

She took down the family Bible, and read the 91st Psalm. With what sweet hope and gentle reassurance the family arose after evening worship and retired to their beds!

Such is Religion's soothing balm.

The period for the third annual payment on the house was now rapidly approaching. We had not found our creditor a hard man. The day had passed by in both previous years without the money being demanded, and Mrs. March had been allowed to take her own time. This year was a difficult one for householders, provisions were never known so high, and the number of our boarders (our only pecuniary resource) had diminished. Mrs. March expected daily to hear some dread news on account of the warning Allen had given. But it seemed as if either the youth was mistaken, or that his father had changed his humor, for weeks passed without calamity, and the fear of it at first so appalling, gradually died away. Meantime we were all making strenuous efforts to increase the list of our boarders, to reduce still more our slender expenses, and by careful economy to lay up money for the payment. The event, however, seemed doubtful. The times grew harder, and we were drawing on what had already been saved and laid by. The first day of the last quarter came, and with it another note from Allen:

"DEAR MAUD:

"I have just learned from Mr. Floury that my father has purchased the remaining unpaid portion on the bill of sale of your mother's house. What his object may be I dare not conjecture. Pardon me for presuming to advise that if Mrs. March only meets the payments promptly, as they fall due, there can be no trouble. Hoping I am not destined to be the herald of further exciting news, I remain

"ALLEN MAGROY."

This was frightful enough, yet Mrs. March, while not despairing of making the next payment in time, felt some relief in the fact that Mr. Magroy seemed to direct his malice against her rather than Maud.

"After all," she said, "it may be a mere matter of business between Mr. Articles and Mr. Magroy." The former was the gentleman in whose hands the property had fallen at my father's decease, and from whom Mrs. March had made the purchase.

Every sinew was now strained to meet the approaching liability. With no little reluctance on the part of Mrs. March, Maud, Guilford, and myself were withdrawn from our schools to save the expense of tuition. Mabel declared she would not go either, but insisted on reciting to Maud, and turning her school expenses into the family fund. It was to no purpose that we all protested. Mabel would have her way. And Maud became our instructress for the nonce.

Payment day came. It seemed to my imaginative soul that we were on the eve of some grand catastrophe, that the world was to be in some sudden manner changed, to us at least, for I knew very well that the filthy lucre was not forthcoming. And to think of Mr. Magroy! I represented him to Mabel as a bloody-minded Shylock. After breakfast my mother went down the avenue. She did not return till the dinner hour. It was easy to see that she was disappointed. Her excellent old friend Casher Coiner could have helped her to ten times the amount at any other time, but now the year was just closing, and the bank directors had given orders that not a dollar should be discounted until they saw how the affairs of the institution stood, and whether it would be likely to weather the currency storm just beginning to rage over the country. She had applied to several of her friends among the merchants, but with little, better success.

In the afternoon she put on her widows' cap, black bonnet and shawl, and neat plain collar, and again went out. Soon reaching the house of Mr. Magroy she tremulously raised the brass knocker at the door. Dame Polly Fidgets appeared, dressed in silk.

"Is your master at home, Mrs. Fidgets?"

"I'd like to know who you call my master, mam. I'm as good as any wash"——

"I beg your pardon. Is Mr. Magroy at home?"

"Well, I'll see," said the ruffled hen partridge, smoothing her feathers—with an ill grace.

Mrs. March was left standing on the door-sill, while the dame was gone. Her heart palpitated violently, and in spite of herself already augured an unfavorable termination to her mission.

"This way, ma'am. Mr. Magroy will see you in his office."

"Have you come on business, ma'am?" My mother made no reply.

Worthy Dame Fidgets did not leave the door which opened from the house into the office, but anxious for her prospects, and fearful that a reconciliation might be effected between her master and the Marches, and thereby lead to the return of the disinherited son, she applied her ear to the keyhole.

"You wish to see me, madam," growled the deep voice of the gentlemanly proprietor of the mansion, who, from some unknown cause did not raise his face towards the lady.

"Yes, sir," said my mother, summoning all the composure she could command.

"There is a chair," spoke again the voice.

Mrs. March sat down, or rather sank down, in silence, which she at length interrupted with difficulty.

"Mr. Magroy, there has been some trouble between yourself and Allen, in which, by some unintentional circumstance or act perhaps of"—— Mr. Magroy suddenly sat erect.

"Is this your business, madam?"

Such rudeness in his speech! his looks! his whole manner, aroused all the pride of character of Mrs. March.

"No, sir!" said she rising with dignity and coloring highly. "It was my desire to remove any misunderstanding that might exist between us as neighbors. But since you have so rudely repulsed me at the threshold I will bid that intention go, as best it may, conscious, sir, of the innocence of me and of mine."

"Oh yes, Mrs. March, neither you nor your fair daughter are capable of womanly designs on young gentlemen above yourselves in the world. Women never are!"

"No gentleman—no one but a coward, sir! would thus insult a defenceless woman."

"Do you come to beard me, woman?" he yelled forth with such frenzy as to shake the door at which Mrs. Fidget's ear was pinned, so as to shake that honest woman from head to foot—but with delight at the cheering course of events.

A retort rose to the tongue of my mother, but she remembered the cry of the little ravens in the home nest, and she shrank back likewise from the vulgar war of words, so suddenly and unexpectedly raised. She had expected no such reception, and with bitterness she remembered that this same insolent man had been under no small obligation to her husband in their early business life. Nay, more, she might have recalled the time, further back, when the young Scot conferred upon her the honor of his marked attentions. All this flashed through her oppressed and outraged soul, and left an almost lightning scathe. Then she remembered the words of the Psalmist, "I will rebuke kings for his sake," and quietly resolved to leave the widow's cause with the widow's God.

She advanced to the table at which Mr. Magroy was sitting, and laid upon it a package of money.

"Payment on the house, hem! Let me see," said he, "how much is due." The dissembler! had he not been feasting his eye on the little note all day.

"Three hundred dollars!"

My mother kept silence as he then proceeded to count the bills.

"Here are but two hundred."

"Yes sir! I thought that if convenient to you"—my poor mother paused. To beg any favor of this creature was too humiliating. Then she endeavored to look upon it as a matter of business and went on, under the scowl of her creditor.

"If as convenient to you, sir, a few days delay would I think enable me to procure the remaining hundred dollars."

"Possibly your expected son-in-law, that penniless scapegrace of mine, might assist you," he said sarcastically.

My mother bit her lips till the blood flowed. At length she was able to reply calmly.

"Mr. Magroy, you have repelled my explanations, you have added insult to insinuation, you would drive me to madness and to ruin. But know, sir! that there is a higher tribunal where justice shall be meted out to the oppressor and the oppressed. You will learn some day, perhaps on this earth, the vileness of your calumnious insinuation. And now, even though you appear to triumph, I fear you not. No," she added murmuringly, "I fear not what man can do."

Mrs. March's calmness had by this time excited the inflammable character before her, even as oil the burning tow.

"What the devil has got into all of them?" he cried jumping upon the floor, and stamping fiercely with his foot and striking his cane. "My villainous son and this washerwoman preach to me! yes, a woman preach to me! Is that the way you converted him? caused him to raise his arm against his indulgent father? drove him away from the fire-side of home; filled his head with fine notions of equality and virtue; a pox on both you and your preaching! Please begone from my roof, madam, you contaminate a once happy home with your hypocritical white visage."

"When you have endorsed the amount of that package on the note, Mr. Magroy."

My mother was remarkably cool and self possessed. A timid bird even will fight for her nest and young.

"No such thing, madam! I'll do no such thing!" said he tossing the money on the table.

"Bring the whole amount due, and that in coin, or I'll turn you out of your house, bag and baggage!"

Mrs. March gathered up the package, and went out by the office door. Happily this for Mrs. [illegible]gets, who was so fascinated by the scene, that she was not prepared for my mother's exit by the door at which she was admitted.

Mrs. March passed through the little orchard fronting the office, and turned her steps towards the business portion of the city. It was past banking hours, and most of the merchants had either deposited in the banks or locked away their specie for safe keeping; so that it was no easy matter to exchange the bills for the legal tender upon which Mr. Magroy insisted. She succeeded in exchanging a part, however, but as for borrowing the additional hundred dollars that was entirely out of the question on that day. She remembered that the law allowed her until twelve at night to make the payment, and so went heavily homeward. As she walked down the little lawn in front of the dear old mansion that looked now like a blessing brightening as if on the eve of flight, she was almost thrilled at the loud cheery notes of a robin perched on top of a leafless lilac bush. A momentary gleam of hope seemed to quicken her steps at the sound.

"That robin wouldn't sing so if the little hands that fed it were going away: no! the angels would not let it."

So half smilingly half sadly thought the little care-laden woman.

Now what to do we all did not know. Our tea passed in silence. Tea, that had always been the liveliest meal, where our mother presided over the softly exhilarating beverage with such infinite good humor, and when she told our fortunes from the tea leaves in our cups in the manner of her New England grandmother, and fine happy fortunes they always were. Now, with what tear-moistened faces we sat round the board, raising our eyes timidly to each other, and casting them anxiously towards the head of the table.

Tea was not over when a knock was heard at the front-hall door. Guilford arose and went to answer the call. He did not return. After waiting some time we marched very solemnly into the library, where we found him looking soberly yet singularly into the fire before which he was sitting. It was evident something new had happened, and that it was not of an unhappy nature was plain from the boy's countenance. Yet as no one thought it could be connected with the terrible cloud overhanging us and keeping us all so silent, no one thought of questioning him. Finally the restless little Mabel ran over to Guilford, took his face in her two hands, turned it roguishly towards her own, and said:

"What is it, Guilford? Don't torment me any longer. You are provokingly deliberate in your movements, sir knight."

"Mother," said Guilford, now clearly smiling, "it was a friend."

My mother looked towards Maud, who was intently regarding Guilford's further words.

"What friend?" cried Mabel.

"He had seen you accidently in a shop inquiring for

specie and thought by your manner you were in trouble, On my going to the door he took me down to the gate; said, I was the very one he wanted to see. He inquired what was the trouble. I told him all. "Tell your mother," said he, "I have that amount in specie at my lodgings; not to perplex herself any more about it. I will see Mr. Magroy before nine o'clock and pay it."

"Heavenly Father!" said my mother in a low voice. "I thank thee," and the tears streamed down her cheeks. The others were too much touched by her agitation to interrupt it.

At length I broke the silence.

"You haven't told who it was, Guilford."

"I know! I know!" cried the delighted Mabel.

"Who do you think, canary bird?"

"Allen Magroy?"

"No! he has the heart, but I fear not the means."

"Then who?" demanded the disappointed child rather petulantly, for Allen was her hero.

"Major Fontenoy," quietly replied Guilford March.

CHAPTER XVI.

THE YOUNG ORATOR.

> Methought I heard a voice,
> Sweet as the shepherd's pipe upon the mountains,
> When all his little flock's at feed before him.
>
> OTWAY.

IT was a good custom in our old times, for gentlemen of all classes, young and old, military, political, legal, commercial, and mechanical—clergymen, schoolmasters, and students—to meet for purposes of debate. Eloquence was then a gentlemanly and influential accomplishment; the tricks and chicanery of politics had not yet supplanted it.

The society met in the old Council House.

This venerable building, now no more, deserves a passing word, as it dated back to the most primitive times of the white men on that frontier. Here the chiefs of the tribes gravely smoked Ka-nic-a-nic—or Indian tobacco of the North, prepared from the bark of the red willow—with the governor of the town and the ghostly Jesuit Fathers. The odor of ka-nic-a-nic still clung to its walls. There seemed yet to be a sort of Indian summer reigning in its atmosphere, as the light streamed through the dusty windows, and was reflected from the old yellow paintings.

Here, then, after more stately modern edifices had robbed the building—a long, low two-story affair—of its primitive honors, met the ambitious young men and worthy literary rabbis, to hold high debate.

How well I remember the chief speakers! Not the least attractive among the young men was Allen Magroy. His tall person, his long, black hair, his musical voice, the slightly sarcastic, yet ever-softening, smile, and graceful gesture; he stands before me now, pausing even at the tumultuous applauses beating in the hall of my heart.

In the chair, presiding with urbanity, sits Major Fontenoy. Here is Maud by my side, an attentive, nay a rapt listener, at least to one voice; and there, with his chin on his cane, sits old Growl himself. While over yonder, under the shade of the gallery, I espy Dr. Oliphant, with his face and whiskers wrapped in the folds of a white handkerchief.

Who may listen without emotion to the enthusiastic heart-wisdom of Youth, when glowing with the light of eloquence? He kindles his torch, not at the baleful fires of the world as it *is*, but turns it towards the world as he thinks it *was*. Brutus is his justice, Leonidas his patriot; his father is Regulus, his mother, Cornelia, his sister, Virginia, and Greece and Rome are his native country.

The question to-night concerns the rival merits of

learning and virtue in the welfare of a state. The learned and witty Counsellor O'Mar, with his drollery, and mixture of pathos and ridicule, has just sat down beneath the roars and shouts of the meeting.

Allen rises, to answer him on the side of virtue. You wonder at his temerity. His face is crimsoned with genuine modesty. He alludes deferentially to the superior judgment and greater experience of his predecessor, and pays a compliment to his art and learning Before proceeding to unfold his own argument, he attacks the weak points of his adversary ; and in less than five minutes, you are quietly astonished at the ridiculousness of the Irish counsellor's position, deemed a moment ago impregnable. But you console yourself with the general absurdity of Irish blarney, and are not yet ready to give the stripling before you credit for overthrowing them. He now proceeds to state the question on his own side. Where did the once indolent idler get hold of this principle? where pick up that fact? Now he warms into the argument; his body seems to dilate into the ample proportions of a man; he stands a head taller than before; he waves his hand with a new grace; his eyes beam with a new fire; you watch them with intense interest; they seem fairly to light up the hall, with its dusky galleries. Men lean over on the backs of the benches in front of them; a pen dropping from the secretary's table, sounds like thunder, and you are ready to devour the secretary for venturing to stoop down and pick it up. In the heat of the argument, at the top of a climax of power and beauty, the tables are suddenly turned again on the counsellor. A sudden sally takes everybody by surprise, and brings down the house with peals of laughter. You look at the adversary, expecting to see him faint, or get up and leave the hall, and are surprised at his *nonchalance;* nay, he himself looks with admiration at the young orator.

Then came the peroration. The debater's long locks are brushed away from his temples. His eyes have a far-off gaze; and even your own thoughts are not at home now. You see the Acropolis, the streets of Athens, the prison where Socrates sits drinking hemlock, and conversing calmly with his friends. Or, by rapid movements of the fancy, you are a spectator in Independence Hall, and behold Franklin and Washington; or on Bunker Hill, amid the fire, and smoke, and shock, and war, and groans, and shouts, you lean over the dying Warren. Then solemnly you gaze, with the pale, husky, agitated champion, on Calvary, and see the cross, and victim there nailed between the two malefactors, while Rabbis are contending in the Sanhedrim over their books of ancient lore, and ignorant of the Light that has come into the world.

Allen sits down, and all eyes are turned on old Mr. Magroy; but mine regard only the sweet, trembling, delighted Maud at my side. It seemed to me that when the speaker spoke of learning, he addressed Mr. Magroy, and when he grew so eloquent in the cause of virtue, his great, burning eye-balls shone only on Maud. The question is carried by acclamation in favor of virtue. The meeting breaks up, and everybody shakes the hand of Allen Magroy—everybody save one. Yet their eyes have met, and in that one look is Allen's chief laurel.

How cruel that destiny seemed, which, like an impassable abyss, divided those great twin hearts. There they stand, like two tall cliffs, asunder, with their sunlit faces fixed, the one upon the other, in steady constancy, sublime to contemplate.

Time, the river at their feet, rolled down many a golden sand for others, yet brought no happiness for them.

The scrupulous Maud pursued her conscientious path, and, so far as outward sign might show, was no more to Allen Magroy than other gentle maidens of the city.

Thus years flowed wearily away. The river was widening towards the ocean.

Meanwhile Allen passed the bar, and Mr. Floury took the eloquent young advocate into partnership. Allen mingled with society; he often met Maud; she was generally attended by the devoted Major Fontenoy, who lived only in the light of her smiles.

CHAPTER XVII.

WILD OATS.

During the period which has passed, Maud has been teaching school, helping no little towards the purchase of the homestead, and Guilford has been placed in a store with the understanding that the nights shall be his own, and his wages go scrupulously into the common fund. Yet with these aids Mrs. March has been forced to sell a portion of the large grounds belonging to the place, as with each year, according to the terms of contract, an additional hundred dollars over the last payment is added.

Meantime we have frequent letters from John. During the annual vacations at college he goes into some New England town and teaches school, thus he contributes towards his education and aids his mother in carrying out the views of Mr. March. College conceits are gradually wearing away beneath experience and maturing reason. He has lost his heart beyond redemption, every summer during his absence, till now he begins to talk wisely of the world, and slightingly of the softer sex. It is thought that John will marry a rich wife and become a solid man of Boston.

As for myself the memory of my father is yet green in my heart. My love for him is the little shining river meandering through my days, and on its banks are clustered the fair flowers of beauty and the rich fruits of love. I am not sure that my poetical efforts do not date back as far as this period.

It was a melancholy happiness to take Mabel with me Sunday afternoons with baskets of flowers, which we braided and laid all over his grave. Sometimes my mother went with us, and looked on with an abstracted air, while we twined garlands over the sorrel, which like little crosses waved amid the grasses as the gentle south wind swept along. On one occasion a tall elderly man, a stranger, who said he came all the way from Nova Scotia, accompanied my mother to the church-yard, and they two knelt down together and wept. He did not make himself known to us, but only said:

"He was my friend, where is his grave?"

This person may have been once a fur trader.

My wanderings in the woods formed an ever fresh source of pleasing ruminations. Here I led a life all my own. The noise of the school, the sports of merry companions, and the pleasures of home, where my mother and Mabel were—and yet where care, though in gentle guise, stood in the midst of us—school-books, and the little every-day duties which fell to my share in the common object to gain—all these were forgotten in the woods. The rustling of the branches, the singing of the birds, the distant sound of a gun, the bark of invisible dogs, the lowing of far-off cattle, the soft mottled sunshine, the cool shade and fragrant atmosphere, charmed my half melancholy senses. Perched in the crotch of some tree on Wednesday or Saturday afternoons—when there was no school—I would sit with a pleasing book, a romance, or the homelike songs of Burns, even Addison's Spectator and Johnson's Rambler were devoured with sober satisfaction: but my delights were the Vicar of Wakefield and Rasselas. In the one I compared Mrs. March to Parson Primrose, in the other, Guilford to the Prince. I thought it good to be a philosopher. Then I did not know but a poet would be the thing. Then I compromised between the two, and resolved to be both.

But a few times going to the theatre, I remember the first play—The Forty Thieves—and reading a book of plays, put me in love with the drama. With reluctance I confess that many a night I would kiss my trustful mother good night, go to bed only till the house grew still, then rise and steal off to the theatre. At last I resolved to write a play. For this purpose I selected an exciting novel of the day, and worked the whole winter changing it into dialogues with acts and scenes. Finishing to my taste, and to the recommendation of a young gentleman boarder, my confidant, I lounged around the purlieus of the theatre, principally at the drinking-shop, where the actors congregated, waiting for an opportunity to place it in the hands of the manager. For weeks I watched with the play buttoned up in my coat. The manager came and went occasionally, but he was a repulsive looking man, who acted the parts of cruel tyrants and bad fathers, and my heart always failed me. Finally I summoned sufficient courage to address one of the principal actors—a kind-hearted man—he may be living yet, his name was Marsh. Noticing that jokes always seemed to please the actors, I asked him waggishly:

"Are you sure, sir, that your name is Marsh?"

The gentleman stared, and his companions laughed.

"Well, sir!" he said at last, "suppose it be, then again, suppose it be not, what then?"

My waggishness all vanished and left me in the lurch.

"Only please, sir, my name is March, and I thought possibly yours might be too, and that you may have changed it."

"Why, you little rogue, do you think me ashamed of my father's name?"

"No, sir," said I, quite frightened, "only I have heard that actors frequently change their names."

"You are a curious little fellow: won't you take a cigar or an orange, or something?"

"No, sir! I thank you very much."

On the following occasion of my visit to the place I found Mr. Marsh alone, sitting on a bench in the garden attached to the theatre.

He accosted me with great cordiality, and called me to a seat by his side. After begging his pardon for prying into his private business the other day, I took my play from my breast. He glanced at it very carelessly.

"Who wrote this, my little friend?"

"I did, sir." He gazed doubtingly.

"You are not telling me a story?"

"No, sir. I never told a story in my life." And I colored deeply, and was a little offended.

"Well, what do you want done with this?"

"If you would only be good enough to look at it and see whether it can be acted?"

"Oh! certainly, certainly. If it can be brought out you will see it announced in the bills."

"But I say"—— I had risen, and was about to leave him, "I wouldn't write any more tragedies."

I stopped, and looked at him inquiringly.

"It's poor business, even for a grown man, my little author. If you want to be a happy man, don't write plays. If you want to escape having all your nights and days plunged into the inky depths of despair, don't write plays. If you wish neither to envy nor be envied, if you do not want to live on the rack, to be a haunter of green-rooms and taverns, to stand in fear of miserable, capricious, besotted, starveling stage managers, and crochety critics, for God's sake don't write plays!"

The kind man seemed to be very much in earnest. I thanked him with tears in my eyes, shook hands, and as soon as I had passed through the drinking-rooms, I ran with all my might.

It must be remembered, in justification of the words of the actor, that at that period the drama was at its lowest point, and a very different institution from the now-flourishing temple of Thespis.

For weeks, I looked at the bottom of the play-bills for the announcement of the forthcoming appearance of a "new play, 'The Outlaw,' by a young gentleman of this city."

The season terminated, the company went away, the theatre gates closed, and I was disappointed. During the four or five weeks that intervened, I lived, as the good actor predicted, fairly "on the rack." But that was nothing to what my fate would have been had they attempted the performance of my tragedy. In fact, I am not sure that he is not a good man and a benefactor, who declines to perform your first play or publish your first poem.

Shortly after this air-castle tumbled into blue-tinted ruins, one of the class of persons called revival preachers favored our city with a visit. It became the fashion at once to "get religion," as it is called, particularly among the young people. The uncouth eloquence of the Rev. Holifernes Brimstone, was physically captivating.

After all, there is something picturesque in the wild descriptions and familiar allegories of revival preachers. My heart fell a willing sacrifice to conscience, aroused by the roaring of the lion of Judah. With a firm step I advanced to the bench known as the anxious-seat, and full of the frenzy, as well as the language of those around me, with my arm uplifted, I exclaimed—

"I have been a soldier of Satan, and I enlist under the banner of the cross!"

And straightway fell upon my knees, and poured out torrents of tears. I remember that while on my knees, I fancied myself a sort of martyr to early piety—possibly my name might yet figure in some new Fox's Book of Martyrs. The extreme susceptibility of emotion, however, soon wore away. My religion was an imaginative principle, creating a new world. I desired to do something out of the common way. No ordinary missionary life, even, would do. I inquired of my mother whether there were not some Jewish blood in the family? Possibly I might be a Hebrew of the Hebrews; nay a lineal descendant of David; perchance the intended restorer of the Jews—nay the very Messiah! or, at least, a very near connection—a sort of right-hand man, an earthly instrument, his sword-arm—destined to overthrow kingdoms and achieve the victory of Armageddon.

The "young converts," as the good deacon called us, were examined for admission to the communion of the faithful. The number of questions propounded was as great as the sands on the sea-shore, and more various.

I failed beyond redemption on the following question:

"Do you feel it to be your duty, my young brother, to urge upon sinners the danger of their souls, in all places and under all circumstances?"

"What!" I demanded, "if I chance to meet a young lady on the street?"

"Exactly."

"Then my answer is, no."

My name was placed on the list of doubtful cases. What! notwithstanding all those dreams of philanthropy and Hebrew visions, could the wise men of the church hesitate? I began to suspect their fitness.

But, it seems, the worthy committee had a shrewd method of their own. Time proved its wisdom. In less than a month, I shudder to think what a reprobate I became. I attended a juvenile ball! there were fiddles and flutes, a bass-viol and triangles, sponge-cake, lemonade, and a glass of wine in an ante-room. Guilford and Mabel, Maud and Allen were there, and Major Fontenoy and M. Latrobe looked on with beaming faces. The floor was chalked, and I plead guilty to dancing! nay, to being one of the managers! and wearing a blue rosette, made by —— alas, not Mabel! And here it is time to confess to another delinquency. During this memorable summer I had fallen desperately in love. My Dulcinea was much older than myself, yet quite as ardent a lover. Did she not return a bashful kiss I ventured to steal at that very ball? and did we not tramp the streets of the city, and the border of the river a mile above town, of nights, night after night? and did not her step-mother—cruel woman!—scold her, and call me "little boy," one day when I had my newest pantaloons and tightest straps on? and did not her father send her away East to boarding-school? and was I not sent by Mrs. March to rusticate at Farmer Jumps's? and did I not catch the fever and ague? and did I not recover and write Dulcinea a letter, vowing fidelity and constancy towards her, but hatred to all step-mothers, and chiefly *one?* and did I not receive a silly reply, saying she had not time to write me, because she had just made an engagement to ride with "such a love of a young man?" What better proof of love than change? What better proof of fever than a chill? How Mabel laughs at me to this blessed day about it!

From the frenzy of religion to the frenzy of love; from love to fever and ague—what a fall! I recovered from the latter to plunge with new ardor—more than the ardor of youth—into a little sea of politics! The ship of state was a juvenile debating society, over whose interests the members strove with a valor worthy a higher place than these chronicles. The question at issue was the welfare and increase of our collection of books. Parties formed, divided, fought. Caucuses were held in kitchens, garrets, cellars, fire-engine-houses, anywhere. Oaths of secresy and union were administered. Various sagacious methods were adopted to draw over the wavering. Speeches were delivered not contemptible for manner, matter, or success. Duels were fought—fortunately with cork bullets. Thus sagacious politicians sprouted in the fertile fields of the tumultuous West. Thus tact, invention, secresy, combination, and the power of concerted action takes early root, and bears at no late day a goodly crop of heroes and statesmen.

Hands once in, as the saying is, our mischievous thoughts were turned into new channels. We played tricks on honest citizens and their houses at night. We conspired against the peace of the city. We interrupted public meetings, and charged upon singing schools. We dived into forbidden places in disguise, and came out—at the Mayor's Court.

Thus feverishly, thus ignobly were consumed some of the most precious years of my life. Yet in common with other staid old gentlemen who look back with pity—if not pleasure—on the foibles of youth—as at the worst but the rank weeds of a fertile soil—I sometimes like to recount my wild oats. That a certain religious tone, like a vein of gold running through Plutonic regions, preserved its course through this unhappy period, may seem strange, yet such was the fact, trifling as may be the value set upon it by those who know little of the human heart. How sweetly have I prized it since! The bare consciousness of wrong-doing may be the slender thread connecting man with divinity. It may be the clue that will lead him through error and transgression to the final light.

How the thoughts of Walter March came to take a military turn I do not know, unless it was the unbounded admiration he felt for Major Fontenoy. It was during my sixteenth year that the candidate to re-present our newly formed State in Congress proposed to Mrs. March to send me to West Point. This gentleman seemed so delighted with his elevation, that like the clown in the farce, he stood ready to marry all the widows, and father all the children amongst his constituents. In fact this virtuous politician gave out significantly—before election—that his reign should be known as the paradisaical period for such poor folk; that Widow March's son should go to West Point, and the son of another widow should have a midshipman's warrant; he would fill the post-office with indigent blind persons, and the custom-house with deaf and dumb. Our worthy friend and patron had lately visited the East, where he had been conspicuous in the assemblages of public philanthropists.

My application was drawn up in due form by Major Fontenoy, himself a military graduate. The newly elected member, Hon. Oliver Hazzard Perry Hustings, took the paper with many recommendations accompanying it, to the seat of government. We heard no more of the matter until the return of Mr. Hustings, who told us with evident pain he had not been able to secure the appointment, but that had the application been for a midshipman's berth he could have got it. My friend the navy candidate, however, fared no better. Mr. Hustings told him it was a pity he had not applied for West Point!

In a short time we learned that the benevolent and

disinterested statesman had appointed the sons of two political friends.

It was then that M. Latrobe offered to take the matter in hand.

CHAPTER XVIII.

THE JUMPSES.

"Bless my stars!" exclaimed Bowes, rubbing her hands on her clean apron. "If there ain't farmer Jumps! and Joram! just as sure as I'm a livin woman!" Bowes always did delight in strong expressions. The two worthies were seen walking up the lawn carrying each a basket, and between them a seal-skin covered trunk. Their persons were adorned with new garments, evidently meant to serve as fashion plates by the village tailor.

Since last we made mention of the worthy farmer, philosophizing with Guilford in front of his cabin and giving utterance to country complainings, time had not dealt churlishly with him. He had now a less care-worn expression of countenance, a freer air, and was more portly in person—in short was a justice of the peace for the township of Green Run.

"Wall, Widow March"—he always reminded my mother of her widowhood in the manner of those who call you Squire, or Major, as aware of your dignity.

"How de dew?"

The Messers Jumps senior and junior were cordially

shaken by the hand, and invited of course into the library. Mr. Joram Jumps sat down charily, with but the edge of his person on the corner of the lounge, while Mr. Jumps senior made himself quite easy and comfortable at once in the arm-chair—as any squire should. Trunk and baskets were left in the hall. Reassured by his father's confidence of manner, Joram gradually gained ground on the lounge, till he felt himself sufficiently secure to lean back, as imitative of his father as the back of the lounge permitted.

"Picture of the old man, s'pose?" said Squire Jumps, pointing towards the portrait of Mr. March.

Joram cast two pencils of what little light was reflected from his diminutive eyes upward towards the picture, without presuming, however, to turn up his face sufficiently for a full view.

Those eyes!

They were set a league back in Joram's head.

But that nose!

Picture to yourself the least possible bit of red flesh turned up, and overlapped, as one may say, by two round, prominent cheeks, so as to throw the cut-water of this noble human bark back between the bows.

But eyes and nose together!

Fancy a railway tunnel. Through the long conical vista, behold an object—that nose—yet doubting whether you actually see anything but two lights above—those eyes.

In fact, it seems as if the good old fairy lady who

presided over Joram's face, was a capricious painter—capricious even for a painter, nay, even for a woman—and had drawn that part of the picture intended for the foreground of this human form divine, all perspective. Nature and true art always go together; and Joram's shirt-maker had heightened the view of this perspective by the altitude of the advanced points of Joram's collar, which was starched stiff withal, and held Joram's jaws so straight to the front, and his neck so immovably erect, that you wondered whether Joram was not afflicted with one of Job's comforters on the neck.

"I have brought you a little garden sarse, Widow March, not knowing how's you mightn't be pestered in the city to get fresh vegetables."

Joram, by a stupendous effort, turned his erect person towards the open hall-door, through which the baskets were visible, and caught an indistinct view, I dare say, of the edge of the greater basket.

"You are very, very good, Mr. Jumps."

"Folks always calls him squire to home!" was heard from the far end of the railway tunnel, in a nasal twang.

"Keep your peace, Joram!" sternly ordered his indignant sire.

"Wall, as you're justice peace, s'pose I must." These sounds, I must not forget to say, issued from the tunnel; but Joram's cheeks, and chin, and collar, were as immovable as the rock through which railway tunnels are usually pierced.

"My hopeful son there," Mr. Jumps went on to say,

without deigning to notice the witticism just perpetrated—" my hopeful son there thinks he must have an education. Wall, the course adopted by my father in Vairmont was just to let common sense do the business, for he always thought common sense the chief end of life, especially on a farm. Then says I to Joram, says I, 'I'm your natural-born father, I believe,' says I, and Mrs. Jumps she nodded her head, 'and I'm not goin' to be stingy with you, and spoil your education, just 'cause your gran'daddy spoilt your daddy's. So just adopt your course. What is it? Speak up like a man.'

"'Then,' says Joram, says he, 'I've been thinking ever since that ere Guilford March was out here, and Suz she thinks so too, that an educated man knows more than an uneducated man!'

"'Hain't got any more common sense, Joe,' says I.

"'Wall,' says he 'Guilford knew more than all on us put together, except you and mam. Then thinks I to myself,' says Joram, says he, 'there ain't no use of education unless in the learned professions. And that's the reason why I have wanted to be a minister ever since that ere March boy came out here.'

"I tried a long time to beat this notion out of Joram's head, for I thought he never would make a minister worth going to hear. Still I was willing to give the critter an education to make a man of him, but—

"'It won't be any use on a farm,'" says Joram, says he.

"'Why not?' says I.

"'Cause it didn't do Guilford March any good, and I

kinder guess on the contrary it made him sick of farming.' "

"Did too! true as preachin," issued from the tunnel.

"Wall now, Widow March, I've brought him in to see what can be done, and all I ask of you is just to adopt a course."

"Please explain yourself, Mr. Jumps—Squire Jumps I mean," said my mother, looking apologetically at Joram.

"Yes marm!" said the immovable centre of the picture.

"Wall mam, if you can take this ere boy of mine"—the "boy" was six feet tall and twenty-two years old—"if you can take this ere boy," he repeated, "do his boardin, lodgin, and washin, and ironin, and mendin, and send him to Doctor Oliphant's school, I'll do what's right."

"To tell you the only trouble in the matter," replied my mother, "I've no room to give your son."

"Sleep with the boys, thick as three in a bed, don't care a darn, by Golden!"

The canvas of the picture shook a little as these sounds were emitted from the vanishing point of rays.

At this stage of the negotiation, Guilford came in for his dinner, and he and I readily agreed with my mother that a new bedstead might be set up in our room for Joram Jumps.

"Wall," says the good farmer, rising, "now mam adopt your course. Say what is it?"

"What is what, Mr. Jum—I mean *Squire* Jumps?"

Mrs. March did not venture to glance at Joram. The tunnel was regarding the lady, however, and said solemnly again:

"Yes marm!"

"Why, say how much you ask, mam, set your own price; so it 'taint onreasonable I'm ready to adopt"—

"Oh! as for that matter, Squire Jumps"—the little lamps seen through the tunnel twinkled—"the terms shall be the regular price."

Which being arranged to the satisfaction of all concerned, Squire Jumps arose to go. My mother invited him to dine. The farmer excused himself on the plea of business.

"Stay to dinner, dad!" spoke Joram rather eagerly for a picture.

"See how they live. Want my money's worth."

The old gentleman was unchangeable, however, and Bowes was called to empty the baskets. There was quite a bill of fare. To wit: A turkey nicely dressed, a half peck of meal in a pillow case, three quinces, one squash, twelve apples, a tenderloin of fresh pork, three carrots, a string of silver-skinned onions, two dozen eggs, one blood beet, a little coriander seed in a bit of muslin tied up with pinkish ribbons, two rolls of fresh butter, and a little kitten from Susannah to Mabel.

"I came into town in the cars with our new member," said Mr. Jumps senior. "He larfed at me considerable about these two baskets, and asked me if I wasn't carrying my dinner into town? I told him no; I wasn't a member of the legislature."

The tunnel now laughed outright, suddenly checking himself and coughed like a locomotive just going out at the far end of the perspective.

Farmer Jumps had kept up a friendly intercourse with us, ever since the Guilford affair, concerning which he often laughed loudly.

"Your mother's the woman for the money," said Jumps. "She knows how to adopt a course. Now if she'd said 'no!' and kept your brother back from goin onto a farm, he'd never have been satisfied, and might at last have run away and gone out West, and you never have heard more on him. But she just told me, says she,

"'Don't spare my son a little labor, Mr. Jumps, let him have his heart's content. He won't bother you long.'

"'Trust me for that,' said I, catchin her idea in a second, and larfin ready to bust myself. 'Only take care on his health,' says she, but just show him what farming truly is.'

"Now that's the way to break in wild colts.

"Now my two boys took it into their heads there was nothin like playin cards. So I just shot 'em up in the old cabin—that was arter we moved into the new house—with two of the hands to work on the farm, and sot 'em all to playin high low jack and the game, or whatever they liked. Wall, they thought it fine fun for a while, but by and by grew tired and wanted to come out. 'But no, boys,' says I, 'you love the crittur—just you stay where you are till you are satisfied.'

"I guess I kept 'em in with nothing but their meals for four days and nights, and they hain't touched a card since."

"Never will!" muttered Joram distantly.

This conversation took place at the Jumpses, when I was sent there to rusticate after my love freak with Dulcinea. The family were living quite comfortably in a new house built of hewn logs. The neighborhood was settled more thickly. The O'Gradys had been driven out by the intolerable force of public opinion, the American civilizer; the school-house was standing on the road-side at a mile's distance from the Jumps estate, and here prayer meetings were held weekly, and school in the winter time.

Little as we may commend the reputation of rustic schools in that country, and at that dim twilight period, this we may say—the prayer meetings were *unique*. Far be it from us to speak irreverently, much less with ridicule, of those private assemblages of the good. The rude attempts at religious services on the part of those benighted pioneers, may perchance bear more glorious testimony at the judgment seat than the more refined and sumptuous worship, vacantly and with wandering eyes, conned over in velvet pews, and chanted from the throats of gilded organs, or trilled with operatic effect by hired musicians. In the East, good honest souls are hired to mourn for the dead. Why may not we employ proxies to sing for the living? 'Tis doubtless sweeter, in the ears of cherubim and seraphim on high, to hear the well tuned voices of professional sweet singers, than the inharmonious concourse of rude utterances from a promiscuous congregation of saints and sinners.

Mew me my good pussy cat. Coo me my soft turtle dove—I'll fain do my own roaring in the streets.

And since we have descended to the animal creation, it behoves us to speak at once of certain young crows, or gentlemen of the cloth, as they are softly denominated, from a certain Theological Seminary not many leagues distant from that State in our grand confederacy where swine are wont to be fed. In the woods, through which they disseminated their doctrines, and quartered themselves on the simple farmer folk, they were known as *perfectionists.* The incumbent of the Green Run circuit was the Rev. Mr. Milkwhite. On the occasion of my attending "meeting" in the little log school-house by the road-side, this gentleman, a youthful prophet, sat behind a little pine table, serving the purposes of pulpit and desk, with his eyes of milky blue raised, or rather voluminously rolled, up to the ceiling. It was after the regular morning service—a special gathering of the Just, making or already made perfect. Here sat on low wooden benches a few of the choice spiritual dames and fathers of the Church Militant, settled in the neighborhood of Green Run. As it did not seem to be expected or desired that sinners would be present, it was with no little difficulty I had prevailed upon Joram and Tobias to remain with me. In the brief interval between the two meetings they pointed out the parties assembled, and gave me their names, with a glimpse here and there of their characters. I found them to be chiefly the termagant wives and hen-pecked husbands of the township, with an honest exceptional old grey headed saint—ready to worship God with sheep or goat.

To my own discredit be it acknowledged, that Walter March was there from motives of idle curiosity.

"Brother Pipelegs will lead the meeting in prayer," quoth the Rev. Mr. Milkwhite, lowering his eyes towards the side of the house occupied by the female benches, but raising his mortal incumbrance of a body, turning with a heavenly sigh, and kneeling down with much devout emotion—in short, a groan.

Brother Pipelegs' prayer was not very edifying. He had become familiar to the ears of the neighborhood, at Jumps's and elsewhere, for years. But he was followed by young Milkwhite himself. Oh! what a happy season: those excited hearts leaped for joy; their joyful groans, their shouts of Hosannah! Amen! come Quickly! Jordan! and Canaan! were heard far through the green old cloistered woods. Yet I, who had not long since passed through some excitement—not such as this, however—in a religious way, God forgive my shortcomings—I was not completely overcome, but wondered at the manifest discrepancy between natural cause and supernatural effect, for Mr. Milkwhite was not in my worldly eyes an exciting young man, but a feeble, rather, I thought. Be that as it might, here was the emotion of a host under the thunder claps of a Wickliffe.

Amid the rapid rustling of palm leaf and turkey tail fans, a hymn was then sung to the tune of Peter Street, for the refreshment of those devotees.

Rev. Mr. Milkwhite's eyes were no longer on the ceiling. Doubtless the dove for which he had been looking had come down. And that dove, it appeared to my sinful mind, Mr. Milkwhite found rustling amid the muslins of the good dames before him, for there were his eyes now also, during the singing of one of Watt's beautiful hymns.

Brother Peppergrass was then called on for a prayer, and the meeting knelt again.

Mrs. Peppergrass was deeply moved; her sighs choked into gasps, her gasps grew into sobs, her sobs fell into tears, her tears dried into moans, and Mr. Milkwhite noiselessly arose to comfort the afflicted dame. He knelt down by her side and softly placed his arm around that buxom waist, while with the hand of the other arm he tenderly brought the cheek of Mrs. Peppergrass on his own shoulder. In this heart-moving, this comforting position, he gently consoled the afflicted Mrs. Peppergrass with the words of hope and joy, till Mr. Peppergrass ceased praying.

"Will Brother Dandelamb pray?"

Mrs. Dandelamb now fell into a similar state of

tribulation, to that lately betrayed by the now calm Mrs. Peppergrass, and Mr. Milkwhite vouchsafed a no less touching condolence.

"The meeting will now," he said, as Mr. Dandelamb closed his hearty, honest, simple appeal, "the meeting will now have a season of silent prayer."

And the benevolent Mr. Milkwhite moved like an angel of mercy from man to man, and from woman to woman, to comfort and relieve the o'erfraught heart. How gently he laid his hand—a hand of pearl—on the shoulder of each distressed brother! How tenderly he communed closely, face against face, with each sad sister! A chapter in the New Testament was then read. The attention given would be a mild reproach to any city auditory, it was almost breathless—except from the palm leaf and turkey tail fans.

At length the reader, with much emphasis, came to the words—"Be ye perfect." No sooner was "perfect" uttered, than prone upon the floor fell three sisters and one brother, and so far as I could see, they were all in a swoon. There was some slight spasmodic action here and there, but in another moment, they all four lay pale and motionless.

To my astonishment, this did not frighten Mr. Milkwhite.

"Where," said I resentfully to myself, "where now that tender care which, when the bodies of these simple people could sustain themselves, was too freely granted? Oh! Milkwhite!"

I then whispered to Joram, "Why in the world don't they do something for the poor creatures?"

Alas! Joram's ears seemed buried beneath his shirt collar; his eyes fixed reverentially on the milky azure eyes before him.

"Toby!" I shouted in that young gentleman's ears; "will none of them move? Shall we let them die?"

"Nothing but the 'power,'" whispered Tobias.

I moved forward myself, towards the nearest body. Both Joram and Toby held me back. There they lay, extended in syncope during the rest of the chapter, during another prayer from Mr. Milkwhite, a concluding hymn and the benediction. We went away and left them still lying there, stiff, white and motionless.

Toby told me, after leaving the little log temple, that the four persons who had fallen before our eyes, were thought to have arrived at the coveted state of perfection. The proof of this consisted in their trances. The stout Mr. Pipelegs, and the gaunt, sharp-visaged Mrs. Peppergrass no sooner heard the sound of certain charmed words, such as Perfection and Holy Spirit, than away they swooned. Mr. Peppergrass at the plough, or Mrs. Peppergrass at the churn, would sink down at no further notice, and remain insensible for an hour.

On our way homeward, that still sweet Sabbath evening, feeling that Nature had been violated, and God profaned in the solemn courts of the pure wilderness, I said to Joram—

"You are very affectionate in these parts! Do all ministers embrace the good sisters of the church in this wise?"

"Don't call that anything, do ye?"

"Why at home you may kiss a French damsel, or madame—on New Year's day—but this sort of thing, you know" ——

"Brotherly love," quoth the walking tunnel-picture at my side.

"But I wouldn't bear it! Do you intend to marry a wife here, and permit such liberties?"

"No! I intend to be a minister myself!"

CHAPTER XIX.

MABEL AND JORAM.

Mabel Latrobe! the cricket on our hearth, the canary-bird of the house, our bright little star-flower. Maude was the fringed gentian of the prairie, sometimes our lily of the valley. In what colors may I paint thee, Mabel! my life's darling!

Every artist knows how difficult it is to take the likeness of a child, and it seems as though Mabel always was a child, and ever will be a child. And I fear lest the patient reader of these leaflets of memory grow tired of child history. O! reader, companion of my journey so far up the hill of life, dost thou weary of the tender growths of plant, and tree, and grassy violet bank? Seekest thou impatiently the dark pine and rocky crag alone? Bear with me, gentle sir, a little while, ere we depart from the sweet scenes of childhood. One look more at the village green over which you tripped to school and sanctury in days when —— well, no matter; but look at that little locket, and those scraps of old notes treasured away, and sigh with me o'er boyhood and your own Mabel Latrobe.

Such a medley of folly and wisdom, vanity and

modesty, smartness and *un*common sense, tenderness and ridicule, sympathy and irony, such a little determined coquette of a creature never sat beside me on a fair summer's day.

"Ah, Walter, you are slandering me ungallantly," she exclaims now, as I read her the above sentence in manuscript.

"Sweet Mabel, every lady is at heart a little bit of a coquette—and you cannot deny it."

"But what do you think of gentlemen, you shabby old fellow?"

"Do not bother me over my story, dear Mabel."

I scarcely know whether Mabel was beautiful or not. I never saw anything but her eyes, so soft! and yet a most enchanting wildness—as if the spirit of her Indian grandmother had come from the grand old woods and cataracts, and the broad, free, and beautiful prairies, and asserted her spiritual supremacy over Mabel's cultivated nature.

"Walter, you are a prozy old dreamer."

"Beshrew me! Mabel, sweet, what is the memory of early dreams but the spiritual presence of better things in a material after life?"

"Go on! go on! you are so dull."

Mabel knew everything as if by instinct. She read everybody as if by necromancy or astrology. Yet although she knew so much, and read so many, everybody loved Mabel. One said she was so queer, another thought her funny. It was universally acknowledged that Mabel could keep a secret, and this gave her a world of confidants, so that she knew everybody's secrets, my own, always, of course. Yet Mabel was pure in heart, and she loved everything really pure and beautiful, with a perfect love, a vehement love, a love that made her happy, a love that knit her to me for ever.

But then, how Mabel would ridicule everybody and everything. No one knew it except we at home. In truth, nobody knew Mabel at all. No one thought that such a quiet child could be the life of the house: no one dreamed that she chirped and sang from daylight to midnight: no one knew that she could dance on her tip-toes, jump over chairs and a-top of tables, and perform all the tricks of the gymnasium.

So you perceive what a nondescript I have to describe, for nobody either knew anything or would believe anything about her. They thought her prudent, believed in her, confided in her, trusted in her, and she was true to them all, and laughed at them all, and loved them all—but alas! not as all would have her love them!

Thus she grew up a little charming Sphinx, a riddle to us all, and a fairy delight. Mabel was quite independent in her notions; neither Maud nor even her father could judge for her, and she believed in them to the skies, too; yet she had a sharp, joyous, innocent way of seeing and judging for herself, that, I must confess, though her conclusions were often at war with my own, amused me beyond measure.

I wish I could have reduced Mabel to a sober, steady love for me. She was as capricious as any weathercock. She would have her little flirtations with her eyes—that's as far as Mabel ever went in that quarter of female frailty—so that her eyes were quite celebrated all over the city. The awkward country student, the pale young Presbyterian divine, with lemon-colored hair, the licentiate at the Catholic Presbytery, with dark eyes, the shabby genteel lawyer, the dandified young dry-goods' man, the queer old bachelor judge, the youngest boy and the last beau from the East—each vowed there was a peculiar meaning in Mabel's eyes which he alone knew how to solve—the deluded self-flatterers, as if *I* did not know who alone Mabel Latrobe deeply loved, notwithstanding her caprices and shy flirtations.

Joram Jumps had not been at Mrs. March's house a week, ere he had fallen a victim to her eyes; and Joram was as confident of his power of pleasing and of his conquest over Mabel, as young gentlemen frequently are who have had but little intercourse with the sex.

Joram Jumps was a source of endless fun to Mabel, although to save her very life, she could not help using her conquering eyes on the tall, green sapling. She would mimic him to the life—though of course not so rude as do this before his face. Mabel never wounded the feelings of a dear creature in the world. The sly mischief would set all sorts of little traps into which Joram would fall, and the catastrophe appear so very like accident that Joram never suspected any one, and least of all the quiet little tender-eyed Mabel.

Joram often stumbled over objects in the dark hall going to bed, when the lights were all extinguished, accidentally, of course. Joram sometimes complained that Mrs. Bowes had made his bed in a very uncommon manner. Joram found notes in the post-office from young damsels dying for him. But Joram always brought these soft missives straight to Mabel, and to please her in a delicate way, would cut them to pieces with his jack-knife and throw them on the fire in her presence. He never to this day has suspected Mabel Latrobe of all the flattering attentions bestowed upon him from such diverse quarters.

Joram was not destitute of natural ability. He progressed rapidly at Dr. Oliphant's, but now his studies begin to flag. In truth, Joram is in love. Mabel sees it, we all know it, and Mabel is the only one that does not seem to enjoy it after all. Mabel grows grave, alas, has she lost her heart likewise? No, Mabel is really too good to enjoy any one's misery, and Joram is evidently in tribulation. Yet the son of stout Farmer Jumps is no weak dangler, no persecuting step-slave. Joram is independent in his feelings.

On one evening, seeing Mabel alone in the library after tea, he glided in, and seated himself stiffly. He closed his hands on his lap devoutly, and then folded his arms across his breast thoughtfully, and then clasped his hands behind his head boldly, and then coughed a short, embarrassed, starting cough, as if not sure the train would follow; the little lamps shone in the far end of the tunnel with uncommon briskness.

"Miss Latrobe!" at length he said, bending a trifle the stiff shirt collar on the side towards that demure young lady. "Have the pleasure spending this evening with you alone?"

Miss Latrobe was fairly frightened to death. Then she thought she would comply, merely to see what this oddity would say and do. But she was a very coward in all but eye skirmishing. The onset she dreaded—in fact she had never thought over such foolish things. And so Miss Latrobe vouchsafed, after a little hesitation, during which Joram Jumps sat on pins and needles, without moving a muscle—the following reply:

"I came in for a moment only, Mr. Joram, and am waiting for Miss Maud. I—I—have a little engagement with her for this evening."

Mabel! Mabel! what a fib! Her very hesitation and confusion betrayed it.

During the reply to his important and delicate request, Joram changed his hands uneasily, and drew out his handkerchief with abstraction, and on the conclusion of Mabel's reply, he arose, faced squarely about, stalked to the door, faced about again, looked from afar towards his poor little frightened enemy, and as he gave a petulant flirt with his handkerchief, exclaimed—

"Don't care a darn, by Golden!"

Then the centre of the picture vanished from the landscape.

CHAPTER XX.

A DENOUEMENT.

READER, had you ever a friend for whom you felt a degree of responsibility "in certain circles?" If so was not your friend sure to commit all his *faux pas*, say all his silliest things, do his most awkward and extraordinary deeds in that very "certain circle?"

Major Fontenoy was always my beau ideal of the gentleman. The point was disputed by Mabel, who preferred Allen, and by Guilford, who was too matter-of-fact to enjoy the Major's sentimentality.

Even Maud smiled at him. Walter felt responsible for his friend, and thought the apparent excess of sentiment, nothing worse than a flowering of the Major's exquisite nature.

"Nor," said I, "is he sentimental on all occasions; it is here, in this house, beneath the eyes of Maud March, that my dear old friend appears to so poor advantage."

But with all reasonings and all efforts on my part, the good Major never seemed to do himself justice at Lilac Cottage. In all other places the gallant soldier captivated right and left.

We were sitting one evening after a summer rain,

upon the porch, enjoying the fresh fragrance of the earth, and the awakened perfume of the flowers, when Major Fontenoy came up the lawn. He advanced towards us in a sprightly manner—a little too sprightly for his years—the hypercritical Mabel thought. This peculiarity was noticed afar.

"See!" said Guilford, smiling, "I suppose Walter would term that, 'graceful motion.'"

"No," replied Walter "the major never will be graceful, or in any way himself, when Maud is within view."

I went forward to meet him.

"How lovely the evening after a shower, hey!" said my friend, as he drew near the ladies, and lifted his cap handsomely.

"Yes, major," replied Mrs. March, "will you walk up and join us? we are all out enjoying the freshness."

"It is as sweet," he said taking a seat, "as the breath of cattle on the lea, hey Walter? your friend old Brindle, hey!"

The breath of cattle is charming, yet altogether the comparison did not quite suit—some people are *so* fastidious. I warmly replied, "Yes sir," with a smile of appreciation.

"What has the fair lady Maud been doing to-day? Sitting in her bower, hey!"

"Yes, major, if by bower you mean my school."

Maud was innocent of offence, yet the major blushed, seeing how inapropos was this second comparison.

"Temple, I might say with more propriety, hey! sweet goddess, hey!"

"No, no!" said Maud laughing, "I should rather say plain old school-house."

She stepped down the porch, plucked a sweet pea blossom, and handed it to Major Fontenoy.

The old gentleman joined the laugh, with his heart full of simple ready glee. Then he grew silent. It was only in Maud's presence the agreeable talker ever was silent.

Guilford then spoke of meeting a soldier of the garrison, who told him slily he had got on the sick list by playing old soldier with the surgeon, and came down in town to have his fun.

The major had an anecdote ready in a moment.

"Of course you all remember Surgeon Prim, stationed here a few years ago, hey! Well, a soldier came into the dispensary one morning with his tongue whitened with chalk, hey. Doctor asked him what's the matter? 'Fever, sir,' hey! touching his hat, hey! 'How do you know that?' 'Felt of my pulse,' hey? 'Felt of your own pulse, sir!' thundered out the doctor, hey! 'How dare you feel you own pulse? Let me see your tongue,' hey! The man showed his tongue; 'Much coated, much coated,' said the doctor, hey! Then he drew a little of the whitening on the end of his knife-blade, dropped a drop of acid—fumed like slacking lime, hey? The doctor caught the man by the throat, heigh! and thrust him out of the office, hey!

saying, 'You are a rascal, hey! you feel of your own pulse, hey! and coat your own tongue too, hey! get out of my office, hey!' "

No one could resist one of the major's stories, his own excitement and drollery seemed to make the dullest story good. He never put "hey!" after a real inquiry, and that made it appear the more ludicrous.

Of course we all laughed; Mabel, as was her wont on all such occasions, fairly shouted.

The conversation turned next on books. The major was a great reader. He kept us supplied with the latest works. On the whole, what with his books and his beautiful cameos, that payment affair, his flowers and his fun, we all loved the major—though in different degrees, and for various reasons.

"Does Maud love the major?" Guilford inquired of me, as we went around the outside of the house towards the barn, for a look at Brindle's calf.

"Why do you inquire of me?"

"Oh, you are something of a connoisseur in love matters; 'Dulcinea,' you know!"

"Oh! ahem, yes; I don't think the major has asked her."

"Then why so many costly gifts?"

"Because he can't help it, I suppose.'

"But why does Maud take them?"

"Why, for the same reason, I suppose."

"You may think as you please, Walter, but I never did quite believe in these purely disinterested Platonic affairs. Wherever there's so much smoke, you may be sure of fire."

"He think of getting married!" I cried. "Nonsense! his one hand, an old bachelor, at least forty-five. Nonsense! nonsense!"

"I hope it is so, that's all. Let's go in."

Mrs. March had retired to attend to household matters, and Mabel had gone to tell Bowes Major Fontenoy's last story, and so it fell out on that fair, fresh summer's evening, that the major found himself alone with Maud March.

They rose from the porch and walked about the flower beds, and among the rose-bushes, and beneath the lilac trees, and the leaves and flowers all around them distilled sweet odors as they passed.

"The flowers seem to know you, Miss Maud, hey?"

"Yes, they ought to, major; I train them, you know."

"Very good, hey? very good, hey?" I dare say you train them even to talk, too, hey?"

"Certainly!" answered Maud, laughingly.

"Then Miss Maud—*dear* Maud—tell me, hey! what you would have this sweet pea blossom say to Major Fontenoy, hey!"

For the first time in her life, my sister attributed a feeling to the poor old officer, stronger than friendship. And yet, thought she, the next moment, how could such a thing be? Her passion of self-depreciation drove out the suspicion.

"It must be a mistake," thought Maud.

"If the little flower," she now hastened to say, "does not speak volumes of gratitude for my mother, and love for all the rest of us, I'll not own it as my gift."

They now stood in a closely shaded part of the garden.

"Love, Miss Maud, hey! love, hey!"

"Yes," faltered she, "such love as" —

The major dropped upon his knees. He took the listless hand of the young lady in his own, and while he held over it the poor maimed arm, he poured forth his love.

"Love me, hey! Love me, hey! Behold me at your feet, delighted, hey!"

Maud struggled in bewilderment.

"Beautiful! lovely! angel! Maud, hey! My heart has been yours for years! long, sweet years, hey!"

With difficulty the afflicted girl wrested her hand away. Covering her face she exclaimed—

"Oh! Major Fontenoy! dear old friend, this is indeed painful, unexpected, too bad! too bad!"

Bursting into tears, she left him, and hastened into the cottage.

The moon looks calmly down. It shines upon the flower that has closed its petals since the god of day, its life and light are gone. It reaches through the leafy covering where the bird sleeps securely and fondly with its loving mate. It discloses the bare stem on the lilac tree, where spring blossoms have fallen off, and left a withered thing. It lights up the dew-drops hanging on the point of a thorn projecting from a beautiful rose. It sees the grass covering the earth where hopes lie buried.

And down through the vista of the lawn, behold, shrinking beneath the friendly shade, one goeth with a maimed hand and a blighted heart!

Alas, Major Fontenoy, it is indeed too bad! too bad!

CHAPTER XXI.

MILLBROOK.

Our path towards the bush went by a beautiful farm through which ran a winding rivulet, overlooked by a little green bank near the roadside. In the spring time this bank was carpeted with a multitude of wild flowers, dandelions, aster flowers, violets, and anemones. It was canopied overhead by the profuse branches of a grove of young butternut trees, up and along which the fox grape climbed and trailed its vines, forming many a graceful festoon.

Here it was often our delight to pause as we strolled out on pleasant Sunday afternoons after old Brindle—Guilford could not leave his business on week-days. To sit or lie here on the grass and build air-castles, each in his own way, was for years our romance and delight.

"Come, Walter," said Guilford on one of these memorable times, as we lay extended at full length, with straw hats covering our faces from the sun, "come! let your kite fly!"

It was no sooner suggested, than Fancy took wing. Away it soared into regions of love, religion and poetry, changing almost momentarily, with capricious humor.

"But," said Guilford, "come down a little from the sixth and seventh heavens: you are to be a soldier."

"Ah, yes," and Fancy took a fresh start, careered through an ideal life, as little like probability as possible, and insensibly gained an apex on some pink cloud, silver trumpet in hand, blowing a blast of mingled fame and philanthropy.

Then said Guilford, laughing in his hearty, pleasant way—

"Walter! Walter! you are the least belligerent knight-errant I ever knew!"

"Brother," replied Walter, "I would draw sword to deliver damsels, conquer Palestine, or overthrow oppression in any form."

"Dare say! dare say! but by herald and flag, or rather by poem or metaphor!"

"I hope, Guilford, you don't doubt my courage?"

"No, but I do doubt your common sense."

"Common sense!" I cried, resentfully, "there never was a good cause, or mighty achievement yet, but had to encounter common sense as its enemy."

"Do you know why?" quoth Guilford.

"Tell me if you can."

"Because common sense is a machinist, genius an inventor; common sense looks to the means, genius to the end."

"Yes," cried I, "all things are possible to genius, all things impossible to common sense. Your common sense is born with a 'no' in his mouth."

"There is something in that, Walter. Genius points the way to common sense. Common sense clears the way for genius."

"Well, well, Guilford, what would you have me think of? what do?"

"Tell me first your motives in seeking West Point? What preparation are you making? How much mathematics have you got in your genius? Can you govern men? How would your nerves stand fire? Do you think your soldiers can hear you? Jump up now and give a command."

"Anything to please common sense," I said, rising.

"Shoulder arms!"

"Pretty good," said Guilford, laughing; "you've frightened off the bobolink."

"Charge bayonet!"

"Better yet."

"By regiment, right wheel!"

"Yes, yes, 'by regiment;' but begin by squad or platoon—a long time before you will command higher."

"By squad—by squad ——

"Pshaw!" I exclaimed, "I would rather wheel the world into line by kingdoms and empires!"

Guilford roared with laughter, and said, "begone, brave army, and don't kick up a row! Now for your views on the subject I have mentioned, Cadet Walter."

The Dreamer was silent.

The Doer spoke.

"The chief object, the great demand of your nature

is education. West Point will afford this—so far as elementary books may go. Then, I've no doubt it is your honest wish to do all the good you can in the world—that is, provided your wild oats are all sown. Now the army, it appears to me, affords as ready a field for cultivation, as fruitful a soil for tillage, as any other field in life."

"How may one do good in the army, pray?"

Monsieur Common Sense went on.

"By example—the silent magnetism of life, far more powerful, perhaps, than the electric shock of astonishing doctrines."

"I must confess," said Walter, "that to astonish would not be disagreeable."

"Those who strive to astonish the world, most generally succeed—that is, the world is astonished at their folly!"

Walter now grew weary of the conversation. His notions of philanthropy were rather vague, and tended more to speculative enjoyment than to practical operation.

"Now, Guilford, I've flown my kite. Suppose you let yours slip?"

It was near sun-down, we were sitting upon the bank, enjoying the beauties of the landscape.

"Do you see that farm-house?" asked Guilford.

"What, the miller's?"

"Yes. I would exchange all other earthly success for the ownership of that habitation and these green acres. I would ask no better fortune than just to live out my days here—the mill below clicking in my ears—to look out upon the green meadows at our feet, with their pyramid haystacks—the grand old oaks and sycamores looming around me like guardian giants—those waving fields of grain—the white sheep dotting the hills sloping down to the brook—the cattle yonder more precious to me than Egyptian Apis—the barns—the poultry—the orchard—this rivulet—a silver thread upon which to string my necklace of jewels—grant me these, with my mother to dwell in yon house, and you to live in a cottage of your own upon this very bank" ——

"Large enough for a library?" I cried.

"Yes, with you over here I would be the happiest man in America! Walter."

"But Maud and Mabel—what's to become of them?"

"Mabel!" my brother Guilford uttered abstractedly.

"Yes Maud and Mabel," I repeated.

"Oh! I'd like a fortune for their sakes, or rather for *her* sake"— Guilford looked at me in a puzzling manner.

"As for Maud," continued he, "she should marry Allen, and I would buy a library for him—a law library."

Guilford then proceeded, as we arose and started away after old Brindle, to speak of the present.

It was now nearly three years since Guilford became shopboy. His experiences had been various. His first employer was a grocer. His wages twelve dollars a month. Mr. Sortem was a pinching tradesman, wore a pin head on his shoulders, and you would think a pin hole in his bosom; for his heart was as diminutive as his head. This man was a widower, and had a little needle of a daughter—she was so sharp tongued. My mother took her as a lodger, but she darted out so dreadfully her little fiery serpent of a tongue, that Mabel was driven half crazy, and my mother was obliged to send word to Mr. Sortem that it was inconvenient to keep his daughter. This enraged that gentleman, and in retaliation Guilford was discharged.

He then went to measuring tape and ribbons in a small dry goods establishment, a little further up from the market. Here he lived with a worthy gentleman, who treated him very well, but the skeleton now was an elder brother who had crazy fits, and exercised, sane or insane, unbounded influence over Guilford's master. It happened one day that the young clerk found a lost pocket-book in the street. It was advertised, and no owner appearing, the skeleton took possession. Boys are supposed to have no natural rights—of course—besides this was a sort of supernatural affair. Guilford had spirit to leave the establishment, and found employment better suited to his early tastes. He is now a clerk in the warehouse of the great steamboat owner, Mr. Mayflower. Guilford never has felt that high respect which is due shopboys—"Little fellows," said Guilford, "who for the sake of dressing well pinch their souls as well as their bodies." It must be borne in mind that he was prejudiced.

Nothing is wanting now but the prospect of some day retiring on a farm, to render Guilford March "the happiest man in America." This end to attain is the ultimate hope, the grand climacteric of his day dreams.

Besides supporting himself, Guilford paid no little pecuniary tribute to the lady paramount, our excellent mother, to secure whom in the unembarrassed possession of Lilac Cottage was the first object in the youth's heart.

"But one more payment to make, "quoth Walter, as the two went searching the wood, pausing occasionally to hark for the sound of a cow-bell.

"But one more, and then the cut off lot to repurchase."

"If we *can!*" said Guilford, emphatically.

"Why may we not?" I inquired.

"The gentleman who bought it has gone away, leaving his business in the hands of Maud's friend, Mr. Magroy."

"What, Old Growl?"

"Yes, Allen told me so yesterday. He came down to the counting room."

"But were we not promised the refusal of it?"

"Mr. Magroy may interpose some friendly obstacle," said Guilford ironically.

"That old man is our evil genius!" I cried.

At this moment I had taken hold of a branch lying across the path, and was drawing it back in order to pass by. The branch broke and I fell.

"Guilford!" I demanded, with increased wrath, rising from the earth, "if you had the power, to what fate would you consign the persecutor of our house, the maligner of Maud and mother? Would you not hang the wretch?"

"No."

"Would you not force him to do justice where he has wronged? To take Allen back?"

"No! No!"

"Would you not reduce him to rags? fling him on the wide wide world, an outcast and a beggar? a by-word—a reproach—a hissing?—a"

"No Walter. He should marry Mrs. Polyphemia Fidgets!"

The distant though welcome tinkle of old Brindle's bell was heard. We left the wood ere long, and the trees with their briarean arms arched over the little cow-path behind us. The leafy wilderness grew musical with the twitter of insects and solemn toll of night birds. The sun had already sunk upon the western prairies, where the Fringed Gentian closed her blue hood, and watched like a nun in the chapel of the dead. Nature lay down in stately repose.

And Doer and Dreamer went pensively homeward, passing from the present into the future.

CHAPTER XXII.

MAJOR FONTENOY VISITS MR. MAGROY.

> But gentle heaven
> Cut short all intermission : front to front
> Bring thou this fiend of Scotland and myself.
>
> MACBETH.

AUTUMN came with its crimson-spotted leaves and Indian summer sky, a beautiful, hazy, smoky, dreamy, indolent carnival for all the forces of nature. Night and day seemed to have crossed orbits and confounded each other, or like two tired wrestlers, were lying down peacefully together. The clouds seemed toppling over with drowsiness, like the dizzy old Leaning Tower at Pisa, or those ancient minarets whose bases are wearing away by the wasting flood of Egypt's Nile. The red windmills on the river shore looked as if standing beneath an incessant rain of dim fire. My body went about tenantless of its spirit, which methought was likewise absent in cloudland, dreaming with sister spirits.

The thought, the possibility even of leaving home, rendered doubly dear to me the enjoyment of my favorite season in its favorite haunts. I lay down by my father's grave, in the long, dry grass. The banks of the river and the sound of the woods—where the leaves falling made music like that of showers on straw-thatched cottages—grew sweeter and sweeter every day, as with melancholy pleasure I paced along. The thought of leaving Mabel weighed a little upon my listless spirits.

"If I do go, dear Mabel," said Walter to that beloved creature, as we walked the lawn together one afternoon, "if I do go, I never shall forget my little madcap sweetheart."

Mabel changed color and looked away

"Ah!" thought I, "her grief is great."

"You may be sure of my constancy, Mabel; I shall be ever true to thee."

"You will have many things to think of more important than a little girl," she said, still looking away.

"No! nothing so sweet, no one so dear as you. In the palaces of the great, on the field of renown, at the top of Fame's ladder, Mabel shall claim the first place in my heart."

Walter's manner was a graceful blending of loftiness with condescension. But it was not so fascinating in its effects upon Mabel as one might suppose.

"Had you not better begin to think of your mathematics, Walter?" said she in a quizzical manner. In another moment she had fled from my side, and vanished into the house.

"Mathematics!" I exclaimed. "The valley of dry bones! 'twill be the death of me some day."

"My thoughts now were fully turned on West Point. The son of Mr. Hasting's political friend had failed, leaving a vacancy. M. Latrobe was going to the United States Senate the coming winter, and promised to urge my appointment.

Guilford has gone up rapidly in the esteem of Mr. Mayflower. He has just been promoted to chief clerk. He has been able to assist his eldest brother, John March, in the pursuit of his legal studies, though John requires little—ere long, none at all, as he will soon go into practice.

Townspeople began to remark—

"The Marches are certainly a rising family."

As for the coming payment, six hundred dollars, there will be no difficulty with reference to that; for between Guilford, Maud, and Mrs. March's savings during the year, it is to be paid when due. Our hearts swelled with emotions of pride and pleasure as we thought the great burden of our lives, especially that of our mother, was so soon to be rolled away.

But one thing seemed wanting to fill our cup to overflowing—the happiness of the unselfish, conscientious, glorious Maud. And even here an unexpected light came breaking in just at this time, cheering us—or at least *me*, for Guilford was less sanguine—with hopes for the dear lily of the valley.

There are some souls in this rough world who are capable of a height of magnanimity inconceivable to the vulgar. Major Fontenoy, dear reader, was one of those souls. He no sooner learned the secret with reference to Maud and the Magroys than, to use a military phrase, he advanced to the rescue.

"I will see Old Growl myself, Walter, hey!" said he.

The buoyant spirit of this noble man, in the immortality of its vital goodness, enabled him to bear the burden of his grief more lightly than one might look for in a man of feeling.

A sudden grey streak about his temples, showed like the ashes of unquenchable fire smouldering beneath, or that the lightning had passed. Beyond this there was no change in the outward man. The bouquets, the beautiful cameos, the music and books came as ever from the "unknown friend"—alas! never to be known by dearer name!

I had been brought more into the company of Major Fontenoy of late than usual. He claimed the right to fit me for West Point. We became as knight and squire, rather than master and pupil. This intimacy led to his pouring out his secrets to Walter, and to that youngster telling the excellent bachelor, with an attempted fine stroke of consolation, how matters stood in the heart of Maud.

One day then, in the hazy October, behold Major Fontenoy at the entrance of the kennel.

A knock.

A growl—"Come in!"

"Good morning Mr. Magroy, hey!"

"Good morning! good morning. Take a chair Major Fontenoy, take a chair sir."

"Thank you sir, hey! The plum trees begin to look bare, hey! in the sere and yellow leaf, hey! Melancholy, melancholy, hey!"

"Course of nature, major, course of nature; no use going to bed because leaves fall—so Dean Swift thought, you know."

The major was pleased at finding the canny Scot in so pleasant a mood.

"Hearts like yours so stoutly bound up, are not easily disturbed, Mr. Magroy, hey! but with me, destitute of ties of any fleshly nature, with no soft eyes to look into mine for sympathy; the leaves sir are children, hey! my only children, hey!"

"Not so much to be pitied major, after all. Real children are a bother, sir. Nay, friend Fontenoy," he added, leaning over the table, and slightly stamping his cane on the door, "children are a grief! a grief, sir! a grief, a grief."

"Ah yes, hey! But might there not be new channels dug to turn the waters around the work, hey! —imprisoned heart, hey!—so that pity and forgiveness may march to the attack of grief, and deliver the heart from its dungeon, hey!"

"You allude to a sore subject, a sore subject, Major Fontenoy. Pardon me, sir, but we will leave it."

"Oh, ask pardon, hey!"

"Yes, sir!" said Mr. Magroy, looking dark already from the pine forest about his eyes.

The good old gentleman was confused, not knowing which of the two was asking pardon. The gentlemanly major was quick to detect the dilemma.

"I ask pardon *myself*, hey! ha! ha! Beg pardon, hey! ha! ha!"

Though the major still laughed, Mr. Magroy did not cease to frown, not yet set right.

"Do *you* beg pardon, or do *I* beg pardon, sir?" he thundered, at length.

"I beg yours with all my heart, my dear sir, with all my heart, hey!"

"Granted, granted," said Mr. Magroy, gruffly. "I always thought you a perfect gentleman. Officers of the army generally are, sir."

"I am afraid," said the major slowly, "my dear Mr. Magroy, that I am about to jeopardize the reputation of the class which you have so politely complimented, hey!'

"Yes, I mean to compliment them, sir." The learned Theban did not yet *quite* perceive the major's peculiarity.

"Be good enough, sir, to try me now," he said, in a manner which encouraged the major at once.

"Well sir, your son, hey!"

"My son, sir, what of him, anything happened! but no matter, he is no longer my son. They have robbed me of my Joseph, and carried him away into Egypt,"—the tender hearted father half-sobbed.

"He is a splendid fellow, hey!"

"He is a disobedient, rebellious brat, sir!" exclaimed the classic Mr. Magroy, very unexpectedly to the diplomatist, who had just bgan to flatter himself with his progress in this delicate negotiation.

"Were you aware, dear Mr. Magroy," asked the major, "that in keeping your son under the ban of your displeasure, you are breaking the heart of one of the divinest of human beings?"

"Breaking whose heart?" demanded Mr. Magroy, with a weak glance out of his strong eye.

"The heart of the daughter of one who was once your friend, hey! I will not say more, hey!"

Now the fact that Mr. March had assisted Mr. Magroy when a poor man, was a lasting monument to his disgrace—for Mr. Magroy the rich, thought poverty a disgrace—and this unhappy fact always enraged Archibald Magroy, LL.D. At least so we easily accounted for the mystery.

"The Marches! the detestable Marches!" he shouted jumping to the floor, and setting cane and feet in motion. "The cause of all my troubles, the Egyptians that stole my Joseph. I demand of you, sir, a professsed gentleman, sir, what right have you, sir, to meddle in this business, sir?"

He stopped to shake his cane in the major's face across the table.

"Gentleman! by St. Andrew no gentleman are you."

Again he went on stamping on the innocent floor, as if it were his enemy. Suddenly he cried out more violently—

"To enter a man's house, a man's castle, sir, and remind him not only of his domestic misfortunes, but sir! of his—sir—his poverty, his youthful folly, his disgrace, his beggary, sir."

The major had risen from his chair, and calmly yet sternly confronted the madman before him.

"Sir," said he, "sir, you are making a fool of yourself, hey!"

"This in my own house, sir? to *me*, sir? villain! low born"—

"Who are you, sir?" interrupted Major Fontenoy, "that dare attempt to stain the escutcheon of one born and bred a gentleman—a *Virginia* gentleman, sir? And who, I demand too, sir, are you, that claim to be above the decencies of life, common gratitude for favors, for aid notoriously the groundwork of your fortune? And who, sir"—the major's voice rose and his manner increased in sternness—"who, pray, are you, sir, that dare to profane the name of mother and daughter—in every respect your superiors—and, sir, so far above the conduct you have lyingly attributed to them, as to have renounced all intercourse with your son, and what is still more to their credit for true delicacy of feeling, have never made that mention of your conduct which its infamy deserves. I will proclaim it, sir. Why! were you not an old man, sir, this single arm "—

Astonished, rebuked, alarmed, Mr. Magroy had listened to this address, striving momentarily to interrupt it; but, yielding to the resistless energy of the *true* gentleman before him, he had quailed again and held his peace, till now he sank down in his chair with a groan, uttering faintly:

"Oh! God of Israel, Esau my eldest brother has came up against me, de-liv-er me."

And the wretched old man gasped with terror.

Major Fontenoy stood regarding him a while in silence and undisguisedly contemptuous pity. He then rang the bell, Mrs. Fidgets appeared—so quickly that the major thought her within surprising proximity. Fidgets, who had heard the greater part of the conversation, assumed a look of innocence, and running up to Mr. Magroy with an officious zeal, cried out,

"Good lud! sir, what is the matter?"

Despite Fidgets' affection, her countenance expressed so little pity and sympathy, that the major, with a look of disgust, ordered her contemptuously to bring in some wine and water for her master.

On her speedy return with the required beverage, her master drank with the docility of a child, and sat up in his chair refreshed.

"Leave, hey!" said the major to Mrs. Fidgets, as she lingered caressingly over her master.

The woman obeyed.

"I am very sorry, Mr. Magroy," spoke the major, again sitting down, "that circumstances should have brought about this scene, hey!"

"Please proceed, Major Fontenoy, proceed," replied Mr. Magroy meekly, sipping his wine and water.

"My object in calling, sir, was in a friendly way to reconcile you to your son, the best young man I ever knew, hey! as well as to set the conduct of other persons, the subject of our late conversation, in a fair light before you, hey! you will please perceive that I had no vulgar desire of meddling with your affairs, hey!"

"I will apologize," exclaimed the old man in a whining tone.

"No apologies necessary, hey!" continued the major, somewhat gentler in manner, and less dry and cold in tone.

"What I wish, sir, is more ample satisfaction, hey!"

"What, sir, do you want!" demanded Mr. Magroy peevishly—for an LL.D.

"That you heal these unhappy differences by a simple act of justice."

Mr. Magroy sipped his wine and water, and tapped his cane on the table in silent abstraction a long time. Finally he said,

"Major Fontenoy, you will pardon me for bringing this neighborly conference to an end, sir. But if you please, I will confer with the parties. In short, sir, I would rather see Mrs. March herself."

"Certainly, hey!" growled the major rising, "you will promise me not to insult"—

"Trust me for that, trust me for that. My honor for that, sir!"

"Very well. Good morning, hey!"

"Good morning, *good* Major Fontenoy."

When the major related this scene to me he said,

"I'm inclined to think the old fellow has some honor, too, hey! Walter, hey!"

And the dear major did verily believe that everybody had *some* honor.

I do not know but that he was right.

CHAPTER XXIII.

MR. MAGROY HONORS LILAC COTTAGE.

"Yes; I don't know but he was right," quoth I to Guilford, "or else there's some mystery in it."

"Mighty little honor," quoth he.

"There may be some in his heart," said I.

"I don't believe in fire till I see either smoke or blaze," said he.

"Not if you scent it out?" asked I, returning to the rescue of charity. "The old fellow evinced shame at least, and when Shame goes before, like a Nubian slave, you may be certain the noble Roman, Honor follows after."

At this moment, happening to look from the library, through the lilac trees, upon the mottled lawn, who should we behold but the old Scotsman coming over the grass, stamping his cane, and looking down like Winter trampling on the lingering train of Autumn. Guilford seized his hat and departed for the warehouse. He met Mr. Magroy. That good-natured gentleman stopped and shook hands—rather warmly I thought, for an evil genius.

The two parted, and Mr. Magroy's cane being heard on the steps of the porch, I went to greet him welcome—a feeble welcome to be sure.

"Is Mistress March within?" he asked.

Mr. Magroy sat down heavily in the arm-chair.

I called my mother.

Mr. Magroy arose and bowed profoundly.

My mother went up to him, and held out her hand in a friendly manner.

"I am happy to see you once more in our house, sir."

"Ahem! yes, madam. I reciprocate. In fact, madam, my heart is touched. There have been some differences, madam, between our families, a long time: yes, madam, a long, long time," and Mr. Magroy leaned his breast on his hands, which covered each other and the head of the cane, and looked fixedly at the fire—or something far beyond it.

"I hope, sir," said my mother, "that the hour is at hand when we shall resume our old neighborly intercourse. Yet, sir," she added, "the difference between our circumstances in life" ——

"Say no more, madam, say no more. I've been thinking that all over, madam, on my bed, madam, in my heart, away from that pest of a housekeeper," he added fiercely. "But thank God! that's ended."

My mother thought the distressed old gentleman wandering in his unhappy mind.

"But I cannot live alone, madam. Is that tall, fine boy your son, Mistress March?"

"Yes, sir. Walter, Mr. Magroy. You have not met since—since" —— My mother faltered and glanced reverently towards the picture of my father.

"No, no, Mistress March. Be good enough to request the young gentleman—a worthy, fine-faced boy he looks—please request him to withdraw."

My mother looked surprised! "If you have any matter to communicate to me, sir, do not mind Walter. We have no secrets but what are common to my family."

Mr. Magroy looked a little blank, and then a little displeased, and then somewhat embarrassed. He turned on his chair. He changed his hands on his cane. Finally a thought came and shook him by the head.

He spoke.

"Well, madam, perhaps there is a slate or blackboard that the young gentleman may find for me to write my communication on, for madam, to save my life, I do not feel strength for words. My heart has been wrung, madam. I am a feeble old man, madam. I seek light, consolation, and peace—yes, let him get a slate or a blackboard."

Walter suggested "paper."

"Ah! that will do—quite a bright lad!"

I went to the desk, and drew thence a little folio—in whose pockets scraps of poetry were lodged—and laid it before Mr. Magroy, with some stiff old English paper, such as we then used, and a pencil.

"This will do, my fine fellow, this will do."

10*

He took the pencil, and after a moment's deliberation wrote a few words, then handed the paper to my mother.

Mrs. March handed it to me without looking at it.

"Read it, my son."

"Aloud, mother?"

"Yes."

Mr. Magroy looked vexed, but held his peace.

The communication was as follows:

"Mrs. Fidgets = gone."

I read accordingly,

"Mrs. Fidget's equal to gone;" and felt much pride, too, in my newly acquired knowledge of algebraic terms.

"Never mind the sign of equality," he cried, with his usual cane accompaniment. "Mrs. Fidgets is gone! madam."

Mrs. March said, "I am glad to hear it, Mr. Magroy. I quite congratulate you."

Mr. Magroy took the paper again and wrote—

"She abused my confidence, madam, she had designs on me, she has lied to me about Allen, about you and your worthy daughter; and only last night, madam, she bearded me, threatened me, Archibald Magroy, LL.D., demanded a provision in my will or she would expose me, for what, God only knows, madam. I rose in my righteous indignation and drove her from my house—wish I had kicked her."

Over the last five words the pen had been drawn as if the amiable gentleman had suddenly repented.

My mother read the communication this time, and

handed it to Walter, who read and returned it to Mr. Magroy.

"I am very sorry," said Mrs. March.

"Sorry for whom?" he asked abruptly

"For both of you, sir," replied the kind hearted lady.

"You have it in your power to console," was now written.

Mrs. March wrote in reply.

"I would be happy in my humble way to oblige an old neighbor."

"Thank you madam." The old gentleman paused, handed the paper to my mother, who returned it in silence.

A long time Mr. Magroy paused, with his chin now fastened down to his knuckles, clasped over the head of the cane. Two or three times he nodded approvingly to himself—or the fire—then shook his head immediately afterwards. At length he took paper and pencil and wrote as follows:

"Will you be my housekeeper?"

My mother's face crimsoned as she wrote in strong characters,

"No, sir."

Mr. Magroy read this reply without looking at my mother. He made a peculiar gesture with his head which I interpreted to mean—

"Humph! I thought so! I thought so!"

Then he suddenly wrote more freely, as if he had thought of it before—contingently, but now, decidedly.

Meantime my mother had risen from the lounge, the color on her face deepened and darkened. There was an angry, excited motion of her lips. Her bosom heaved with emotion. She walked hurriedly towards the door as if to flee from a pursuiug enemy. Then, as if changing her mind, she staggered to the window, against the frame of which she leaned.

Mr. Magroy handed me the communication. I handed it to my mother. Her appearance startled me. Never in all her lone widowhood, never in lowest penury and desperate distress, had I seen my mother look so utterly woe-stricken as now.

"Oh God! oh God!" she uttered, "if thou hadst but spared him but to save me this trial!"

I placed the paper in her hand. She struggled to appear calm and control the passion and wretchedness contending as it were for her very life. With a blanched cheek and quivering lip she read,

"I will forgive Allen, let him marry your daughter, and settle on them my fortune, if you will be my—wife!"

"Never! never!" murmured my mother. Her form glided down the wall. I sprang towards her and caught her ere she fell.

"Fiend!" I exclaimed, "fiend! you have killed my mother!"

"I have! I have! oh God how innocently!" he exclaimed in a wild, despairing voice. "I thought to make amends for all, and by my rashness have murdered the wife of my old benefacter, the only woman I"—

He hastened to assist me, but I brushed away his outstretched hands and bore my mother to the lounge.

Bowes, and Maud, and Mabel, rushed into the library at the violent ringing of the bell.

My mother's head lay in the lap of Maud, whose white face and fair hair gave her the look of a statue. Mabel was on her knees, weeping silently. Bowes was opening the fastenings of my mother's dress. Yet Mr. Magroy stirred not.

"Some water!" whispered Maud. I saw him as I turned to bring water from the adjoining room. On my return there he stood, stock still. I took him gently by the arm.

"Old man—go!"

I led him towards the door.

"My son," he cried, as he raised his wan eyes to me, "she's right, she's right."

I led him compassionately and tenderly down the steps of the porch.

As he walked away with difficulty on his cane I overheard him say,

"A wretch once more, a wanderer on the earth, a childless, wifeless, friendless old fool—Oh! oh!"

CHAPTER XXIV.

JOHN MARCH IS ABOUT TO RISE AND BECOME A MAN OF THE WORLD.

"CAMBRIDGE, *November* 30th.

"MY DEAREST MOTHER:

"I crave a thousand pardons for my negligence this fall—I have been so busy. As my letters have been hasty and mere scraps of notes to Guilford, Maud, and Walter, I will now give you a connected account of myself and my various doings since leaving Law school. I had scarcely got up my shingle, as we say West, ere the fall campaign for the presidential election began to rage in New England. The political friends of my excellent patron and partner demanded his services in the field. Detained at home by family afflictions, he requested me to "*take the stump*," as we say at home. Accordingly I commenced operations at Cambridge, the scene of my college and mock court achievements, such as they were; made a happy hit; my fame was noised abroad through the Boston papers—my tour through New England, though laborious, was like a triumph. I would say so to no one but you. My friends and the friends of Mr. Lucklaw, my partner, flatter me that my efforts have had no little to do with the triumph of our candidate in the New England States.

"Now comes another sort of story.

"My partner has a daughter, tolerably pretty, well-educated, no fault to find, though no great personal attractions. My attentions have not been lost upon her. I have offered myself, and been accepted. The old gent's approval warmly given, and I only wait your approval to become one of the—I will not say happiest of men, for I have not staked my fate upon domestic happiness—but one of the most fortunate.

"How melancholy that I have always been forced to forego—by pecuniary straits, the pleasure of a visit home! The means for my electioneering tour, of course, were furnished by political friends. Mr. Lucklaw has come down, or is to come down, handsomely. His first gift in money will enable me to visit you, and bring my bride.

"You must not expect too much. Remember she is neither brilliant nor beautiful. But she is good, amiable, affectionate, educated, and as you already know, last, but not least—rich. She is a good Episcopalian, so that you will like that, although Maud having thought best to be a Presbyterian, may find less congeniality. These things make little difference to me yet awhile, till I get my fortune and reputation made. But I thought you women might feel an interest. (This part of John's letter did not please.)

"You don't know how much effect any ordinary Western orator may produce in these parts. Accustomed to prosy old fogies, the life and animation of young men—they are not much accustomed to listen to young men—excites their astonishment.

"How they wondered at my youth. I think my policy will be to attach myself to the cause of young men, and raise a crusade cry for their rights. Unless one be a substantial business man of thirty-nine, or a grave old professor, they think him nobody. The consequence is, that they are all behind the spirit of the age. My public aim is to bring up young men to the consciousness of their rights, their numbers, and their power. Of course I shall *lose* nothing by having such a party to support *me*. But so that the good of the public is advanced I feel no scruple about advancing my own interests.

"The health of both aunts is very good. Aunt Virginia is a fine specimen of the old-school spinster lady. Her society is as much sought after as ever. Aunt Carrie sees well enough to do almost everything but read and sew. But she thinks she would give up everything else now to enjoy them. Thus it is always. I continue to live with them, although my office is in the city. I owe everything to them, especially to Aunt Virginia, who has been so ambitious for me. But Carrie has taken best care of my clothes, and made me read the Bible to her every day. I hope the day may come when I can give better heed to the precious doctrines she, and you, and Maud love so well. But like everybody else who has said everything there was to say, I am beginning to preach, so good night. God bless you all.

"Thine, ever,

"JOHN.'

CHAPTER XXV.

THE YOUNG COMMODORE.

On returning to his castle, did Mr. Magroy notice Mrs. Polyphemia Fidgets' face at the window? Did he see her shrink away? Did the good man of the house know that his worst enemy still presided over the concerns of that abode of peace and happiness?

Mrs. Poly had but one eye, yet Mrs. Polyphemia saw a long way. For instance, she saw that the illumination of her master's mind concerning a variety of little matters, was nothing more than a rift in the cloud, which must soon close again, making darkness darker. Meantime, she saw it was her policy to keep out of his way—she would soon render her services, her very presence, nay, her counsels, necessary; for even that massive, compact mind must put forth little tendrils, feeling for sympathy.

Mr. Magroy closeted with his will and his Bible; he changes one and consults the other daily. Now he is seen busy writing, and again he compares himself with all scriptural characters, from outcast Adam to the stricken widow of Nain.

By artful and gradual approaches, the spider Fidgets,

drew the great blue-bottle fly Magroy, into the toils of her mazy net. In less than a month she had gained an influence over her victim, more powerful than ever. It may be needless to say that the light which had lately broken in upon his troubled soul with reference to the Marches, the fear, the shame and the self-reproach, all gradually vanished, and left him a blind listener to the insinuations of Mrs. Fidgets. A new element soon mingled in the blindfold war raging within him—avarice. Mr. Magroy never had been an avaricious man—never since the period of his youth—Money was lavished upon Mrs. Magroy more profusely than that prudent woman required. Allen knew no stint until he left the paternal roof. Even Mrs. Fidgets had, until now, lived in silks and clover.

Now, Mr. Magroy is a miser.

This interesting change in our neighbor's character first came known to us, on the occasion of Guilford's calling to pay the last installment on Lilac Cottage.

"Mr. Guilford March, I believe, sir," said Mr. Magroy, as my brother entered the office.

"Yes, Mr. Magroy," replied the latter respectfully.

"Your mother, sir?"

"Is well, Mr. Magroy."

"Is a what?" he cried.

"Quite well, sir."

"My son been to your house of late, as much as ever I suppose?"

"No, sir, he has not entered our house for years."

"All the same! all the same!" he muttered, "understood thing, conspiracy, waiting for the old man's shoes.—I'll fool them yet," he exclaimed, looking fiercely at Guilford.

But happily he caught sight of the little canvas bag in which Guilford had brought the silver and gold for the payment. His eyes glistened with unnatural fire as he looked, forgetting everything else.

"Ah! I know you want to pay, sir. Let me see the coin! the coin, sir! quick!" and the poor creature—poor with all his wealth, learning, and honors—hurriedly advanced to clutch the object of greed.

Guilford drew back, saying firmly—

"Stay Mr. Magroy, you forget yourself, sir. The papers first—the bill of sale, note, deed."

"Oh! yes," he answered, in a plaintive tone, that ancient over-bearing temper humbled to the dust.

The papers were delivered as soon as the trembling miser had counted, weighed, and inly devoured each piece separately, as he took it from the bag. Guilford felt a thrill of pleasure as he took in possession the evidences of Mrs. March's sole estate in Lilac Cottage.

He gave notice to Mr. Magroy, that he should ere long repurchase the cut-off lot, and bidding him good-morning, he went home to make holiday with the family.

Not long afterwards, Guilford was surprised to see Mr. Magroy enter the counting-room of the warehouse. He passed through the office without deigning to notice my brother, and held a long conference with Mr. Mayflower in the private business apartment. Shortly Mr. Magroy passed through again, went out; Mr. Mayflower came in, rubbing his hands.

"Guilford, what do you think old Mr. Magroy has proposed?"

"What, sir?"

"Why, to enter into a co-partnership with me, ha! ha! ha! as if I'd have such a glum old fur-trader prying around my establishment."

"Why, sir," replied my brother, "under the present state of the finances, his money bags might help you out of your difficulties."

"I thought of that too. But what do you think was the condition upon which he was to favor me with his assistance?"

"I cannot imagine, sir," said Guilford, nibbing a pen with his knife.

"On the easy condition that I discharge you."

At that moment the edge of my brother's pen-knife went through the pen, and almost through the thumb nail.

"What, sir?"

"That I discharge you."

"Mr. Mayflower, if that is the only obstacle I pray you not to hesitate to"—

"Not a word! not a word more, my dear fellow. I've known you from childhood. Your father was my early model, sir. I reverenced him. Your mother, sir, has a name more precious than her lost fortune. But what do you think I told my old Scotch friend?"

"That your friendship for my father and mother"—

"No, sir, not a word of it. I said you were the best clerk in the city, on dock or street, and destined to become one of the first business men in this community, and that it was my intention next spring to take you into the concern as partner. That is if you"—

"My dear Mr. Mayflower!"

"Not a word my dear friend"—Many gentlemen would have said my dear *young* friend, and looked the patron. But Mr. Mayflower was a gentleman of simple—perhaps plain manners.

"If you are willing to share my *hot water* awhile, Guilford, I think that, with your young blood fully roused, we may weather the present storm. The sun will come out—must come out—my dear fellow."

"Yes, I dare say we'll do very well. Egad! we'll begin right off."

And the firm became Mayflower & March.

There were not a few things in Guilford's present mode of life—to say nothing of its contrast with his experience with Sortem and the Skeleton—that gratified my brother. His senior, Mr. Mayflower, was an ambitious, sanguine, though practical man, who delighted in "hot water," as he called it. That is, having a new steamer or sail vessel on the stocks while yet embarrassed with the last dozen outfits, pushing ahead of all competitors on the lakes, giving employment to thousands of needy sailors and ambitious artisans, challenging sister cities for competitions, and carrying, or rather staggering under pecuniary burdens that would crush a score of less able men together. All he wanted, he said, was a little more "young blood," and now he has it.

These excitements aroused the best energies of Guilford March. If he had genius, it lay in contrivances, or fetching things about, and now all the powers of his mind were drawn into play by a business demanding great ability. It had likewise its pleasures. The rivalry, the patronage, the launch, the contract with sailors and shipbuilders—frank, hearty, honest, friendly, often disinterested classes both—quickened and ennobled the pulse of life. His early fondness for the water, too, was gratified in a modified, but agreeable form. He went at times from port to port, crossing the wind-tossed white caps of Lake Erie, or the many-hued surface of Lake Huron; he dashed down the rapids of the St. Lawrence, and sailed beneath the picture rocks of grand old unknown Superior—passing on his way, or pausing to gaze upon the Arch Rock, and Sugar Loaf, where the mythologic Indian gods once dwelt in Mackinaw—the Mount Olympus of the Red man—but still more nearly interesting to Guilford as the scenes of his father's gentle intercourse with Indians and Frenchmen.

By degrees my brother acquired a sort of a sailor roll in his gait; the people called him the young commodore. His firm regard for truth, together with the frank heartiness of his manner, rendered the good-looking young fellow both estimable and popular.

Dock life, so to call Guilford's present career, gives rise to a peculiar species of men. To be sure, there is a flavor of tar and oakum perceptible, yet tar and oakum are often valuable to fill the chinks of leaky vessels; and bluff, hearty, even rough usages may tend to stop the small crevices of a weak nature—the better able to buffet with the waves of life. A man on the dock is apt to be sound, and tough-hearted for the right, and independent, combining part of the bluff honesty of the sailor, and part of the thriving industry of the landsman. He launches vessels, on whose decks little communities live and labor, and do battle with wind and wave. He hears of them in distant ports, and his interests and sympathies stretch abroad to them. Hundreds, perhaps thousands, with their wives and little ones, depend upon his enterprise and calculation, his prudence, foresight and humanity. And he feels a sense of power. *Power*, that necessity to a human being, the element which tries him, the scale which weighs him, and makes known what manner of soul he is. Under such influence my brother Guilford developed gradually into the full stature of a man. With less favoring gales, less refreshing dews, a less life-darting sun, Guilford might have come short of the standard, but some sort of a giant he would have been, though a stunted giant.

Guilford became the *acknowledged* head of the family.

"Walter," said he, one day, as he came in to dinner, "you must go to Washington."

"How so?" I inquired, with a thrill of surprise and hopeful expectation.

He took a letter from his pocket.

"M. Latrobe says so—here is the letter."

I took it and read.

"My Dear Guilford:

"Things are in such a state of hodge-podge here (he meant hotch-pot) the Member and each Senator his favorite, and none of us having *l'entente cordiale* towards the administration, that I think your brother had better come on himself. I will help him all I can. It is his only chance. Make my compliments to the ladies, and believe me with lively sentiments.

"Your friend,

"Jacques Latrobe."

CHAPTER XXVI.

THE DRUM BEATS.

M. Latrobe's letter was submitted to Major Fontenoy, my military and mathematical friend and adviser, in a council of war held in the third story of the warehouse, whose window fronted on the beautiful straits, whence in summer-time the cool breezes came in, laden with the freshness of the lakes.

"My advice, my boy, is to go, hey!"

"The only obstacle I see, lies in the pecuniary circumstances of my friends. I cannot bear to encumber them with the expense."

"As for that, Walter," said Guilford, "I think we'll manage it for you."

"Who? what 'we?'"

"Well, myself."

"No! no!" said I, "you have just put on the harness of responsibility"—I always liked to deal in metaphor —"and you'd better not pull yourself out of the traces on the first stage."

"What do you mean by that rigmarole?"

"Why, have you not come into this concern of Mayflower & March, without a penny, and is not the establishment embarrassed? What would your partner say to your plunging your arm into the purse first thing? Besides you know there's the lot to purchase."

"Commodore," said Major Fontenoy to Guilford, "step this way, hey! Any bank checks in the counting room?"

"Major!"

"Never mind, old patriarch, hey! all right one of these bright sunny days ahead, hey! you are in deep water now. Walter is my boy, hey! romantic youth, rather flighty. I was once, myself, hey! But my boy, *my boy*, hey!"

The end of the stage whisper was that the major soon came back to the council of war, with the military chest full, *i. e.*, a check for two hundred dollars, which he placed in my hand with the remark,

"There is the sinew of war, my Walter, hey! We allies must subsidize each other, hey!"

"No, sir." I said firmly, returning the check. Then a tear came straining its way through my heart to my eye. I turned towards the window and looked out on the water.

"Julius Cæsar! what does the boy mean?" said the major, coloring and dropping his snuff-box from the crook of his maimed arm.

Guilford respected my emotion, and was grave and silent.

"Major," I said, turning round and taking his hand

between both of mine, "I know your heart. I shall always love you next to my brother Guilford, but sir—I will walk to Washington."

The major started back amazed.

"Long march, Walter. Forty days. Snow on the ground too, hey!"

Guilford placed his hand over the major's and mine.

"Do not say a word to deter him, sir."

"Walter you are a *man!*"

We all three shook hands.

The council of war broke up.

I walked up home and communicated my resolution to my mother. She turned very pale but said nothing till afterwards. Mabel came in. When she heard the news she threw her arms around my neck and kissed me.

"Walter, dear Walter," she said, "you will never come back to little Mabel."

I was confirmed at once in the opinion that my floating doubts of Mabel's love were mere fleecy figments of the brain. My mother left the library.

"Darling Mabel," I said soothingly, "I shall see thee again in thirty months. I will be true to thee."

"Don't talk so!" she shudderingly cried. "She refers to my being absent so long," I said to myself.

"Nay darling," quoth I, "it will pass more slowly to me than to thee."

Mabel withdrew from my arms.

"Walter," she said, "when you are away from home

in the great world, it may give you pleasure—if they do not spoil the dashing young officer"—she parenthesized mischievously—"it may sometimes give you pleasure to think of your little Mabel, whose doll houses you made long ago under the lilac bushes."

"Shall I not always think of thee, dearest?" I cried.

"Walter," she said, "don't be theatrical."

"What!" said I on my knees, "may I not call thee dearest? Are you not my own divine little"—

At this moment who should appear at the door of the library but Joram Jumps, the tall young candidate for divinity—of another sort and a better.

I saw nothing through the perspective tunnel, but thought I heard a locomotive whistle.

"Whew! whew!"

And the train was off.

Mabel burst out laughing. "What a delightful thing a duel would be between the rivals!" she cried as she ran to the door, and flew through the hall, leaving me to recover from my astonishment and regain my feet.

"I never did see such a provoking little flirt!" I exclaimed aloud with bitterness. "And such a weather-cock! At one moment she is on my neck; at the next she is mocking the deepest and holiest of feelings. Now she looks pale, and trembles at my coming; now she avoids me, now she runs up to me, and now she has ran away from me. By Jove! I vow I'll give her up. But that," said I to myself benevolently, "would break the child's heart. After all she's nothing but a child."

"Who, Walter?" inquired a soft voice.

"Maud can you unriddle that little sphinx?"

"What, Mabel?'

"To be sure."

"What is the matter between you? you always got on nicely until lately."

"Ever since that Joram Jumps affair between them, she has blown hot and cold, been one thing to-day, and another to-morrow. If I seek those affectionate caresses formerly my wont to enjoy, she teazes me to death."

"How so?"

"One moment she weeps and the next she laughs."

"Why, Walter, since your grand affair with Dulcinea, don't you understand the sex yet?"

"No!" said I, bluntly, "not the Mabel Latrobe part."

"Do you want my opinion?"

"Yes."

"People who interfere between lovers generally suffer for it."

"You shall not suffer—at my hands at least, dear Maud. I really need some sisterly counsel."

"Well, Walter," she said, as we seated ourselves together on the lounge, "you think yourself in love?"

"I am in love!" I exclaimed. "I can scarcely recollect the formula $x^2 y^2 = \frac{x + y}{2}$ for thinking of her."

Maud laughed. "You test it mathematically," she said. "The next best test is analogy, but as analogy does not always lead to certainty" —— I said, quoting from the book.

"Why, you remember very well," said Maud, laughing. "But come, let us look soberly at this problem, if you please. You think you love Mabel."

"I know it! I know it!"

"You thought—nay," she added, looking slily at me, "you *knew* that you loved Dulcinea."

"Dulcinea!" I exclaimed, impatiently—"what a comparison! a sheep to a gazelle!"

"The only difference is that then you were *sheepishly* in love with Dulcinea, and now you are *gazelle-ishly* in love with Mabel."

"Maud, you will drive me mad!"

"The soft, wild eyes of your gazelle will probably haunt your dreams, and kindle your imagination as those things generally do with poets"—

I inclined my head to acknowledge the compliment—being reckoned among poets.

"But you have never had the yearnings and sympathies of your heart unfolded to you by the pitiless hand of time, or the chilling influences of experience, or even the heat of passion! so that Walter, my dear brother, you have no sort of idea what will or will not make you happy."

"I have been in the habit of studying my own heart since a child; I have looked into its deepest depths, and see nothing but Mabel ever reflected there."

"Pardon me, Walter, but that depends upon your

humor, or the train of your fancies. Looking down into those awful and mysterious depths is no trifle. You may once have had them moved to the very bottom when he died"—she glanced at my father's picture—"but since then your thoughts have played more sportively, and now you see in the dark, deep reflector nothing but phantasmagoria of fame—a poet's, a hero's, a philanthropist's fame."

My sister had read me exactly.

"Why, Maud, how did you learn all this? I never thought of it myself, even: your hand has removed the veil."

She went on.

"You are the simplest of the simple—a child—to those who give you credit for a little genius."

I actually kissed Maud warmly.

"But," said she, "your greatest enemy may prove this very genius. Above disguise, working out its wild, yet simple nature, in acts at war with all worldly people's notions of propriety, you will be alternately mistaken for a madman, a simpleton, and a rogue."

"Why, Maud! Maud!"

"Remember the warning, Walter: it will come up many and many a time unless you begin now to impose a wearying burden upon yourself."

"What is it?"

"Every sort of self-restraint—over your temper, your fancy, your reflections, which will always be tinctured too warmly with the inner glow to enable you to see clearly the cold, grey substance of matters of fact. You must keep down your heart, your good impulses, yes, your very religion itself, which will be but too apt to oscillate from the extreme of emotion to the opposite extreme of skepticism. Finally, your sympathies must be rigidly restrained."

"My sympathies!" I exclaimed, "the sweet sources of my happiness?"

"The sweet sources of your transports, which you must learn to moderate, and the sweet sources of your love affairs, which you must not indulge in too far."

"Not too far?"

"A certain amount of experience in love's extravagances will be useful, in fact necessary to your settlement in the land of content."

"Where I never care to, and never *would* settle if I could," I cried. "A sort of discontent is the source of all effort, all progress, the load-stone to heaven itself—discontent with the low—aspirations after the lofty."

"Wait Walter. I mean in plainer terms, that in order to be contented with a wife, one must first enjoy—with such a ranging thought as yours—a pretty extensive acquaintance with various women, and no little heart experience mixed with it. Now I'll venture to say, that you never, in all your life, have gone so far as to inquire what sort of companion would be best suited to your temperament."

"Yes I have."

"Who, then?"

"Guilford."

'But you stray from the subject. Of course I mean by companion, a wife, since you will thus prematurely vex your soul with subjects of this nature."

"What a pity, Maud, you are my sister! I would drop down on my knees before you this moment and sue for your hand."

"There! there!" cried Maud rising from her seat, "you have forgotten Mabel in half an hour!"

I must confess that I blushed and stammered.

"You must study yourself, Walter, learn the wants of your peculiar nature, those things, I mean by wants, which shall not only produce enjoyment, but promote peace, self-respect, and sober, deliberate satisfaction."

"But do you think Mabel and I are suited to each other?"

"You said just now that Guilford was the sort of temperament for you."

"Yes."

"Guilford and Mabel are very different. Besides, are you suited to Mabel?"

"What a cold reasoner you are!"

"Dear Walter!" said Maud reproachfully.

"Well, go on."

"Two things divide a man's life and thoughts, a career and a home. I know not which is most important, but if he is so careful in selecting the former, is governed so completely by his idiosyncrasy, as one may say, the latter deserves at least deliberation."

"Unless," said I, "unless accident does the business."

"Yes," replied Maud gravely, "accident has much to do with such things, chiefly the accident propinquity, as for instance in this case." She looked at me archly.

"But speaking of temperaments," Maud.

"Well, Walter, do you think Mabel could ever love and respect you as she might, Guilford?"

"No I don't," said I frankly.

"She *ought* to," said Maud musingly, "but I fear, I fear"—

"Dear Maud!" I kissed my sister again. "You are not only an angel, as I have called you a hundred times, but you are—as somebody else once said—'a goddess.'"

Maud blushed and looked pained, as any allusion to Major Fontenoy always made her look.

She was going.

"Stay one moment till I return," quoth I.

In a moment I was back with my hands full of laurel leaves and holly, that grew in the garden.

"Let me make a wreath for you, Maud, I will twine it around your hair; the contrast between its fair color and the dark green leaves, will have a pretty effect. They are ever-green, and the wreath will last long after I am gone."

"What! are you going?"

"Yes, to Washington. If I succeed as I hope to, I shall thence to West Point."

"God will bless you, Walter, you are one of his lambs."

Maud dropt a tear, which added a bright diamond to the wreath.

"I will weave a chaplet for you, Walter."

"What shall it be, Maud?"

"Laurel and Bay."

I brought in the leaves from the garden and laid them on her lap. In a few moments I had plaited the wreath and placed it on her head. She looked more beautiful than the purest work of Grecian art.

"Now kneel, sir knight!" she cried, raising the chaplet.

I knelt before her.

"Laurel and Bay," Maud said with simplicity, "Soldier and poet. Be this thy motto:

"*Moderate your transports!*"

CHAPTER XXVII.

IN MOTION.

The busy note of preparation resounded through the house. There were clothes to make which Maud and Mabel sat up nights to help my mother finish. Major Fontenoy took me to the saddler's and ordered a knapsack, which fitted nicely on my shoulders, and contained my wardrobe and simple toilet. There came up to the house one evening two pairs of shoepacks from an unknown quarter—probably Allen Magroy sent them. My mother put in the knapsack the smallest copy of a Bible to be found at the Sunday School Repositories. Guilford gave me a purse for incidental expenses, and Major Fontenoy slipped there unknown to me a draft on the bank.

"A plaster in case he should be sick on the march, hey!" he said to Guilford.

The Rev. Mr. Cradle gave me a letter to a brother clergyman in Washington.

There was a snow-storm the night before I was to leave. Allen came up through it to Lilac Cottage, inquired at the door for Walter. Bowes came and told me, rubbing her hands upon her apron, that a gentleman wished to see me. Allen took a little pearl breastpin from his shirt-bosom, and pinned it on mine, then wished me a safe journey and good luck, and departed, wringing my hand. The major spent the evening with us, looking at Maud while he gave me my "orders," as he called them. I was to commence walking no more than ten miles a day. I was to beware of politicians, except M. Latrobe and Colonel Sedgefield—who were not politicians. I was to take a letter he gave me to the commander-in-chief. I was to see the secretary of war. I was to ask M. Latrobe whether it wouldn't be useful to see the President of the United States. Perhaps the letter to the clergyman might be useful. I was to tell my business to nobody but those who it was necessary should know it.

Allen had told me I must try and hear Mr. Clay speak. Maud told me I must not be too much of a man, but treat everybody with the respect and courtesy that my mother had always required.

"You may be surprised on being thrown among strangers for the first time, to see many older and richer than you," Guilford said, "who appear to know less. But keep your own ground, and listen with open ears, for you will soon find a vein of substantial ore of good sense by which you may profit."

Mabel said I must see the pictures in the Rotunda, and she wrought a little book-mark for me, which I was not to look at till the first night of my tarrying on the road, which I then found embroidered with her hair in beautiful, small letters, "Dulcinea."

Bowes said I must bathe my feet in ice-water every morning. My mother said I must read my Bible every night.

I took leave of all the family except Guilford: neither of us slept any that night. The stage came before daylight next morning. The driver blew a tin horn. I was to ride with him ten miles for nothing, for it was Abe. Guilford and I, though great youths, kissed each other. I jumped on the driver's box, and was off with a heavy heart. A few miles out, I wished I had slept more during the night, for there was no catching a nap now with Abe, who whistled, and sang, and blew his horn—though he kept me covered up with a horse-blanket.

Abe, on reaching the end of his drive, consigned me to the care of the next stage-driver, whom I found cross-grained, unsociable, and cruel to his horses. So I declined his surly offer of being "turned over," as he called it, to the next driver, but walked the rest of that day. I had ridden twenty miles, and easily walked ten more. The snow diminished in depth as I advanced, so that I found little on my second day's route, and easily walked fifteen miles. Gradually my days' journey increased in length till I could accomplish my thirty miles a day, except through occasional snow-drifts through northern Ohio. But then I was sometimes favored with a ride on top of a load of wood or flour, driving into market towns; but most frequently the teams were going the wrong way, or I, not liking the looks of the driver, would not ask to ride with him. At night, I slept in the bar-room—for nothing—when there were no noisy men smoking or drinking in it. Sometimes I called for a room, but rarely, they put me with so many bedfellows. I generally read my Bible a little on the road, and said my prayers in the barn, or in the woods, on the wayside.

Thus I travelled all through Ohio, and by the Cumberland road, which led over the Alleghany Mountains, through a part of Virginia, into Maryland. A mountain! how I had longed to see one! It wore as picturesque a form in my imagination as an Egyptian Pyramid. I was disappointed in them at first. They were not so tall, so conical, so steep, so triangular, as I had thought. Few had snow-tops. Here and there I saw a cascade half-congealed. I wished it were summer, so I might wander from the road, find a mountain stream, and trace it up to its fountain spring. Laurel Top was grand.

On reaching Cumberland, I first saw the railway, just completed from Baltimore. I did not like walking over the dead level track so well as winding over the uneven roads. I took any by-road which I learnt, on inquiring, lost me no great distance. I took great interest in the appearance of the fields, and negroes, and houses, going through Maryland. Everything was different from Ohio, looking older, more dilapidated, and more respectable, as if people there had once known wealth and hospitality.

At length I drew near Washington. Possibly, a more detailed account of the journey might be acceptable, but our story is too far advanced, dear reader, to detain you concerning boy-adventures with inn-keepers, bar-maids, travellers, peddlers, drovers, Boston tailors, New York dandies, philanthropists with patent medicines or Mormon tracts. Nor shall we wait to tell much of the man who put me out of my seat in the coach, when driving through a snow-drift, and made me ride under the driver's seat, with his—the new-comer's—valise, until the passengers held a sort of an indignation meeting in my favor.

"He is only a boy!" said the oppressor.

"He has his rights!" replied one.

"He shall come inside?" cried another.

"You shall ride outside yourself!" exclaimed a third—a tall, dark looking fellow, who had labored in the silver mines of Mexico—to the oppressor.

Accordingly I was re-instated, and the gentleman forced to ride on the top till the drift was passed and the storm abated, when I left the coach.

Nor shall we dwell on that happy meeting I saw between a young husband and wife, after a month's separation; during most of which the bride mourned her bridegroom lost in the snow with the cattle he was driving. Or upon the burial of that little child who died in the emigrant's wagon, and was buried in the forest at evening, and on her little grave a white pall of snow from heaven had fallen in the morning, when the emigrant's family went weepingly away, leaving their little one there.

Many I met were curious to know who I was, with my shoepacs, and white blanket coat with a hood, and red stripes around the borders of skirts and sleeves, and my knapsack—too young for a soldier, and going the wrong direction for an emigrant. They took me for a Mormon, a mail carrier, a tract distributer, a juggler, an Indian Theological student. One swore I was a Greenlander sent on special business to Washington, to see about the annexation of the Arctic regions; another swore I was a Chinese. I have no doubt I was very green, and many must have amused themselves at my expense.

How my heart throbbed as I came in sight of the great buildings of Washington! Elated by pleasure and pride, I exclaimed—

"See!—there are the proofs that I am no longer a dreamer, but a doer! Who knows but the next time I approach this proud city, instead of being afoot and alone, I may be riding in some triumphal procession, the cynosure of every eye?"

It was about noon. I walked up the steps of the capitol, found my way through the rotunda, to the Senate ante-room, and sent my name to M. Latrobe by a tall, benevolent looking gentleman, whom I was astonished to hear called the doorkeeper.

I hoped to pass among the crowd unnoticed, for my shoepacs made no noise, but my knapsack and long hair, and even the shoepacs themselves, the chief source of my feeling of security, must have caused many a stare.

M. Latrobe greeted me with cordiality and affection. He even embraced me in his arms, and took me into the Senate chamber. He had heard I was on the road, through Mabel; expressed the greatest surprise at such an undertaking, and said—offering me his snuff-box—

"You are very unfriendly, Waltair."

"Why so, M. Latrobe?"

"Not to draw on me, and ride to Washington in a coach, like a gentleman."

I took a pinch of snuff which made me sneeze, and frightened me to death lest I should disturb the Senate, and be called to order by the Vice President of the United States. A tear came into my eye, I thanked him tenderly, for his kindness touched me, but said with some pride,

"It may be more gentlemanly to ride, but it is more soldierly to walk."

M. Latrobe put on his hat and a blue cloak, which gave him a senatorial air. We went out the eastern doorway of the capitol, took our seats in a coach, and drove to M. Latrobe's lodgings.

"Who keeps the house, sir?" I inquired.

"A widow lady. I always find one good enough to take care of me."

I admired his benevolence, and have always since

followed his example, boarding, when I could, with widow ladies. But some widow lady boarding-house keepers, are—well no matter.

"You will stay here with me, Waltair?"

"Pardon me, sir!" I said, "this is too splendid and expensive for me." I secretly feared, too, I might be in the way of the good gentleman.

"I shall feel injured in my feelings, if you refuse me the pleasure of being my guest, Waltair!"

And so a room was assigned me not far from his own. He then left me, and returned to the Senate.

I locked the door of my apartment, and read in comfort my little Bible, and knelt down to thank Him who bringeth travellers safe on their way. My father seemed bending over me with a smile in his mouth—that sweet mouth, now freed from the old look of power repressed. It was like a vision.

After changing my garments, I went into M. Latrobe's room, which he had invited me to make my head-quarters as he called it; and where I found some choice books. Racine, Montaigne, Montesquieu, and some English philosophical and statistical works, which I found had been well thumbed. I buried myself in the arms of that old literary dry nurse, Montaigne, until the reappearance of M. Latrobe.

We went down to dinner. My friend took me to the lady of the house, and introduced me in a very cordial, polished way, as if I were his own son. She was a pleasant little Frenchwoman. She gave me a seat next my friend, who sat near herself, at the head of the table.

I soon learned that the lady had known my father, and this had the effect of making me feel at home.

It is unnecessary to detail all the steps we took in the business for which I had come. There were several difficulties to be encountered. There was but one member of Congress from our State. The unrepresented faction of the constituency, however, was so large that we were allowed two cadets. It was the custom generally for the member to *nominate* the cadet, but as there were two, the matter was shared between the member and our two senators. Yet neither senator had the power of nomination. Thus all depended upon the member. These facts we learnt by visiting the secretary of war, the engineer bureau, and the commander-in-chief. To the last I delivered Major Fontenoy's letter. The commander-in-chief expressed much pleasure at hearing from the gallant major, whom he called an ornament to the army. But he said he had no influence in the administration of army affairs, was consulted in no appointments or other matters of moment. My eyes filled—I had such weak eyes—as they gazed upon this man, one of the two pyramids of our military history, briefly and calmly expressing himself as a cypher in the War Department, a department which he had invested with power, and covered with glory.

With M. Latrobe then I went to the member. He received us politely, seemed somewhat preoccupied, had nothing to say with reference to the previous application, but was rather favorably touched by the fact of my zeal and labor, coming so far.

"Quite a feat, sir, for a mere stripling," he said.

"Yes," replied M. Latrobe. "I think he deserves the prize for it."

"Hem—ah—yes—of what politics was your father, Master March?"

"A Jefferson man, sir."

"Ah! I did not know that. Your New England brother, sir, is a whig, sir, he has done us some damage."

"Yes, sir," said I, somewhat uplifted by talking politics at the seat of government, with a congressman, and hearing my brother's name complimented. "But John never agreed with my father, or Guilford, or even me in politics."

"Pray what are *you*, sir?"

"A Jackson man," I said, stoutly.

"Good! very good!" Mr. Hustings laughed and rubbed his hands—a slippery-looking pair of hands "Now, sir, what is your mother?"

"My mother, sir!" I echoed, with surprise.

"Yes, sir, her politics?"

"Pardon me, sir, if I decline the honor of bringing my mother's name in question."

Mr. Hustings began to look displeased. Fortunately M. Latrobe came to my rescue.

"Ma foi! my friend," he said, addressing the

member, and handing his snuff-box with the air of a courtier of Louis XIV., "you must not endeavor to convert Mrs. March to democracy. She belongs to *our* party, sir! She is a member of the party for home industry, sir!"

This lively sally silenced the batteries of my cross questioner; and the editor of the organ of democracy in our city, happening in at the moment, and greeting me with unmistakable warmth, our friend Mr. Hustings, throwing himself back in his chair, perching his heels on the stove, at the same time spitting a stream of tobacco juice over the carpet, said in a loud, patronizing voice,

"Well, there's no resisting widows and orphans. I suppose I must give him a letter." We arose to depart.

"At what time shall my friend call for ze lettar?" inquired M. Latrobe, as if addressing the king of France, or his own idol, Napoleon *le grand.*

"He needn't call, senator," the gentleman said, "I will send it to your rooms." We left.

As soon as we were in the street, M. Latrobe gave vent to his disgust and contempt, in words which would have edified any professed politician to hear. He ended his complimentary discourse by saying, "I know ze breed, Waltair! we will watch him. Closely, closely," the senator repeated, as he forced a large pinch of snuff into his nostril.

That evening Walter called on his excellency, the President, in company with the clergyman to whom I bore Mr. Cradle's letter. His excellency was very urbane, but Walter was both surprised and disappointed: surprised at himself being not overwhelmed in the presence of so great a man, and disappointed in that the President was not overwhelmed to hear Walter had travelled so far on foot. Walter came to the conclusion that there was nothing now to astonish or be astonished at in Washington—but I had not yet heard Mr. Clay speak. The evening passed off very agreeably, however. There was a distinguished man present from the South, with a noble, frank, easy manner of address, reminding me of some of our home gentlemen. The conversation turned principally on political reminiscences, and a good many not entirely new anecdotes of John Randolph. My business was not then brought before the President, as that would not have been the etiquette.

M. Latrobe had no faith in our decorous friend, Mr. Hustings, and it was now thought a matter of prime importance to gain the ear of the executive, and as sharp political differences prevented intercourse between that high functionary and my zealous friend, I must needs go alone to the audience chamber.

CHAPTER XXVIII.

THE KITCHEN CABINET.

Arrived at the White House next morning, I rang the porter's bell with a trembling hand. The keeper of the king's gate was an Irishman, illustrious under the reign of Andrew the Great, and not unconcious of his importance under the present dynasty.

"I wish to see the President."

"What a lad!" he exclaimed, with assumed amazement; "in that white blanket coat, with a what d'ye call it, a night-cap on the shoulders!"

"No, sir!" retorted I, with no little spirit. "I shall take off my overcoat."

"Well," he resumed, looking with well-feigned fright at my shoepacs, "d'ye think to see his excellency in those" ——

"Yes, sir," I exclaimed, now angry; "these shoepacs are the gift of a friend, and for that reason I value them above the handicrafts of the first cobbler in Ireland."

"Arrah, my boy! you're a spirited fine fellow, but you can't see his excellency to day." He closed the door on me, but re-opening it immediately, thrust out his head, and added,

"Nor to-morrow, mi lad, nor" —— just at this critical moment of my life, I caught a glimpse of a dog in the vestibule.

"Cap!" I cried joyfully, "Cap!" for the sight of any acquaintance at the forlorn moment was joyful, and it was an exquisite stroke of policy—to seize sudden use of whatever advantage my familiarity with any object inside the White House might afford."

"I defy common sense to have done it," said I to Guilford afterwards.

"Arrah, mi lad, do you know the nager?"

"Certainly," I replied, with perfect coolness.

"Come in then, come in. You're a broth of a boy, any way, whoever ye are."

I walked in triumphantly, and after getting beyond the Irish gentleman's sight, Cap along with me, wagging his tail, I loitered in the hall until the "nager," whom I felt sure of knowing, made his appearance. For my complete relief and joy, it was the sheriff himself.

"Mason or Anti-Mason?" I cried.

He paused, and looked doubtfully at me a moment—everybody seems to suspect you in Washington—then cried out,

"Walter March! why I'm so glad to see you."

Cap began to frisk around us, as if himself overjoyed at the recognition, the hesitation of which had doubtless surprised him. Dick had been absent from our city several years.

"Then you've turned politician, eh?"

"Yes."

"What do you want? to see the President?"

"That's it exactly."

"I'll manage it. Come this way, Massa Walter."

Dick led to a little apartment cheered by the warm rays of a large wood fire-place, placed in front of which stood an immense armed and cushioned chair, with leather coverings. Dick planted me in the chair. A table stood near, covered with newspapers, letters, and documents. Dick took a paper-knife, and cut off the wrappers of several fresh-looking papers, which he shook out in front of the fire, and placed on my knee.

"Now make yourself comfortable, Massa Walter, and read the news till I come back. I'll be back soon."

And Dick took my name on a card, and went out of the room.

I found myself in the office of the President's private secretary; at least I judged so from the papers and letters lying on the table, addressed to him.

It was a sharp, cold day, and I was glad to warm myself for an interview which I regarded so decisive of my fate, as to send a chill creeping over me. My eyes wandered vacantly over the columns of a gazette, until Dick returned.

"All right, Massa Walter; wait a few minutes."

"Why do you call me 'massa,' Dick?"

"'Cos that's the fashion down these parts."

"But old friends—you know, Dick."

Dick came close to my chair, and almost whispered,

"I'd rather call you massa, than some *big* folks Dick knows."

I laughed, and the rest of the hour was spent by Dick's inquiring after Guilford, and Allen, and Abe, and telling his adventures, and much entertainment did I find there in the private secretary's room.

I wanted to ask Dick to sing,

"Come hither blue-eyed stranger,"

but rather doubted the propriety of such a request, considering the place and circumstances.

"But," said I, "Dick, you haven't told me yet what office you hold here, nor how you got here."

"Oh, keep dark!" said he.

At this moment a little bell tingled, and my warm-hearted friend said very quietly,

"Time to go, Massa Walter."

My heart leaped as though it would break its barriers.

We went through a corridor, and entered a wide lobby, along the walls of which settees were arranged, and occupied by a crowd of well-dressed gentlemen, old and young, most of whom wore a fagged expression on their lengthy jaws.

"Some of those gentlemen been waiting since last Friday," whispered Dick—this was Tuesday—"and some on 'em will never get in!"

"Why not?"

"Never you mind! keep dark!" replied Dick, with a wink.

He stopped a moment to inquire of a messenger in waiting, whether any one had gone in since the bell rang. The messenger shook his head.

Dick then advanced boldly to the door, which he opened, and announced, with a loud voice,

"Massa Walter March!" and I found myself in the audience chamber.

The President recognized me, and inquired after the health of my reverend friend of the night before.

Then he said good-humoredly,

"Well Master March, what emergency of state affairs brings you to Washington?"

My story was soon told.

"You say, then, that this appointment was promised you a year ago?" said the President kindly.

"Yes sir—unsought."

"And that you collected testimonials which were delivered to your member, for filing in the office?"

"Yes, sir,"

And that neither your application nor the testimonials are in file at the engineer's office?"

"Neither, sir."

"But now this member promises you a letter to the Engineer Department?"

"Yes, sir."

The President wrote a line; touched the bell on the table. Dick appeared.

"Give this to the messenger—to deliver immediately—an answer required."

Dick bowed and withdrew with no little grace, keeping his face towards the President till he was gone.

The President took up a document which he perused. Soon came a knock at the door, and Dick announced

"Chief engineer—War Department."

That gentleman, with his colossal head, advanced towards the President, who greeted him with republican simplicity. The chief engineer did me the honor of a bow, and took his seat.

"General, our young Western friend, Mr. March, has walked all the way from the State of Michigan, after a cadet's warrant."

The chief engineer bowed.

"I regret," continued the President, "that my own list is already filled. Is there any other means within our reach?"

"The member from Mr. March's State can nominate him, your excellency."

"He has already promised our friend a letter," said the President.

"A letter, your excellency knows, is not always decisive. Many are written with studied no-meaning."

"I dare say," said the President.

"Then, sir, all we can do for you, my brave lad, is to put the most favorable construction possible, on any letter your member may give you."

His excellency extended me his hand, which I shook with good Western warmth, and then withdrew.

Dick held the door open before I had fairly reached it.

"What luck?" said Dick as we passed down the hall, the gentlemen waiting audience regarding me with peculiar looks.

"Good, I hope?" inquired Dick, noticing that I could scarcely speak.

"Yes, I think it is good."

"Did the President promise?" asked Dick, as soon as we were out of hearing.

"No, but he'll do all in his power, I've no doubt."

"That's good. I believe he will. He's a good gentleman," said Dick—"that is," he added, in a whisper, "for a politician."

My friend did not lead me back to the room in which he first installed me, but said the secretary would be returning soon. We paced the far end of the lobby together, talking in an under tone till the morning hour expired, and Dick was relieved from his duties as door-keeper to the audience chamber, and taking me to a room in another part of the building, he introduced me to a very handsome and bright complexioned mulatto woman, with blue eyes. Dick's wife.

"One of my old prisoners," said he, to the young woman, who curtsied.

"Why Dick," I said, "you've found your blue eyed stranger. What shall I call her?" said I, taking her hand—for I never knew Dick's surname.

"Mary," quoth Dick.

There was a pretty olive and pink blush, on blue eyed Mary's cheek.

"You will stay to dinner, Massa Walter?"

"With the greatest happiness," I replied, and Mary went out to prepare the meal, which she served up on a table in the same room, and I must acknowledge myself indebted to that honest couple for a dinner of herbs, sweeter—though simpler—than any banquet.

Meanwhile Dick told me that he had left our ancient city, because with the ingress of a more money-making community, though they professed greater love for his negro brethren of the South, he found himself sinking individually, and meeting with a sort of contempt. There never was a nobler fellow than Dick, white or black, and you should have witnessed the mingled condolence, pity, and pride, with which his Mary regarded him over this part of his story.

"I left, Massa Walter, because I was worse than nobody, and made up my mind to come South, where the negro man is somebody, everyone knows what, where there's no rubbing against white folks, no chafing negro's spirit."

"But have you never regretted it?"

"Well, Massa Walter, I often regret the old town where Abe and I used to play with the boys, and fight for them, too, you recollect," he added, showing his pearly teeth.

"Mary ever hear of that?" I asked, laughing, too.

"Oh, yes. That's the poetry of my life, that and

sitting down on the grass with the boys all around me. She's heard it a thousand times. Wouldn't wonder if that's what got her for me, eh, Mary?"

"Don't know, Dick; you used to talk mighty eloquent 'bout those times."

"Well," said Dick, "next to that sort of life, give me Southern life, where a nigger's a nigger, and everybody don't think he's as good as a white man, and make him unhappy 'bout it, then leaves him to starve in the back alleys."

"But how did you bring up in these comfortable quarters, Dick?"

"Owin' to that gal," said Dick, looking fondly and brightly at the pretty, blushing Mary. "She was a children's maid in the old general's family. I used to wait on our old governor when he came here to the cabinet, and that's the way I got acquainted with Mary."

"Well,"—said I.

"Then," said Dick, "I couldn't help falling in love with her, you know."

"Ah! go 'long, you Dick!" exclaimed the bashful Mary.

"Don't believe Massa Walter could ha' helped it himself," said Dick, "if he'd seen you then."

"I can hardly help it now," quoth I.

"Then," continued Dick, "old massa governor was very good, and when the old cabinet went out, he asked the new President to give me a place, so I might live with Mary."

"Then you were married before that time?"

"Yes," replied Dick, "but did it seem like marriage when I lived in one place, and Mary in another? and that's the whole story."

"But how does it happen, my friend, that you have so much discretionary power at the President's door?"

"Well, Massa Walter, I've lived in Washington long enough to know almost everybody, and some I know the President don't want to see, and some, he tells me, he *won't* see, and some I don't like the looks on myself, no how! You ought to seen our house about the 4th of March; such a wolfish looking set. Ki! worse than hungry niggers!"

"How so, Dick?"

"Well, Massa Walter, they'd bow and scrape to the old Irish messengers, and whine around me, and boot-lick everybody they thought had anything to do with the ropes."

I now rose and took leave of Mary with much friendliness of feeling, and Dick escorted me to the front door, where the porter stood, ready to open the king's gate with great alacrity.

"Arrah! my lad, it's fooling wid ye I was, entirely."

"Better look out how you fool with my friends 'nother time," said Dick, rather good-humoredly, as he shook hands with me.

I left.

"Bad 'cess to the chocolate-face nager," muttered Pat,

as he ushered me out. "'Twasn't so in the ould gineral's time."

That was true, for in the ould gineral's time this fortunate son of the Emerald Isle had the abuse of petty authority in his own hands—and used it less discreetly than my glorious friend Dick.

CHAPTER XXIX.

THE FIELD WON.

SENATOR LATROBE appeared delighted at the result of the diplomacy, and laughed heartily at the account of my adventure. He took a letter from the table, and handed it to me.

"GENERAL ———

"*Chief Engineer Department.*

"SIR:—I have the honor to address you on the application of Master Walter March (belonging to my constituency), for the position of Cadet at West Point. This young gentleman is the son of a widow lady (politics unknown), who lives in the city of Detroit, the relict, I am told, of the late Wingfleet March, who died immediately after his election as Deputy from the then Territory of ——— a Jeffersonian democrat. The present John March of Boston, is a prominent New England whig. The young man himself is a democrat—so the editor of the *Detroit Gazette* states—but as I have said, his mother's politics are unknown. The claims of the humblest widows and orphans of my constituency, are uppermost in my mind, and I take decided interest in their peace, happiness and prosperity.

Yours, in the bonds of democracy,

"OLIVER HAZZARD PERRY HUSTINGS, M.C."

Sealed with the goddess Justice, holding a pair of evenly suspended scales.

"Well, Waltair, what you think of that?"

"Think, sir! why that there's not a peg in it big enough to hang a hope on," I exclaimed, almost ready to weep.

"Don't despair, my boy," said the good old friend of my father, in a soft, sympathetic voice. "Take the lettair to the department to-morrow, and see what the general of engineers will say."

Accordingly, at the early office hour next morning, behold me in the engineer department. There was a very mild, gentlemanly clerk—he had been a clerk a century, I thought, from his clerkly manner and red tape finish—who seemed to take great interest in me.

"Good morning!" he said, with a flourish of his pen over the desk.

"Good morning, sir."

"Take a chair, sir," he said, getting one from his chief's room, and smoothing the cushion—as he would smooth a document with a paper folder.

"Cold weather," he said, resuming his place at the desk. "For two weeks, thermometer ranging between six and thirty above Fahrenheit, paving-stones on the avenue yielding fine silicious dust, intersections of the avenues wide, great sweep for wind from the mountains," and thus he continued, only pausing to wipe his pen, and dip the point of it in his mouth, talking as if copying the report of some officer on the eligibility of site for a proposed fort.

I must have enjoyed the conversation of my queer friend a full hour before the general came in.

He invited me to a chair in his own office, while he glanced a few moments at some letters on the table. Then he moved his spectacles on the top of his head, and turned towards me, asking,

"What news from your member?"

"A letter, sir."

The general dropped the spectacles on his nose, read the letter, raised the spectacles on the top of his head, looked at me, dropped the spectacles again, read the letter again, and finally asked me, looking with a troubled expression through his spectacles,

"Who the devil can make head or tail of this?"

I had nothing to say.

Then he seized his pencil in an irritated manner, and endorsed something on the back of the letter, which he handed me, saying,

"Ask Mr. Hustings, to please write that over in ink, and sign his name to it."

"Yes, sir, thank you," and I left the office.

My good friend the clerk followed me into the hall, and said,

"Which way's the wind?"

I showed him the letter, which he read with a rapid mumble, as if casting up a column of figures.

"These members," said he, "are as slippery as eels."

I then pointed to him the general's endorsement, which he read with more apparent satisfaction, and said as he handed me back the document,

"Foundation bad! superstructure good! chances

even! Keep to the work! Let me see you to-morrow!"

Those dreadfully long Washington to-morrows! I never shall forget them. Such purgatories, such heart sickening under hope deferred by them.

I found the honorable member at his dinner that day, and waited. When he came in, he said,

"Here yet?"

"I have not waited long, sir."

"I mean here in Washington, yet. No need of your staying longer. That letter of mine will fix your flint."

"I delivered your letter, and the chief engineer has endorsed something on it for you to put in ink and sign."

"Ha!" said he, changing color slightly, "let me see."

He read the endorsement aloud. "I wish the within to be distinctly considered as a nomination of Master Walter March for a cadetship from my district."

The honorable member frowned, took up and laid down his pen. A thought seemed to clear up his brain. He took the pen up again, and wrote in the pencil traces, signed his name below, and handed the document to me, saying,

"There! I hope that will satisfy him."

I thanked him very warmly, and withdrew.

The hoped for morrow came. M. Latrobe shook hands with me as I departed from his lodgings, and said,

"Let me welcome you back as Cadet March."

"I hope so, sir."

There was not the least doubt now on my mind that the goal was within reach, and the prize ready.

The general read the endorsement carefully. His face grew humorsome in expression.

"He is satisfied," I whispered to myself. He finally laughed. I did not fully like the tone of that laugh. Still I thought he would not laugh over another's misfortunes; it must be all right.

"Mr. Tapes!" he cried.

My friend, the clerk, made his appearance.

"Can you read that word, sir?"

"Yes, sir, quite plain, *recommendation.*"

"Just so! just so! I knew he would try to dodge it."

"What!" I exclaimed with affright.

"My dear sir," said the general, "your worthy member has written the word 'recommendation,' which is of no account, in the place of 'nomination,' which is the whole thing in one word."

"How?" I exclaimed, dismayed.

The general made the explanation again.

"Then what is to be done?" I cried, that same little weak, womanish tear that so often persecuted me, rising now.

"The only thing you can do, my dear friend, is to carry the document back to him, point out the discrepancy, and ask him to correct it."

The benevolent clerk followed me out to the hall again, quite excited, too, apparently forgetting for the nonce, the site of that new fort.

"My dear friend, be cautious! don't get mad, that sort of thing, you know, don't pay. Throw the blame on the office—on me if you please—tell him it's a mere rule of convenience—do you understand?"

"I could throw the document in his face," I exclaimed—that little tear coming out.

"No! no!" said he, looking at the tear, "'twould spoil all."

"Guilford never would consent to my stooping to dog the heels of this person so."

"Who is Guilford?"

"My brother, my friend, my father, my proud, good, generous brother," I said.

"But what would he say if you should lose it?"

"Better lose it, sir," said I, in a softer tone to the gentlemanly clerk, "than to degrade myself."

"No degradation: no such word known here at Washington. Get what you can, and how you can, is the motto here. By Jupiter! I'll go with you."

Accordingly my new ally flew into the office, and re-appeared in a moment, crumpling his hat excitedly on his head. Gaining the open air, he soon recovered his wonted composure, and ere we gained Mr. Husting's lodgings, he was lost as deeply in his field-notes as ever. Once or twice he brightened up as he turned towards me—probably noticing my look of forlorn despondency—and said,

"Cheer up, Mr. March, we'll view the work!"

The House of Representatives had adjourned over,

and the member was fortunately at home. I introduced Mr. Tapes, clerk in the engineer department.

"What now?" asked the member, rather tartly, for so small a matter to a statesman.

"The rules of our office, sir," said Mr. Tapes, "are very precise. I may say, sir, *absurdly* precise."

"I should think so, too!" sneered the honorable M.C. "But what's wrong now?"

"The endorsement, sir: all right but one word, not of much importance, easily mistaken for the one written, but the rules of the office, sir, require"——

"Let me see what you refer to."

"That word 'recommendation,' sir, should be 'nomination.'"

"Pshaw!" said the honorable member, representing a constituency of seventy thousand, as he pushed back the paper, "is that all? the words mean the same thing, or nearly so."

Mr. Tapes was evidently at a nonplus.

"You will pardon me, Mr. Hustings," I said, "but surely you cannot allow the great friendship you have shown me in this matter, all to go for nothing now?"

Mr. Hustings looked, or rather leered at me, with a doubtful, inquiring, half-shut eye.

"The cause of widow and orphans, sir, which you justly assert to be uppermost in your thoughts is one, the peace, happiness, and prosperity of which you would hardly sacrifice on the paltry consideration of a word."

"I cannot encourage this sort of dictation from the departments, sir," he replied, uneasily, as if wishing to divert me from a manner of speech impossible to interpret.

"Sir, you are too noble! too liberal! to take issue with them on the difference of a shade of meaning in a word?"

"Well, give me the letter," he said, petulantly. Mr. Tapes handed it to him eagerly. "There," said he, as he erased the objectionable term, and wrote the necessary one over it, "I believe this office of chief engineer should be abolished, and the business of fortification controlled by a committee of Congress, as it was in the French Revolution."

Mr. Tapes and myself beat a hasty retreat, leaving the member to arrange the details of his committee.

"Does that secure it beyond a doubt?" I asked.

"Unquestionably," he cried with joy. I called for a carriage.

"Take this gentleman to the War Office," I said to the driver, with exultation. "What is your charge?"

"Two dollars, massa!"

"The villain," exclaimed Tapes, stepping back from the open door, "it's only worth"——

"Never mind the price," I said, pushing him in, and throwing the driver two Spanish dollars.

On that evening my warrant was sent to M. Latrobe, whose congratulations were showered upon me with every demonstration of joy and affection. M. Latrobe also handed me a short letter from my eldest brother John, inclosing a bank note of considerable value, and inviting me—pressing me—I may say, to come on to Cambridge and visit him until the June term at West Point should commence. I loitered in the political metropolis of the nation, long enough to study the architecture of the public buildings, hear the most eminent orators speak, and pay visits of farewell to my friends Dick and Mary, the clergyman, and Mr. Tapes —with whom I dined.

Dick said that when the administration broke up he'd like to return to good old Detroit. Mary told me confidentially she was dying to go there, too. I promised to find, if possible, a place that might enable them to settle down comfortably, and took my leave of them with a full heart.

Tapes said, coming with me to the door of his lodgings, he had a word of advice that he would respectfully suggest.

"Speak it out, dear sir. I am not the head of a bureau, that you should hesitate."

"Then, Mr. Walter, don't graduate from West Point into the engineers."

"Don't believe I could, if I wished."

"Don't try to, sir. Don't try."

"But what is the objection?"

"O! sir, your brain would turn into lime water, you would be but the carbonate of a man—a walking stalagmite or stalactite—your building materials would go to waste."

Ignorant of what he meant, but profoundly impressed with his manner, I squeezed Mr. Tapes' hand, and we said good-bye!

The secret of the poor gentleman's dislike must have laid in the eternal routine of his own duties, year in and year out, casting up costs, quantities and qualities, of "building materials for works of fortification."

John March's liberality enabled me to travel "like a gentleman," as M. Latrobe would say.

Walter took passage in the railway cars for New York, and in seven days found himself, neither at West Point as he expected, nor at Cambridge, where he was invited, but at Detroit, where he was delighted, with Major Fontenoy, studying mathematics, and with Mabel Latrobe, studying her, himself, and the tender passion.

CHAPTER XXX.

SWEET HOME.

"THE trial is to come off in the May term of court," said Guilford.

"What trial?" I inquired.

We were sitting in the library one evening towards the end of February.

"Did I not write you that we were sued at law?"

"No, by whom?"

"Mr. Magroy. In the first place, about a month ago, I took to Mr. Magroy the amount understood to be the price for the cut-off lot."

"Oh! I'm glad to hear you have secured that so soon."

"Not so fast, Walter. John sent the greater portion of the purchase money, and urged me to make no delay. As I said, I took the amount to Mr. Magroy, but what do you think?"

"Did he say the gentleman wished to keep it?"

"No, he had bought it himself."

"By ——!"

"My son," said Mrs. March, mildly, "did you learn that in Washington?"

"Dear mother, your pardon."

"But, Guilford, what was the old curmudgeon's excuse?"

"Walter," again said my mother—less mildly—"hard names?"

"They do nothing in Congress, mother, but call each other hard names."

"'Tis vulgar, dear boy, wherever you may have picked it up."

"What do they call my father?" asked Mabel, archly. "No one would dare to give him a name."

"The Gentleman from Corsica," I said with a wink at Guilford, "or if they wished to be severe, the Senator from Waterloo."

"The *canaille!*" exclaimed Mabel.

"Well," said I, "this old scamp of a Magroy."

"Call him a good singer," said my mother. It was her rule, when she could speak no good of a person, to call him a good singer.

"This excellent singer then, Guilford, what was his motive?"

"Partly avarice, which grows upon him every day; and partly the fear of a conspiracy; he fancies we have formed one to ruin him."

"Conspiracy?" I echoed, laughing.

"Yes, I believe Mrs. Fidgets has poisoned his mind with the notion."

"Fidgets! the old"——

My mother lost a stitch as she suspended her knitting

on a stocking for my outfit, without looking at me, but waiting to hear if I would ——

"The exquisite singer! mother."

"Fidgets is Fidgets no longer," said Maud.

"She is Mrs. Archibald Magroy, LL.D.," said Mabel, in a mincing manner, imitative of the late brisk housekeeper.

"Is it possible?"

"Yes," said Guilford, "Abe and the Shoepacs were going to *charivari* them, but Major Fontenoy persuaded them not to."

"Guilford had more to do with persuading them out of it, than the major had," said Mabel. I did not very well like the look of pride with which she regarded my brother.

"I don't know," said Guilford, "I only told them they'd better not, on Allen's account. Poor fellow, he was sufficiently shocked to hear of the marriage."

"Well," said I, in a maze of bewilderment, "what about this lawsuit?"

"Oh! there came a harum scarum Frenchman here, from the upper country, a relative of the Fabiens, who once owned this property, claiming not only our land, with the cottage and all improvements, but those of the whole neighborhood, likewise."

"On what plea?"

"Why that his grandfather was out of his head when he made his will."

"And Mr. Magroy?"

"After talking with the lawyers generally, who told him the costs would be great, the Frenchman was about relinquishing the whole matter, when Mr. Magroy purchased his title, took the papers, names of the witnesses, and all that, and is now going to contest the point in an action of ejectment against us."

"The old"——My mother paused in her knitting.

I inclined my head deferentially towards her.

"Who are his lawyers?"

"Counsellor O'Mar is the only one as yet retained on that side."

"And ours?"

"Is Mr. Floury. Allen, of course, views the matter with regret, and thinks his father clearly in the wrong, but motives of delicacy prevents his"—

"Oh yes! I understand that, always the man, always the gentleman!"

"Well, how do you feel about it?"

"Mother and Maud seem to be devoid of fear, but I am not so sanguine."

"Why?"

"Because, money is more powerful than right; because, the avarice and hatred of Mr. Magroy, are stimulated by the jealousy of Fidgets—and jealousy is cruel as the grave."

"What can the creature be jealous of? Has she not married up to the top of her wishes?"

"Yes," said my mother, "she is welcome to look down upon us if she will."

"The worst I fear is, that they may carry on the suit till we are no longer able to pay costs," added Guilford.

"God forbid that he should deprive us of the cottage!" I said.

"Amen," said my mother, in a low voice. She rose up from her seat and kissed me. "When my boy Walter comes back from the strange world, and the cruel wars, we must have a home for him. Maud, my daughter, please sing us *Sweet Home*."

"Oh yes! do Maud! I will join in the chorus," cried Mabel, enthusiastically.

My mother had laid aside her knitting, and gotten the family Bible, which now lay upon her lap, as she sat in the rocking-chair. Guilford laid his arm over my shoulder and took my hand in his own, as we sat side by side on the lounge.

Mabel was on a footstool at the feet of my sister Maud, in front of the fire.

> "Mid pleasures and palaces though we may roam,
> Be it ever so humble, there's no place like home.
> A charm from the skies seems to hallow us there,
> Which seek through the world, is ne'er met with elsewhere.
> Home, home, sweet—sweet"——

Maud's voice died away—Mabel burst into tears—Walter threw himself into his mother's arms—the rest of that evening hymn remains unsung at Lilac Cottage, to this hour.

CHAPTER XXXI.

WHAT WAS SAID ON THE HOUSE-TOP.

Time never flew so rapidly as in the interval between my appointment and my departure—the beautiful spring months.

My mathematics went on indifferently, after the Major told me he felt secure of my passing the examination preparatory for admission. I lay in the grass on the lawn, or with Guilford dreamed away on the green bank under the butternut trees, building more castles, and loftier, brighter, than ever. This place was about two miles from town, from which it was cut off by two or three points of woods. But it commanded a view of the spires of Saint Ann, as well as of the more ambitious new Gothic towers of the Protestant church, which divided the rays of the rising and setting sun, with the venerable old Saint. The river, with its variety of sails, green banks, orchards, old fashioned French houses, and windmills, the distant lake with its light-house, the forest island that stood at its mouth; these, with the woods stretching in a long purple line on our right, and Millbrook farm with its meadows, dilapidated mill, apple blossoms, rivulet, and the cloud-shadows on the waving fields of new wheat, made up a landscape wonderfully charming for so level a country.

While memory revels among those delightful days, I may not pass by an incident which then happened, and its narration may serve to throw some light on the character of our persecutor.

Guilford and I were reclining on Air Castle Bank one serene Sunday afternoon in May, when we observed an unusual column of smoke rising over the spot we always fancied our house to occupy. We started to our feet, and commenced running towards the city, but the column growing more and more slender, and finally dying away entirely, we proceeded home more leisurely.

On reaching the lawn we found articles of furniture lying in confusion on the grass in front of the cottage. There were one or two damped blankets spread out on the roof, which was charred and black for the space of a few feet around the chimney, at one of the gable ends of the roof. On going round to that side of the house we saw the blackened water still coursing down over the clapboards to the ground. It seems that the chimney had taken fire, which communicated by some means to the wood-work around the chimney, and under the roof.

Bowes first saw it, ran in and gave the alarm. There happened to be no person near my mother and Maud, but Joram Jumps.

Mrs. March at once started for the scene of action, taking a bucketful of water with her, and directing

Maud and Bowes to do likewise. They began at once to gather vessels, and fill them at the well. My mother threw up a window which opened on the roof of a wing of the house, where there stood a ladder, by means of which she gained the upper roof, and dashing the water on the smoking crevices around the chimney, stood by waiting for more water.

Meantime Joram Jumps had flown through the hall, flung wide open the front door, and ran down the lawn crying,

"Fire! Fire!"

My mother stood on the ridge of the roof. The breeze was playing with her hair, which had fallen about her shoulders, and while Joram cried fire! Mrs. March cried,

"Water! Water!"

Maud and Bowes, hearing my mother's voice, quickened their movements, and armed with unusual strength by the excitement, soon established a line between my mother and the well. Still the fire gained headway, the smoke rolled out in thicker, blacker, and larger volumes, and the heat began to drive my mother away from the chimney. Joram crying fire! with all the power of locomotive lungs, ran back to the house and began to carry out the furniture in his arms upon the lawn.

A tall, emaciated figure now appeared inside the gate, and came hurrying along up the lawn.

"Water! water!" my mother screamed from the roof, as she caught view of the new ally.

"What the Old Nick are you doing here, you young lout?" exclaimed an excited, strong voice. "Drop that mirror, and go help the women draw water."

Joram obeyed with alacrity, ran around to the well, and by his assistance contributed to an immediate increase in the supply of water.

The tall figure hastened into the house, gained the window, was out on the lower roof, threw away a cane he had hitherto carried, climbed the ladder, and was on the roof between the fire and my mother, now almost suffocated by the smoke. He took her place on the ridge, pushed into the smoke, and dashed bucketful after bucketful of water on the fire as my mother handed the vessels to him.

"There he stood," said Major Fontenoy, "like a prophet of old on a mountain, hey! his tall figure now looming out and anon disappearing momentarily in the smoke, hey! till I gained the roof-top, sent Mrs. March down, and posted myself in front of Mr. Magroy, but the fire began to flag before I came, hey!"

Maud told the story by the bedside of my mother, who was prostrate and nearly blind after her heroic efforts.

"But what," Guilford inquired, "became of Mr. Magroy? did he come in afterwards? did he manifest any other friendliness?"

"No, he hobbled down the ladder as soon as the fire was gotten under, sent Joram up to assist Major Fontenoy in quenching the remains, and was down the lawn and out at the gate before I could thank the dear old gentleman."

"Do you think it was real sympathy for us, or calculation?" asked Guilford.

"I hope it was sympathy," Maud replied, "and I rather think it was, from the kind looks he gave me as he passed."

"I think it was goodness of heart," said Walter. "The old gentleman is impulsive, and impulse is seldom selfish or calculating."

"I don't know," said Guilford, deliberately. "If the house were burned and he gained the suit"——

"It was pure goodness of heart!" said my blinded mother, turning impatiently on the bed. "He said to me when the danger seemed greatest that"—— My mother paused.

"What did he say, mother?" I asked.

"No matter, my children."

And what Mr. Magroy said to my mother on the house-top at the moment she was likely to become houseless, still remains a mystery.

It was during the week following the fire, that the case of Magroy *versus* March came on for trial.

It may be as well, previously to our entering into the narrative of that event, to inform the reader of the state of one of the high contending parties, the plaintiff in the action.

Mr. Magroy's marriage with Mrs. Fidgets appeared to

make the melancholy gentleman no happier, strange as this may appear to the friends of that judicious lady. On the contrary, Mr. Magroy fell a prey to a thousand hallucinations. Major Fontenoy was going to kill him. Guilford March had a mortgage on his princely mansion, and was soon to turn him and his wife into the streets. Miss Maud March was jealous of his wife. The doctor had designs on the hand of Mrs. Magroy.

"Why sir!" expostulated the doctor, "your wife's no buxom lass, no beauty, sir! What do I, already a man of family want of her? The old hag!" muttered Doctor Mendry to himself.

"Sir!" said Mr. Magroy, rising up in his bed, and pointing his long emaciated finger towards the door of the room occupied by his wife. "Let her fix her fascinating eye on any man in America, and he's gone. There's no resisting that eye," he added, falling back exhausted.

Mr. Magroy's most common hallucination was that of the conspiracy. Every morning his money was counted over. That which he held in the bank was withdrawn, and placed in the iron chest in his office, where the haunted being slept. The room was provided with double doors, and the windows were grated with bars of iron. Thus Mr. Magroy had become his own prisoner, and beyond dispute, the worst jailer a wretch can have is his own fears. He fancied, in his darkest moments, that Allen was seeking his life, and his alternate anathemas on the head of his son, and screeches for mercy and pardon, were heard by passers by, and rumored to the world.

"Sir," said Doctor Mendry, taking a pinch of Major Fontenoy's snuff, and laying the forefinger of his right hand in the palm of his left. "Sir, it is a remarkable case. A curious feature is the wonderful knowledge he exhibits in the diagnosis of his own disease. 'Come doctor,' he will say, 'I wish to test the matter of my sanity. Let's take a game of chess, mad or not mad. You are mad, doctor. I am not mad.'"

"Facetious, hey!" said the major.

"No, sir," replied the doctor, gravely, "he means if he beats me he has his senses, for, sir, it takes a well man to do that."

"Very few well men, hey!"

"Another pinch of snuff if you please, major. Capital snuff, capital!"

Allen Magroy became the most sorrowful and pitiable of mankind. He attempted to see his father. Mrs. Magroy glared fiendishly upon the young man, who she yet feared might deprive her of her anticipated prey, and always pronounced Mr. Magroy too sick to be seen, and emphatically said his life depended upon rest and quiet. Then Allen sought Doctor Mendry. He inquired whether *his* course towards his strong-minded father—as he had ever supposed him to be—had served to bring on his present state.

"No, sir, I cannot see that you have acted wrongly. Your father's mind is one of peculiar mould. In fact, his brain seems never to have taken time to cool. He has always been of a violent, headstrong spirit."

"And you have known him how long, doctor?"

"Ever since he came to this country, sir. Ever since he was a mere youth. To dictate is his ruling passion. Your manliness, your independent spirit would have galled him"—

"Doctor! please remember"—

"Pardon me, Allen, my boy, but I speak the words of truth and soberness."

"Can I see my father?"

"Certainly."

"Mrs. Magroy has denied me every day for a month."

"How?" inquired the physician, surprised.

"She has told me he was confined to his bed."

"The lying jade!"

"She is my stepmother, Dr. Mendry."

The doctor was moved. "Allen I beg a thousand pardons."

"You must not speak disrespectfully of one,"—

"Say no more. I never will. You shall see your father to-day. He has been actually confined to bed but once or twice."

Allen went with the doctor. His father was reading the Bible, calm and clothed in his right mind.

"Father," said Allen, kneeling. "I cannot surrender my thoughts of others, I cannot abandon my feelings"—

"Then, boy, what are you doing here?"

"I will act on neither the one nor the other. You have been unwell. It is my hand that should soothe you, here it is—will you take it?"

He laid his hand on his father's knee.

"Allen, my brave boy," sobbed Mr. Magroy. "I know not which has sinned."

"I have father, it is I."

"No! no! no!" cried Mr. Magroy, bursting into wild, hysteric tears.

Allen arose from his knees. He turned towards the doctor, his face streaming with tears. "Shall we go, sir? shall we not leave him now, it is too much, is it not?"

"No, stay where you are," said the doctor, curtly, striving to master his own feelings, and quench his tearful emotions.

At this time Mrs. Magroy made her angelic appearance. She ran up to the chair of her husband, with affected alarm.

"You would kill my husband. You would kill my husband! Mr. Magroy, do you know by whom you are surrounded, what they would do?"

"Heavens!" exclaimed Allen, "this is too much!"

"I'll manage her," quoth the doctor, then going to the ex-housekeeper, he grasped her strongly by the arm, urged her to the door, notwithstanding her struggles and loud sharp remonstrances, and helped her out as gently as her resistance would permit. "It is you, woman, that is killing my patient." He closed the door and turned the key.

"Was not that my wife?" demanded Mr. Magroy, looking up at this moment.

"She has gone, sir," answered the doctor, kindly and soothingly. "She has just stepped out."

"And you with her, sir," demanded Mr. Magroy, with a fearful wild glare.

"Alas! alas!" whispered the doctor to Allen, "that woman has spoiled all."

"'And Nathan said unto David, thou art the man,'" shouted Mr. Magroy. "'And thou too, my son Reuben?'" he cried looking towards Allen.

"Go! go now," whispered Doctor Mendry, "and come another day with me."

Allen the disinherited, the distressed, departed.

Doctor Mendry engaged Mr. Magroy in theological matters, and shortly succeeded in diverting his mind before leaving his unhappy patient.

Mr. Magroy spent the time now conning over Scripture texts, and Scripture stories, applying them to his present circumstances, as wandering fancies led. His food consisted of corn meal and molasses, for Mr. Magroy, in his spectral visions, saw famine and beggary besieging his doors. Mrs. Magroy was not too blind in her pursuit after her victim's fortune, to perceive that she had driven him too far, and now strove to quiet the raging storm over which the cunning witch had presided so long. There where whispers, which did not fail to reach her, hinting that the law might soon step in with an *Inquirendo de Lunatico*, and consequent assignment of Mr. Magroy to the hands of guardians—his property to trustees.

Mr. Magroy then gradually grew better.

Thus matters stood with the plantiff to the suit in the case of Magroy *vs.* March.

CHAPTER XXXII.

THE TRIAL.

"Man is unjust, but God is just; and finally justice triumphs."
EVANGELINE.

THE trial had dragged its weary length along three days and almost ceased to be the wonder of the town. The judge was a Bourbon—that is, his name was Burbon, but his nose was shockingly *retroussé* for a Bourbon. He was a large, heavy-looking man, relieved by a bright eye and fair beautiful hair—a heavy Egyptian column crowned by a lotus. The next conspicuous court dignitary was the crier. He was a Frenchman, and cried *Oyez!* in the original tongue. The jury loitered in and fell into their boxes one by one.

The judge took his seat this morning with the air of one expecting to be bored. The crier opened the court sleepily. A witness was required to be sworn.

"Antoine Lafontaine!" droned the crier, "come forward and take your oats."

While Antoine is on the stand Mr. Magroy enters the court-room, with his cane. Allen has reserved for his father the best seat within the bar, and rising respectfully, bows as his father plants himself there, without honoring his son with so much as a nod. The old man looks haggard, and perches his chin on the two hands crossed over his supporting cane.

The momentary stir caused by the plaintiff's entrance has scarcely died away, when it is renewed with a louder hum by the entrance of a tall, handsome young man, dressed in the tonish mode, whose every motion is grace, polished ease, and gentle assurance, as he makes his way up the middle aisle of the chamber, and through the crowd that hang around over the outside of the bar; he opens the little oaken door separating the learned from the laity, and steps within the bar. Young Counsellor Allen Magroy is seen to rise suddenly from his seat, not far from his father, and spring forward with an exclamation unheard by the laity, as he seizes the hand of the stranger.

"Who the deuce?"

Is whispered inquiringly along the benches.

"There!" said one, "he seems to know the judge. See! he bows to him."

Now he shakes hands with Mr. Floury.

"But neither judge nor Mr. Floury seems to know him," growls one—always opposed.

"Floury shakes him heartily now," says the previous whisperer, "He knows him now."

Attorney-General Floury, a tall thin man, with light curling hair, remarkably wide sweet mouth, and pleasant dark eyes, rises and makes a motion.

"May it please your honor. I regret at this late stage of the case to ask a departure from the ordinary rules of the court. But knowing your honor's obliging character, and the courtesy of my learned brother on the other side, I am relieved from further embarrasment. Mr. John March, a member of the Boston bar, has arrived, and stands before your honor an applicant for admission to this bar."

"If there be no objection on the part of the gentleman, he is admitted, with welcome," replied his honor.

The attorney-general then proceeded.

"We thank your honor, and now your honor, we have to move further, that this gentleman be allowed to participate in the further trial of this cause, as junior counsel for defendants."

The judge looked towards the counsel for the plaintiff, honorable Counsellor O'Mar.

That gentleman arose and said—

"I have not the least objection, your honor; I am only sorry that he has arived at such an advanced stage of the suit. For," added the witty lawyer, "I fear now that not only no Boston lawyer, but not even a Philadelphia lawyer, could prevent my client from winning."

The judge bowed, and the counsellor stepped over to Mr. March, shook him cordially by the hand, and the laity outside saw them laugh together, as O'Mar shakes his head, and they overheard him say something about "saltpetre not saving" something.

The worthy Antoine Lafontaine was one of the last

witnesses for defence. He had not been able in his testimony to help a cause considered quite hopeless. But it seems that the new ally had come provided with succor. For the crier was unexpectedly awakened, and cried out, rubbing his eyes,

"John Baptiste Laflambeau! come forward and take your oats."

M. Laflambeau was a very old man. He now resided at Montreal. Lived on his income. Was once a temporary resident of this city, in employ as part proprietor, part agent, of the American Fur Company. Knew Henri Fabiens. Had heard reports at the time of his temporary insanity. Never believed them. Eccentric man. Honest, clear-headed, thriving to the hour of his death. Knew both witnesses to his will, both were dead. Heard one of them laughingly speak of M. Fabiens' odd ways, and say he acted like a crazy man. Likewise heard him say, that M. Fabiens was no more crazy than himself, and that he would be glad to be crazy like him. Recognized the two witnesses' signatures in the will now before him. The date was about the same as that of the conversations just mentioned.

The court was now fully awake. The judge leaned forward. Interrupted the witness while he wrote down his testimony. Sensation on the benches of the laity.

M. Laflambeau is soon allowed to retire, and two or three other strange witnesses are called, whose evidence goes further and further towards helping out the unfortunate side. Even the jury begin to pay some attention.

Counsellor O'Mar applies to the judge for leave to send for new witnesses, to rebut what he calls new matter.

Judge Burbon says it is not new matter, and refuses the counsellor's application.

The examination of witnesses had ceased.

The evidence seems very evenly balanced.

It is noon. The judge announces an adjournment to two o'clock. The crier cries it to the court, but nobody hears. Everybody has something to say to his neighbor, as their steps are heard shuffling over the floor and down the steps leading to the street.

It is almost two o'clock. The chamber of justice is filled, but people pour in and overflow it. The learned and witty Counsellor O'Mar is to make two of his best speeches, the opening and closing of the case. The eloquent attorney-general is to make one, and it is said that young March has arrived from Boston. He looks exactly like his late father, only more dashing. He has won laurels in New England, and it is thought, but not known, that he too will speak. That tall, gaunt, pale old man, bending moodily over his cane, is the rich Mr. Magroy. Not far off sits his son, the popular young barrister, looking very solemnly. Just within the bar, but separated by a narrow distance from the lawyers, are two ladies closely veiled. They are Mrs. March and her daughter, the great beauty whom everybody loves for her retiring manners. By their side is the good old family pastor, Mr. Cradle. Behind these are the young commodore and his brother, the new cadet—"Wonder whether he'll come back home too proud to speak to his old acquaintances?" one asks; "who knows?" Over there sit Major Fontenoy and Senator Latrobe.

The clock strikes two.

The crier calls out invitingly,

"Oyez! oyez! oyez! The District Court of the United States of America, for the District of —— is now open."

Counsellor O'Mar rises. He is not so merry at first as usual. He apologizes for his own embarrassing position. He was not retained for this case specially. He was the rich man's business lawyer. But the case was one which embraced other parties than his wealthy client and the poor widow, whom he and everybody knew and respected for her virtues. Titles to large possessions in the hands of numerous possessors were at stake.

He then stated the case. Its history. The history and reputation of the original owner, and of owners down to the present hour. He traced the changes. He then went back and struck rock by rock his mazy track through the tortuous current of M. Fabiens' career, from the fountain-head down to that dark troublesome hour of his mind, when he made his will. He dwelt upon the symptoms of his lunacy. He quoted medical works in which those symptoms were clearly defined, and assigned to the cause he wished the jury to infer. That M. Fabiens had certainly been crazy, was frequently crazy, and showed the most indisputable signs of craziness, both just before, and just after, and just *at* the day, hour, and minute, when he made the will, was patent to the spectators, and proof positive to the enlightened jurors. There was not the least doubt in the mind of Walter March, a party concerned. Walter eyed the assembly, their faces bore no shade of doubt. I peered over at M. Latrobe and Major Fontenoy; the honest soldier wore a troubled look. M. Latrobe I could not read. I glanced at Mr. Magroy, and saw the grim smile of satisfaction which illuminated his face. I gazed at the judge; the judge's attention was fixed on the advocate—impassive.

Mr. O'Mar now descended into the reputation of the two witnesses. Proved it unimpeachable. He then picked up and analyzed the meaning of every word proved to have been let fall by those two worthies. His analysis here was masterly—at one moment so profound, and at the next so witty that the jury shook their fat sides, and the laity shook their benches. Having made the most complete and satisfactory statement, and having analyzed and weighed the evidence, he went on to the argument of the points of law. His logic was—to me—irresistible. Finally came his brief recapitulation, and his brilliant peroration. When he sat down, the spectators did not burst into a cheer, as I anticipated, but there were murmurs of applause rippling over the house.

I felt myself that our case was already hopeless, that our title was baseless, and half began to feel that Mr. Magroy was an injured man.

Mr. John March arose.

He complimented the learned counsellor. He had listened, he said, as to a father in the law. He referred a moment to the peculiarity of his own position. He congratulated himself on seeing here among the jurymen, even under such unpleasant circumstances, the familiar countenances endeared to childhood and his boyish years. He spoke respectfully, even tenderly, of the plaintiff, of his learning and public spirit, and was even proud to acknowledge here in public, that by his efforts the cottage, the very mansion forming a part of the property in litigation, was saved from the fiery element.

He then said, he would leave to his senior the answer to that part of the learned brother's address, which touched on the evidence given previous to his participation in the case. It formed the whole of the evidence for the prosecution, but he would confine himself to urging the force of that part of the evidence for the defence which he himself had introduced, and to the points of law in the case. With reference to the evidence, he advanced so boldly, deduced so broadly, charged so impetuously, that I began to fear for him. But how gallantly he sustained himself! He began to compare notes with the construction put by Counsellor O'Mar upon expression after expression—the Canadian *patois* of which he pronounced so exactly that the jury began to smile, and finally roared. His shrewd wordly-wise maxims, addressed to the jury while he held them now shaking with laughter, now looking wise and complimented, with the wonderful intelligence he attributed to them, told with great effect. Then he addressed the judge on the law points. In this part of his address, I do not think John fairly competed with the counsellor. But he did his best. He quoted Story and Greenleaf; he expounded and argued, and illustrated by similar cases, and made it all very clear—if Counsellor O'Mar hadn't preoccupied the ground. Then modestly leaving the further charge of this part of the case to his senior, he went into a frank account of the relative positions of plaintiff and defendant. This portion he addressed of course to the jury. He referred them back—some of them—to early times. Times when Mr. Magroy and the husband of the defendant were young adventurers together. When the world and fortune went against the former, and favored the latter. When—he spoke of it with reluctance, but for the sake of the cause—about the very time Mr. March made the purchase of the homestead now in question, he granted out of his slender means, the first assistance the blunt, ill-favored young Scotchman ever received at American hands. He dwelt not long here, but he did emphasize the notoriety both of Mr. March's *bona fide* purchase, and of the indisputable nature of the title which was derived from the son of old M. Fabiens, deceased, and well known as an eccentric but never, *never* a crazy being; a being to whose foresight the city was even now indebted for the beauty and business convenience of its growth. He spoke of the uninterrupted prosperity of Mr. Magroy after the first stepping-stone, and of Mr. March's more toilsome career as a business man; of the friendship subsisting so warmly between the two families up to the time of Mr. March's decease; of Mr. Magroy's sudden and surprising coldness, and from that day his increasing enmity; his persecution, by getting into his hands the agency of the cottage payments, and exacting such rigid compliance under the most wretched circumstances of Mrs. March, and in the worst times, times when men universally relaxed the rigidity of their just claims; his persecution, by attempting to deprive the family of the assistance derived from the salary of Guilford March; nay, his purchasing this worthless title itself; his contumelious insults to Mrs. March (great sensation among the spectators); his slanderous accusations against the spotless character of her daughter. (Immense sensation, and looks of wonderment and indignation.) It was necessary then, he continued, not noticing the tumult, which soon subsided, to search for the secret cause of this long series of events. The tears stood in the young lawyer's eyes, as he looked towards Allen, his dearest friend, and apologized in a manly, friendly, and delicate way, for dragging family secrets into such an arena. Poor Allen was overcome, and burying his face in his handkerchief, said in a low husky voice—

"Go on. Go on, for all our sakes."

My brother then adverted to the grand motive of the plaintiff's conduct. His laudable ambition for his son, and at the same time his unparental conduct, his harshness, and violence, his fears lest he should marry into a poor family. His malice against the unfortunate members of that family, the innocent, yet lasting monuments of his own days of early poverty.

At this disclosure cries of "Shame! shame! shame!" were heard.

The proud old Mr. Magroy raised his head, and turning towards the spectators, flung upon them fierce looks of defiance and rage.

Renewed and louder, and more numerous cries of "Shame! shame! shame!" arose. Mr. Magroy stood up and faced the assembly.

The judge threatened to clear the court, and John begged the multitude to save him and his family the pain of any expression of their feelings. The jury regarded the scene with amiable benevolence. The foreman thought the people ought to consider both sides, and the other jurymen nodded "yes." Mr. John March resumed.

The highest proof possible of the existence of the feelings he had disclosed on the part of his honored friend the plaintiff consisted in the treatment of his own, his only, son. Driven from the paternal roof penniless, disinherited for ever, this youth had grown up in the midst of the gentlemen of the jury, the child of evil fortunes, as one born under some malignant star; and yet his manner of life was the best guarantee for his innocence and virtues, and his unmerited persecution, along with that of an innocent family, with whom too—such had been his desire to comply with the wishes of his father—he had had no sort of personal intercourse for years, but had been a self-banished man, where he was most loved and best known; a hermit near a garden of roses; an outcast with paradise in view. Some one called out, "Three cheers for Allen Magroy!" The crowd arose and gave three cheers.

The judge's face lightened, the marshal's voice thundered—without avail.

In the confusion the heavy falling of a body was unnoticed by all but Allen Magroy and M. Latrobe, both of whom sprang to the assistance of the elder Mr. Magroy, who now lay upon the floor, his mouth bleeding profusely. They raised him in their arms. The spectators who were nearest to the little partition which separated the court from the laity, made an effort to get within, but were repelled by the marshal and his assistants. The judge pathetically requested that order and silence might be restored, to save him the necessity of clearing the court at a moment when so great and general an interest was felt in the cause.

The spectators complied with his just appeal, and order and silence prevailed.

Meanwhile Mr. Magroy was raised to a chair. He coughed and spat out large quantities of blood. At last he was able to utter in a faint voice,

"Thy forgiveness Allen. I have wronged thee. Oh! God! I see it now. I see"——his voice sank away.

Allen was silently weeping. M. Latrobe had already dispatched a messenger after Doctor Mendry. The clerk of the court brought a pitcher of water. Mr. Magroy drank and grew apparently easier.

"Is she here Allen?"

"Who, my father?"

"Who? who but Maud the daughter of my old friend? The daughter of the only woman I ever loved, and whom I never forgave for marrying him.

"Is she here? quick! good people, quick!"

My mother and Maud stood near the wretched dying man.

"Here is Maud," said M. Latrobe.

"Truly she? I grow blind and dizzy," he murmured, and a new fit of coughing up blood ensued.

More water was administered. His voice came back.

"Give me your hand, Allen. You forgive me?"

"God knows I do, and did long, long ago."

"Now hers, haste!" he cried.

M. Latrobe placed the hand of my sister in that of the cold, quivering man.

He put it in Allen's.

"My children, be hap-py!"

Doctor Mendry urged his way through the crowd.

Too late! Too late!

The hush of death suddenly falls on the assembly. The pulse of Time stands still. A calm sweet voice is heard.

"O God all seeing, all listening, all feeling, all knowing, God! who weigheth not our merits, but pardoneth our offences, receive into thy bosom, we beseech thee, the troubled spirit of our brother."

The low amen was heard like a murmur of the sea. And the pulse of Time went on.

CHAPTER XXXIII.

PROSPECT AND RETROSPECT.

Old Time will end our story,
But no time, if we end well, will end our glory.
BEAUMONT & FLETCHER.

THE period of my furlough from the Military Academy, at the end of two years from admission, was selected for the consummation of two events. It was likewise the occasion of Major Fontenoy's return from Europe, whither he had gone to seek diversion from unrest and loneliness. The better to shake off painfully pleasing associations he had cut himself off meanwhile, even from correspondence with us.

Major Fontenoy.—"Then Magroy left a statement in writing, which has created pity and respect for his memory, hey, Walter."

Walter.—"Yes, it was found with the will. I have been favored with a copy. Here it is:

"'From frequent attacks on brain and body, I am solemnly warned that Archibald Magroy's remaining sands are few and fleeting. Even this moment is but an interval between periods of attack, which drive me mad. I have done injustice to many, and unhappily worse, to those I love best on earth. First, to the relict of my early friend and benefactor, Wingfleet March. She was the only woman I ever loved as a man should love, and the only being I ever hated as a man can hate. Her preference for another stung me to the heart. I never asked the world's sympathy, but my all necessary, my only craving for human love was shipwrecked on her. I quickly married after my rejection, and plunged into business and study. My hatred was dissembled till the death of Mr. March, in whose business perplexities I held an unseen hand. But as soon as he was gone I rushed openly after my prey. From that hour my extreme wretchedness began. There is no peace for the wicked. Amen.'

[ANOTHER DATE.]

"'I feel deeply humiliated and penitent, and have felt so during lucid intervals for years. Yet ever since revenge became dominant, a horrible, irresistible blackness of darkness has enveloped my senses, and covered the light of faith, reason, and conscience, which yet ever and anon flashes out like the lightning. The Bible has at such moments been my solace. Yet in my clouded hours the texts and events of the holy book haunt my gloomy imagination like gibbering spectres, wearing the forms of the dearest ones on earth.'

[ANOTHER DATE.]

"'To God, whom I love when reason sits with me, I commend my spirit for forgiveness. To men I make what reparation lies in my power. My son is beyond the reach of want. He is the architect of his own good name, a true American. I leave him my blessing.'"

Walter.—"This is all that was found written by his own hand. In the will, a tutorship for the classical language is endowed at the University, a legacy of three hundred a year is left to the present Mrs. Magroy, whom he calls Mistress Fidgets, that cunning promptress of evil;' a thousand a year is left to Maud March; that portion of Lilac Cottage premises, which he had lately purchased, is left to Guilford; to the city he devises a large park, to be selected and the grounds laid out and adorned by Major Fontenoy. The remainder, constituting the bulk of his fortune, was devised to my mother without conditions."

Major.—"Had *some* honor, hey! I knew it, hey! And the executors?"

Walter.—"Are M. Latrobe and Guilford March."

Major.—"By-the-by, how does the young commodore, hey, prosper?"

Walter.—"He has risen with the tide of prosperity, which seems to have overflown the banks of the whole country bordering on these inland seas. His activity has kept pace with the demands of the swelling sail of a commerce, whose rapid advance has astonished the world."

Major.—"Rather high-flown speech for a soldier, hey!"

"In short, he is called the Young Commodore of the Lakes."

Major.—"Rich, hey! Good! hey!"

Walter.—"Not yet rich, dear major. Too much at stake yet."

Major.—"Ever think of farm life?"

Walter.—"Yes, it is still the phantom he sees beyond, and follows afar. He has just purchased and fitted up Millbrook cottage, and, with a pony phaeton, will drive into town to do his business. He hopes in a few years to be able to retire, and abandon the exciting world for the soothing employments of rustic life—that is, on a large scale."

The scene changes, and the major and myself stand in the library of Lilac Cottage, in the midst of perfumed bouquets, floating veils, white gloves and flowing robes. Here is the Rev. Mr. Cradle, now D.D., but Doctor Cradle don't sound familiar quite yet. And here is M. Latrobe to give away the brides. And here is the mother—I was going to say—of both brides. And here finally are the major, John and his wife, and Guilford March.

Wedding guests are waiting in parlor and hall. The door is thrown open. Dr. Cradle moves forward in advance, the two happy couples follow after. Allen and Maud first, a splendid couple; she with downcast eyes, her veil and bridal-wreath circling those light waves of hair, breaking into fleecy foam around her shoulders, and he with his long black locks and proud yet gentle motion, graceful as ever. Then Guilford and Mabel. He a frank, hearty, stout youth, with rounded face and girl-like eyes, and she, Mabel! my Mabel——

My eyes swam so whenever I looked at her, and do so now when I think of it, I could not see. I cannot describe Mabel. Then came Major Fontenoy and myself, the two groomsmen, who took our places on the flanks of the line when brought up. Finally my mother and M. Latrobe. No, the last of all was Bowes, rubbing her hands on the cleanest white muslin apron one ever saw.

"But how were the brides dressed?" everybody asks.

Truly that is beyond my knowledge. But if the publisher will wait till I can ask Mabel——

Ah! that was one of the last of the good old fashioned weddings in our city—so I have often been told. They promise me the like of it when I bring my bride. Alas! good friends, that day will never come! Major Fontenoy and I are sworn lovers for life.

"But how did the major come to go to Europe? There is some mystery about that?"

Only three of us knew it. The major, myself, and Mabel.

"What! did the little witch flirt with the good old major?"

No. She never flirts—that is she never *intends* to flirt. But some way or other, the major, silly simpleton! fell into the dazzle of her eyes.

"Julius Cæsar, hey!" he swore to me, confidentially. "I couldn't help it! if there were a whole battalion of Mauds and Mabels before me, all standing at charge bayonet, I couldn't help dropping on my knees to each one in succession, with an offer of my hand, hey! emphatically, *hand*, hey!"

"Dear major," I cried, "this hand is the helper of widows, it has encouraged weakness, and poverty, and distress. It has flashed in the eyes of the oppressor. And," I added, smiling, "it has waved as handsome a compliment to lady fair, as that of any Chevalier Bayard of the olden time."

And again we renewed our vows of mutual fidelity for life.

But on with your story, sir.

Allen and Maud dwelt with Mrs. March until the death of Fidgets, whom my mother prevailed upon—without difficulty—to occupy the Magroy mansion. Allen then took his little bird to dwell among the boughs of the paternal tree. Two fledglings, Mabel and Fontenoy, chirp from their nest.

I returned home again on graduating from West Point, and deposited my diploma in a cylindrical tin box with Guilford, who by this time had built a sweet little house—just large enough for me and my friend the Major—directly above the butternut bank. To this delightful spot Mabel comes every morning, when I visit them on furlough, and sits with her sewing, and little Walter, or little Maud, and the Major and me, while little Guilford blows dandelions and chases butterflies outdoors. In fact, they have been with me while chronicling the events of our family history; and fallen out of patience into a passion over it, so many times, and so often protested they would have no such responsibility in the affair, predicting my utter failure and disgrace in trying my hand at authorship, that I have ceased to consult them altogether.

Meanwhile, the war with Mexico came on. Major Fontenoy got a regiment, and on the close of the campaign again left the service—with the rank of general.

" Walter was breveted twice for gallantry, and is now called Major March."

I protest, gentle reader, that my friend Fontenoy wrote that sentence in my absence. I have no false modesty in the matter, but as I have travelled along with you so far as a stripling, I prefer not to be known as an old fogy.

The youngsters are treading on my weary old heels, and I am innocently trampling on their ambitious toes. It is the hope of both parties, however, that the next Congress, with their young life, and opposed as they will be to the rust lingering on our institutions, it is hoped, I say, that they may pass a law creating a retired list for us worn out veterans.

Though confessedly "the happiest man in America," yet, in one respect, Guilford the Doer's youthtful expectation is not realized. His mother cannot be prevailed upon to forsake Lilac Cottage for Millbrook. She says she must keep up the old house for Walter's sake, and continues to delude herself with the fond hope of my bringing her a new daughter some day. Meantime, she does the honor of Lilac Cottage with old French hospitality. Here the young people all gather to keep holiday, and assisted by Bowes, together with Dick and the blue-eyed Mary, who, with their children, live in a little cottage below, on what was known as the cut-off, Mrs. March dispenses flowers among her neighbors, and charity and gentle words to the poor of the city.

M. Latrobe—now no more—retiring from the cares of state, and the pursuits of business, divided his green old age between Lilac Cottage and Millbrook.

Abe, who was forced to abandon stage-driving, by the laying of railway tracks, for a modern city hack, came at last to Guilford—"his last school-fellow"—Abe said, and besought to be admitted to Millbrook, where he turns out a capital ostler, though but a tolerable farmer. His shining, and high-mettled steeds, with brass-mounted saddles, burnished to the skies, are always at the service of Major—no, General Fontenoy and myself. The general takes a five-railed fence at a leap with his horse, while I am fain to take down the bars by hand.

Poor Tapes is dead.

Gentle reader! If over the dreamy career of Walter March, or the more practical good deeds of his friends, you find aught to feed upon with pleasure, or to sip with the refreshing of useful truth, let this be the acknowledgment of his chief reward, and the response of a grateful heart.

JEPTHA JUMPS' SPEECH.

> Take heed what you say, sir!
> An hundred honest men! why, if there were
> So many i'th' city, twere enough to forfeit
> Their charter.
>
> SHIRLEY'S GAMESTER.

ON my return home from Washington, I saw the name of Jumps in the Gazette. He was now a member of the State Legislature.

I called at his lodgings immediately, and sent up my name to the Honorable Jeptha Jumps. He seemed as pleased to receive me as if he were still a common mortal, for which I felt duly grateful.

"I am in the swamp now, you know!" he said.

"Do you term the House of Representatives of a sovereign state a swamp?"

"Yes," he answered, "worse than any tamarack swamp, a tarnation sight; full of pricks and thorns, and muddy water up to here." He raised his forefinger to his neck—which, by the way, now sported a white cravat.

"How did you get into the scrape?"

"Wall, last autumn, after depositing my hopeful Joram with your folks, I took a tramp out West, to see the oak openings and the pe-rairah lands. And arter I came home the boys in my neighborhood run my name up on the trees as candidate for this ere office. I tried to haul off, but it warn't no kind of use; have me in they would, for, says they, you're the only honest man in the district, soft saudering me up, you see."

"Who was your competitor?"

"The Rev. Mr. Milkwhite; so, you see, I had all the petticoat influence agin me," said Jumps, with a wink. "That feeble pattern of human nater attempted to catch my daughter, too!"

"What!" I exclaimed, "not Susannah?"

"Yes, my little Suz, sir. He courted her off and on for two years, and she refused him regularly every month; he preached to her about having a call to be a minister's wife, and doing good in the world, prayed over her, besieged my wife and half made her crazy, too. Finally, Suz came to me and said she couldn't stand it. I'll adopt a course, says I; so down I goes to where the crittur lives, and says, says I: 'Rev. Mr. Milkwhite, you mustn't come around my house persecutin' my Suz. She don't take a likin' to you, and won't have you no how.' Then the crittur promised as how he'd let her alone on his sacred word of honor. But what should appear at Green Run next day but the whole session? They walked straight into my house, and held a prayer-meeting over Suz—I wasn't to hum—wrestled in spirit with my wife, and made her and Suz both cry, and said it was her solemn bounden duty to marry that ere little snipe of a parson. My wife gin in to them. But Suz, she held out till I cum hum, and the way I made old Pipelegs, Peppergrass, and the rest on 'em, scatter, was a caution now, I tell you—no more of Rev. Mr. Milkwhite at my house, I tell you.

"Wall, since that, the tarnation little crittur has slandered me on all occasions behind my back—told the neighborhood I was a heathen, and dead to the cause of Christianity, and when he heard I was candidate for the Legislature, he up and said he'd run agin me. That was the time I took off my coat, Walter."

"I dare say," replied I, laughing.

"They'd got sick of the village lawyer, and all on 'em owed the village doctor, and the village shopkeeper wouldn't trust most on 'em for cotton calico, and indigo bluen, and so they came down on me."

"How do you feel in your new position?"

"Like a French hunter, paddlin' his canoe among lame ducks in among the rushes."

'How so?"

"Wall, every now and then, in some of my strokes, I hit one of 'em without seein' or thinkin' of the critturs, and he hain't got wings to fly out of my way, but still manages to dive under and come up somewhere else."

Shortly after this interview, I attended an evening session of the House. The measure under consideration was one of general interest; viz. the railway system. After several long and one short speech, from excited members, each in favor of a road through his district,

Mr. Jumps arose, with his honest face and white cravat.

"Mr. Speaker."

The members winked at each other, and many gathered round Mr. Jumps, crowding the seats nearest him, and forcing the occupants and owners thereof to withdraw some of their lower limbs and great cowhide boots from the tables in front of them.

"What few words I shall have to say, Mr. Speaker, I hope will be plum to the bull's eye."

A titter.

"The honorable gentlemen who have jined in the discussion thus far have hunted all around Robin Hood's barn, and missed the crittur after all."

People begin to fill the galleries.

"It seems to me, Mr. Speaker, that gentlemen discuss this bill on the principle of 'you tickle me and I'll tickle you;' you streak a railroad through my village and I'll streak one by your farm."

"I proposed nothing of the sort!" exclaimed an honorable member from a distant village, in an excited manner, "and whoever says so"——

"Lame ducks? Mr. Speaker, lame ducks!" said Mr. Jumps, very composedly. The members cried out generally, "Good! good! hit him again, honest Jeptha. Sit down, Fleece—Sit down." The honorable Mr. Fleece subsided into his seat in sulky, defiant silence.

"Now, Mr. Speaker, if there's any more lame ducks to flutter here this evening, I beg on 'em to wait till I'm done, for they take up the time of the House, and throw it on my shoulders.

"Now, Mr. Speaker, we must buckle into this subject like men working to lay the foundations of permanent institutions, and not like time-serving politicians, looking out every man for himself"—

"And the devil take the hindmost!" broke in a coarse-looking man, with long legs, coiled upon the table in front of him.

"I never use such words," said Mr. Jumps, with real dignity. "I leave them to the lips of my honorable friend over the way. Gentlemen will find it best to let me alone, Mr. Speaker, perhaps, before the end of the session," said Mr. Jumps, taking a glass of water.

"Yes, sir, we must adopt a course, we must act the part of men held to reckoning by posterity."

"What has posterity ever done for me?" demanded a member.

"Nothing! and I kind o' reckon it never will!" returned Mr. Jumps.

The Speaker's mallet descended. The House came to order, and Mr. Jumps was not interrupted again.

"Sir, we have had some experience already pressed home to our hearts and pockets. What do we see on every side of us? Wild-cat banks, sir, howling through the midnight air of these dark and troublesome times. Wild-cat banks, with broken legs and broken heads, and, sir, if I had my way, I'd adopt a course, sir, I'd cut off all their tails as a warning to posterity, and hang 'em on the political landmarks of which gentlemen have talked so loud and so learned.

"Then, Mr. Speaker, look at our schools. Congress donated a harnsome fund of wild lands, out of which, with prudence and foresight, we might, and oughter have raised up a system of schools, with its mother university, that would not only pay their own keeping, but pay something into the depleted treasury of the State.

"Sir! we have nothing in the shape of State schools but broken-down branches of a university that has neither root nor trunk, affording nothing to the people, nothing to nobody, but the old ravens that croak more! more! more! from the nests in the branches which they have feathered themselves into so nicely.

"Now, sir, this will be the story of the railroad, too, if we rush into the same system of reckless extravagance. The intarnal improvements of the State will all run to waste. No, sir, let us begin with moderation and economy, and sure as Dabol's arithmetic, thrift and prosperity will follow. Let us jine hands on some one route most convenient to all sections, and do what we can on that till Congress comes up to our help. And, sir, Congress soon will come. The interests of the West will not be much longer neglected. We have a mighty West! a broad, beautiful West! the tract of our wilderness is wide as the ocean, sir. These States are filling up rapidly, and will have a mighty voice one of these days. Their voice will be heard from Dan to Beersheba, and there'll be a shakin' among the dry bones, I reckon.

"Yes, Mr. Speaker, we have a goodly heritage. I see the West before me now. Her oak openings are like the garden of Eden. Her forests are boundless. The etarnal scope of her pe-rairahs is unlimited. Sir," said Mr. Jumps, solemnly concluding, "we must adopt a course."

THE BATTLE OF WINDSOR.

A FRONTIER EPISODE.

ONE evening, my brother Guilford and myself were out enjoying the beauties of such a blue star-lit sky as King March sometimes canopies himself under after the tumult of a storm. A little way above the city we were overtaken by a sturdy-looking pedestrian, with a knapsack strapped to his shoulders, and a belt around his waist, to which were fastened a bowie-knife and a tin cup.

"That is a patriot," whispered Guilford.

The city was filled with Canadian refugees, together with a promiscuous gathering from various parts of the United States, intent on taking part in the quarrel between the provinces and the mother country. The people along the American frontier sympathized deeply with the revolutionists—and it was whispered among the *quid nuncs*, that even gentlemen connected with both state and general governments contributed secretly to the cause. For these reasons, unless men were found actually assembled in arms, they were not likely to be molested—individuals, notoriously known to be "patriots," came and went openly.

"Shall we accost him?" inquired Walter.

"If you like," replied Guilford.

In a moment we were at the side of the stranger.

Guilford.—"Good evening, friénd."

Stranger.—"Yes! what of it?"

Walter.—"A fine night, sir."

Stranger.—"Fine enough for those who like it."

Walter.—Half provoked—"Fine enough? Like it? Like the stars! like the sweet smell of spring! which you may scent afar, as the horse snuffs the battle, and dilates his nostrils with pleasure and exultation!"

Stranger.—"What do you know about battles, boy?"

The patriot seemed to notice for the first time my youthfulness, and grew sociable.

Walter.—(Laughing)—"It is a subject, sir, in which I take a deep interest."

Stranger.—(In a low tone)—"Then perhaps you can tell me where the encampment lies."

Walter.—"What encampment?"

Stranger.—"The patriot."

Guilford.—"Where were you directed to go?"

Stranger.—"To the second point of woods, I think they called it 'Shane's Point."

Guilford.—"Chene's Point! you have taken the wrong road to distinguish the points running out from the woods. But, by following this road till you come to"—

Stranger.—"Don't believe I can find it, sir, perhaps you might be going part way."

Guilford.—"Oh yes. What do you say, Walter. Shall we go to the encampment?"

Walter.—"It would be quite an unexpected adventure—certainly, let's go."

Guilford.—"I take it, messmate, you are a patriot."

Stranger.—"Yes, shouldn't wonder. What of it?"

Guilford.—"From Ohio?"

Stranger.—"No, Canada. What of it?"

Guilford.—"Are there many Canadians here now?"

Stranger.—"Very few. But we fight in earnest: but what of it? we fight for our country, not for plunder; I wish there were more of us. You Yankees talk a deal in the papers, and make great speeches, but when it comes to actual fighting you'd rather let it out. But what of it? all the same in a hundred years."

Walter.—"Are you an Englishman?"

Stranger.—"No, I emigrated from York State with my father and folks fifteen years ago, and settled not far from Hamilton. We got on very well till this revolution began to make a stir. Then we were suspected right off. What of it? cried I—might as well be hung for an old sheep as a lamb. So I raised all the money I could, and determined to devote myself to the good cause. My father was pretty old, but as many of the people around us were secretly patriots, he thought he could take care of my young wife and the two unmaried girls. The night after I left, gentlemen, my house was burnt to the ground, my father killed, and my sisters and wife"——

The stranger suddenly ceased speaking. His teeth gnashed together.

Guilford.—(After a moment, when the patriot became composed)—"I wish I could help you, sir. Can you not go on with your story?"

Stranger.—"Thank you, sir. There was a camp of volunteers for the British a few miles from our place. Many of the officers and men belonged to our neighborhood, and we had always been on friendly terms till the war broke out—war puts the devil even between friends—But what of it? all the same in a hundred years. Who'd a thought they'd ever permitted a neighbor's family to be treated so?"

And again the distressed fellow was overpowered by his emotions, making such a horrible noise with his teeth, that Guilford and Walter, fearing he might drop down at any moment with the lock-jaw, endeavored to keep him in conversation. Yet there was only one subject. In a moment he returned to it—his family, and threw out dark hints.

Walter.—"The miscreants! how could they dare?"

Stranger.—"Oh! don't you believe it, young sir. The ruffian cowards even killed each other's sheep, robbed all the hen-roosts, shot down the dogs, set fire to corn-fields—caught women, brought them into camp, and ——O God! O God!"

His deep groans of distress moved the brothers to the bottom of their hearts.

Guilford.—"Let us carry your knapsack for you, friend."

Stranger.—"Thank you, you are good fellows, I know; I know my eyes are leaky. I can't help groaning, I make a fool of myself—but all the same in a hundred years."

The brothers unbuckled the knapsack and carried it along between them.

Stranger.—"I had two brothers little younger than the youngest of you. Not near so tall, but honest, hearty lads. Where they are God only knows. What became of my wife and sisters I know too well. The ruffians over there"—he pointed towards the Canada shore—"they know, and they must meet them, and me, too, at the judgment bar of God. All the same in a hundred years!"

Walter.—"Pardon me, but I feel so much interested. Did they kill the defenceless women?"

Stranger.—"Do you think that women of American descent, would ever be debauched alive?"

Guilford and Walter.—"Heavens! Heavens!"

At the next moment the clatter of horses' hoofs was heard behind us. A small party of horsemen soon went by rapidly.

Stranger.—"That's our general!"

Guilford.—"Which one?"

Stranger.—"The last one. He always lags behind. He's from York State, joined us in Ohio, was elected when the band was small, as commander of the expedition. What of it? He's no account."

Guilford.—"Not fit for it, eh?"

Stranger.—"Is a bullfrog fit to drill crows?"

Guilford.—(Glad to divert the late bitter train of thought)—" A bullfrog has qualities considered by many as essential to the soldier. He can strut and swell, grumble and croak, and go slowly enough for any old fogy."

Stranger.—(Laughing.)—" That's just it! sure as my name's Lot! Our general can do all that to perfection. What of it? Meantime, the crows all fly away. Just so. We marched up from Toledo, with five hundred brave fellows. The ladies worked a beautiful silk banner, worth I don't know how many hundred dollars, and presented it to us. Five hundred men thanked them for it. Now we have barely two hundred!"

Walter.—" Why, how is that?"

Stranger.—" Ask him riding on there! Three nights ago there were four hundred of us altogether in the woods, ready to start. Two nights ago, three hundred. But both nights the general had the stomach-ache, or tooth-ache, or something, and said he wasn't ready nor able. So you see they got disgusted; some of 'em out of money too, and had to go to work to earn their bread."

Walter.—" But will he go to-night? will he cross over?"

Stranger.—" He'll have to. They've got hold of him, I see, and they swore last night they'd shoot him, if he didn't go."

Guilford.—" Can't you keep together and prevent desertion?"

Stranger.—" No, we can only meet nights now, since

15

we reached a place where there are United States troops —we don't mind the militia, Frontier Guards and all that. Some of them attend our lodges, then go dress in uniform; and pace the streets all night, pretending to be on the look out to catch us. Well, we rendezvous at some new spot in the woods each night, and scatter ourselves during the day. So if the men don't choose there's nothing to make 'em come."

We had turned off from the main road, and, during many minutes been ascending a lane, which led up to Chene's Point. The camp fires were now visible among the trees—men were sitting or walking around them. As we drew near the encampment, we met a couple of ostlers, belonging to a livery-stable in the city, leading away several horses.

"That looks something like," said Lot, "they're sending back the horses." Our companion pricked up at once. He was all elation.

"Yes," said he, taking his knapsack, "we may cross over to-night. We shall attack Windsor, march straight to Chatham, and from there move down upon London and who knows but we may see Hamilton? What of it? Ha! ha! all the same in a hundred years!"

With a quickened pace we soon gained the woods, and walked from fire to fire, and from group to group. Lot was greeted with those peculiar demonstrations of sympathy which rough men pay spontaneously to suffering. But our friend seemed to stand little in need of sympathy—he was in good spirits.

We found a determined-looking set of fellows gathered here—though few in numbers, nor, with the exception perhaps of the Canadian portion, animated by that devotion which true patriotism inspires. No one would imagine from their looks that a man among them could ever run. Their heavy beards and unwashed faces, long hair, and dogged, sullen, even resolute eyes, gave them a fierce brigandish air, or something more desperate, which the glare of the fire did not serve to diminish.

Invited by Lot, we sat down in the midst of a group who were toasting pork and biscuits at a fire, on the ends of their knives, bayonets, and swords, and discussing the characters of their leaders, the events of the march through Ohio, and the prospect before them. Guilford and myself shared their food; and it was sad enough to think, afterwards, that this was the last meal on earth with some of the devoted band.

The general soon made his appearance, as he was moving from group to group, with a word here and a word there. The men seemed to bear him neither great respect nor good-will—frequently turning their backs upon him. He was muffled up in a camlet cloak, and a white handkerchief around his ears and face. He might have graced a civic procession but here he was evidently out of place.

Next to him in rank, and the real leader of the expedition, was a tall Kentuckian, with a gruff voice, scarred face, and commanding presence; a tower of strength, capitally suited to desperate enterprises. I did not hear his name, they only called him "the Colonel."

Only below the Colonel in favor among the patriots was Major Putnam, an American Canadian, who had abandoned a large property near Chatham, and fled to the United States, misled by the tone of the popular press into the belief that his former countrymen were ready to march in a body for the deliverance of the provinces. Active in forming the present expedition, his hope was set high when it lately numbered five hundred—a sufficient force, perhaps, to march through the Upper Provinces—but even now, with the handful to which they had become reduced, this true patriot was resolved to do so or die."

I remember but one other conspicuous character—Dandy Jack—what a name to die on! Yet none there nobler than Dandy Jack—with his harlequinades, his coat of many colored lists, and his flourishing horse-pistol. He was the soul of jocularity, the life of the camp, a genuine descendant of the true-hearted illustrious Wamba the Witless.

At midnight the order went round for the adventurers to form ranks in the lane by which Guilford, myself, and the brave Lot had come. What provisions remained were tossed into the fires. The men strapped on their kits and knapsacks, took their arms—a promiscuous assortment—upon their shoulders, and silently fell in. It were vain to disguise that their spirits were gloomy. But Lot, and Dandy Jack, and a few others, threw a cheering ray now and tnen along the ranks, and the Colonel, and Major Putnam, whatever their real feelings, disguised them sufficiently to present a confident manner to the men.

On reaching the main road, the column halted. A murmur ran through the ranks.

"What is the matter?" whispered Walter to Lot.

"The steamboat's not ready.

The delay was vexatious. It seemed as though they were to be disappointed again in their wishes to cross, and curses deep not loud, fell from time to time on the head of General ——. Besides, they were now assembled in arms within dangerous proximity to the city.

"The Frontier Guards will be upon us," said one.

"Oh! never fear that," replied another. "Two thirds of them would join us, with half a chance of success."

"The only man I fear is old General Bladey with his regulars," said another. "That old fellow's as true as steel to the government, they say."

"To the devil with the government, old Matty and all! what's the use of their humbuggin?" said a tall Hibernian, who evidently had little faith in the sincerity of the President.

"Faix!" said Dandy Jack, imitating the celebrated sweet brogue of his friend, "if I only had that old fox Matty by the tail, be jabers!"——

A low laugh was heard along the line at this freak of Dandy Jack's fancy, and again all was silent until the figure of the Colonel was seen approaching from towards the head of the column.

"All right, men! The Frontiers are not out to-night, and the regulars are asleep in their barracks," said the Colonel, in a low, husky voice, as he passed by us—the former portion of this intelligence was a mistake.

Soon afterwards another figure moved down the line. It was Putnam.

"Men!" said he, "after we cross over, be careful what you drink. I have intelligence from Chatham that the brandy in the inns, and the water in the wells, are to be poisoned along the whole road." Then pausing, he took out his watch and was lost a moment in deep abstraction. As he recovered I heard him say, "In four hours we shall know our destiny."

This figure disappeared.

"I'll drink nothing but blood!" said the fierce Hibernian.

"And I'll drink nothing but whisky," echoed Dandy Jack, again imitating the Irish ex-patriot.

Ere the laughter died away, the column resumed its march down the road, and having gained a half-mile, suddenly turned to the left. In a few minutes we stood upon a wharf at the end of which lay a steamer letting off steam—an operation it seemed to perform in a low tone, with the spirit of stealthy secrecy which characterized all the movements of this midnight expedition.

The hardy adventurers were soon got on board, Guilford and Walter shook hands with Lot and Dandy Jack—how much sadder we, than they!

"You'll hear of me, boys," said Dandy Jack.

"We hope to hear of your success, old fellow," said Guilford.

"Yes," said Dandy Jack, "this horse-pistol and I were born to distinguish ourselves. I mean to shoot Colonel ——— in person." He spoke the name of the magistrate, who bearing likewise a commission in the Canada militia, wielded both civil and military command in the district about to be invaded.

Alas! we remembered Dandy Jack's words!

There were several long and provoking delays in getting the steamer off. I secretly indulged the hope that something would prevent the further prosecution of this ill-starred enterprise. Some one on board the vessel cut the tiller-rope once, again, and again. Finally a guard of trusty men was established along the rope from the rudder to the wheel. The hawser was lifted off the posts on the wharf, the wheels of the steamer commenced revolving, a low cheer was heard from the few on shore—including some members of the Frontier Guards—answered by those on board, and the "Champlain" moved out into the stream.

We watched the progress of the vessel.

It steamed up the river, finding it impossible, probably, to cross at once through the ice, which was floating down in large thick masses, from the lakes above.

Two hours we waited, watching anxiously. Then thinking it would be morning before the Champlain could land her precious cargo, Guilford and myself returned to Lilac Cottage.

Arising from a troubled sleep at dawn, I looked out upon the river. The Barracks on the Canadian side were in flames—nearly consumed.

"Three cheers! Guilford, they have succeeded!"

We could distinguish small compact parties of men under arms marching on the town of Windsor—a little distance below the British Barracks. Over the heads of one of the parties waved the patriot tri-color. For awhile they are lost among the buildings of Windsor. Now they are seen moving irregularly over a meadow, and into an orchard in rear of the town. It is doubtless their intention, either to await there Colonel ——— with the British, or to take the most direct route to Chatham through the woods.

A small, but well-ordered body, is now seen approaching Windsor, from below. It is the British force from Sandwich. Now they are hid by the town. Now they are seen approaching the orchard. Smoke rises above the tops of the apple trees. A volley of musketry is faintly heard—another—the smoke thickens—there is a promiscuous roar of sounds, swelling and sinking at intervals—small puffs of smoke are twining up as if writhing in agony, here and there from the orchard—sounds die away—the air is no longer polluted—and the battle of Windsor is fought and won.

Meantime there was a vehement excitement among the people of our little city. Thousands flocked to the wharves; some, the better to behold the conflict, others with arms in their hands, with the view of crossing the river to the assistance of the patriots, with whom everybody sympathized—vociferously. The tops of the houses were covered with spectators. They swarm upon the rigging of the vessels at the docks. They fill the streets leading to the river-side. United States troops of the regular service are marching hurriedly from street to street and from wharf to wharf; to prevent our citizens from invading the dominions of a nation with whom we are at peace. The Frontier Guard are out in full feather, with their splendid grey uniforms and fine music, all zeal to close the stable-door after the steed has flown. The multitude cheer them as they pass, but groan and hiss at the regulars. Discriminating multitude! The Frontiers are drawing pay from government on voluntary services—the regulars are marched to the spot *nolens volens.* That plucky little band of Frenchmen, the Shoepacs, are not out on this occasion. They refuse the pay of the government, and resolutely stay at home.

There is not so much ice now running in the water, and a swift little steamer, with a detachment of regulars, and a piece of artillery on board, is plying up and down, preventing boats from crossing to Windsor. The detachment on this steamer have the most odious duty to perform, and are hooted loudly by the mob on shore.

On that long wharf stands old General Bladey, with his thin white hair floating in the morning breeze. Everything to preserve the neutrality is done under his direction. The general watched the battle, as it was fought, with a kindled eye. No doubt his sympathies as a man—even as a soldier—were against the British, for he had fought them himself, was a hero of Lundy's Lane; yet his duty—ah, that is a different thing. That little word "duty," was the general's polar star through life—doubtless it guided him safely into heaven.

A murmur of displeasure began to make itself heard behind and around the old general. Voices were heard calling him

"Tory! Tory! Tory!"

The general turned and faced the tumult. He was alone, a slender man of three score years and ten, and carried no arms but a small rapier. His eyes grew young again beneath those flashes of fearless indignation.

"Pitch him into the river!" was the next cry.

"In with him! in with him!" was heard on every side.

In a moment the general had drawn his rapier, and cutting his way right and left through the crowded mass, he left the wharf before the ringleaders of the mob recovered from their surprise.

After all, I think there were enough left of the *ancien régime* to have protected the general had violent hands been laid upon him; for he had dwelt among us a quarter of a century, and was loved as only a pure, honest, simple-hearted old soldier can be loved. And no sooner, even on this occasion, had the general separated himself from the multitude, than the sky was rent with

"Three cheers for General Bladey!"

It was soon noised about the city that the patriots were defeated by Colonel ——. This unwelcome intelligence was soon confirmed. Small boats—French canoes and others—were seen putting off from the Canadian shore, above Windsor. Orders were given for the steamer which carried the brass field-piece to proceed up the river and arrest the fugitives as they were crossing. Cruel order it seemed! The boats were hailed, some fired at, one hit, when the steamer returned; the captives on board were few, but among them was one poor groaning fellow, who had been struck by a six-pounder ball on the thigh. He was carefully brought ashore on a litter—a blanket stretched over two hand-spikes—and his gory leg was visibly dangling by a shred of the skin. The troops marched over the wharf. The field-piece rattled over the stones. The drum and fife of the detachment struck up a lively air; and the regulars marched out of sight. Yet many a brave heart was bleeding beneath those blue coats—duty! what an easy thing, but for heart-bleeding.

It was not until several days afterwards that reliable particulars of the battle could be gathered from the conflicting rumors. Chance at length brought me into the acquaintance of one, since become a warm friend, who participated in the affair. He was a youth little older than myself, who, carried away by an ardent love of liberty, left his home to share the honors and dangers of freedom's cause.

The "Champlain" landed the patriots just before the break of day. They marched at once upon the Barracks. The few British troops quartered there succeeded, with the exception of one soldier, in making their escape to Sandwich. The building was fired, and the patriots—or rebels, as we must now call them, since the revolution failed—proceeded at once to Windsor, which they captured without a blow.

Instead of pursuing the loyalists to Sandwich, or, according to the original plan, marching at once for Chatham, and rousing the Canadians, who it was thought were only waiting for the appearance of an armed party to rise and rally around the standard of revolt, the patriots lost time in the taverns of Windsor, and were hastily collected in the orchard on the approach of Colonel ——, at the head of a small body of British citizens and soldiers. The general himself, instead of being at the head of his men, was in Windsor when the encounter took place. Hearing shots in the orchard, this impetuous warrior sent his *aide-de-camp* up a lane in the direction of the firing to reconnoitre—discreet leader!

"General!" cried the aid, "they are fighting in the orchard.

Did the chieftain seize a steed, and dash, with bloody rowels, to the field? Did he cry, 'a horse! a horse! my kingdom for a horse?' Did he proceed at once on foot to the critical point?

"General!" exclaimed the aid, with tears, "the men are retreating up the woods!"

"Then we will retreat up the river!" responded the soul of chivalry.

Field and staff; *i. e.*, the general, his aid, and a single staff officer, went hurrying along the river road.

"We'll move up a little way, then strike out towards the woods, and join our forces," said the breathless hero of many toothaches. "The safety of the command, the success of the expedition, depends upon our safety."

A little way above Windsor the general's quick eye caught sight of a canoe drawn up on the shore of the river. The general looked wistfully at the boat.

"What do you say," inquired the aid, a cool young gentleman, "to conducting this retreat by water, general?"

"Certainly! certainly!" cried the accommodating leader, glancing towards the American shore opposite. "Gentlemen, please step into that Frenchman's house, and ask him for his canoe. I'm sure these people can refuse nothing to those who peril their lives for them."

The aid and the staff officer did as they were ordered. But Antoine, the owner, did not easily understand English. Besides, Antoine had shut himself up in his castle, till the heat of the battle should be over—such was the sort of assistance the patriots had relied upon—Antoine did not feel secure that the tide of war had swept by, and was not inclined to leave his castle, to have the object of the two gentlemen's wishes pointed out. Finally, however, he emerged with his indefatigable persecutors.

What was the astonishment of the two at beholding the general, now well out in the river, paddling Antoine's canoe towards the American side.

"Holloa! holloa! ma friend! what you do wiz ma canoe, eh?"

Like an old war veteran, the general appeared deaf.

"I'll make him hear," said the staff officer, quietly cocking a rifle he carried. He brought the gun to his shoulder and shouted,

"General, come back and take us in, or you are a dead man!"

"He has already 'taken us in,'" remarked the cool aid.

The general recognized military language. He turned, and beheld the gun levelled towards him.

"Oh! don't fire, I'll come back."

"I—I—was only trying to see whether I could paddle," said the general, as he returned to the shore.

The two young men seemed in no haste to embark.

"Quick! quick!" quoth the general. "That steamer 'll have us. That steamer 'll have us!"

"Why, general!" asked the cool aid, "don't you intend to pay the Frenchman for his canoe?"

"No! I haven't got any ——; haste, dear fellows, let's be off," the general fairly shrieked.

"Haven't got any money, I dare say," laughed the cool aid, "that's the thing you came to find in Canada."

Then taking off his coat and handing it to Antoine, the young man said:

"Here, Jonny Crapeau, I've no money either, but take this. Remember *all* patriots are not thieves."

The staff officer made a like disposition of his rifle.

"No more need of old Bill now—take him," said the staff officer, "Patriotism don't pay!"

The Frenchman, holding coat in one hand and rifle in the other, looked at them alternately, as if weighing their value in one scale of balance, and his feelings in the other. Feelings kicked the beam.

"Messieurs, Antoine Bellarmy no fight, but take ze coat, ze rifle, of ze patriots? No! sacre! by dam! Antoine is no leetle dog for dat!"

He then threw the articles in the boat, and stood with his hat off on the shore.

"Now general, pull away!" quoth the cool aid.

"For God's sake!" cried that hero, piteously, "don't you intend to take an oar—neither of you?"

"No! you old coward! you have had the benefit of private practice; pull away!"

By the general's labor, they soon gained the middle ot the stream, which here was about a mile in width.

A shot from the steamer came skipping over the water, right ahead of their bows.

The general dropt his paddle in terror, the young men took up theirs, and the boat began to fly through the water towards an island, whose woody cover might afford a hiding-place. But another shot whizzed over their heads, and struck immediately beyond them.

"No use!" said the cool aid to the staff officer, laying down his paddle. "Let them take us. I'm willing to be tried for the sake of seeing the general catch it."

"Very well," returned the staff officer.

They cast their fire-arms in the river, and lay by quietly until the steamer came nigh.

"Pull up to us!" ordered an officer.

"Pull away, general!" said the cool aid, and the leader of the army of invasion made his appearance before the people of the steamer, tugging at a paddle, while his two staff officers sat with their arms coolly folded, in the canoe.

It only remains for me to tell the fate of the Colonel, Major Putnam, Lot, and Dandy Jack. The two former were engaged with the enemy in the orchard—it was they who formed the patriots for battle. A volley or two was fired on each side, when the patriots began to break. "One more round, men!" exclaimed the Colonel, "and the day is ours." He rallied a few, who turned, delivered their fire, and took to their heels. His hoarse voice resounded over the field, as he flew from man to man, collaring one, and striking another with his sword. In vain. True it is that one more volley from the whole line would have sent the loyalists flying—but the rebels flew first. The Colonel rushed with his pistol and sword upon the advancing line of the enemy, and was shot dead.

Putnam, Lot, and a few other Canadians, who composed a little body of their own, stood coolly loading and firing till the line broke, when the major formed his handful of men into a rear-guard, and falling back slowly, endeavored to cover the retreat. Climbing a fence at the same moment with the color-bearer, a ball struck Putnam. He caught the banner in his hands as he fell, and was found rolled up in a glorious winding-sheet.

Lot, who doggedly refused to run, was overtaken, stunned by a blow of a musket, and captured.

An hour afterwards, he was placed against the fence, and shot without trial. Before the platoon fired, he fixed his eyes on Colonel ——, and said:

"I summon you to meet me with the murderers of my father, wife, and sisters, at the bar of God. Ha! 'twill be all the same in a hundred years!"

Our merry friend, the descendant of Wamba the Witless, went into the tavern at Windsor, after his boasted beverage, and came out—half seas over—at the moment when the British were passing on their way to the orchard. Mistaking them for patriots he fell in with them. A moment afterwards he discovered his mistake. Colonel ——, with one or two other gentlemen, was immediately before him. He raised the horse-pistol—"born to distinction," and fired. Struck by an unseen musket, it discharged its contents in the air. The next moment Dandy Jack lay pinned to the green sod by a dozen bayonets.

Alas! poor Dandy Jack!

THE SHOEPACS.

All, all are fled, yet still I linger here!
What secret charms this silent spot endear? ROGERS.

In the sweet month of June, I lately visited my native city. Finding few of the ancient landmarks remaining in the town itself, I strolled out one afternoon and walked beside the river. The old river-road even had been swept away. Its place was, to my mind, but poorly supplied by a broad avenue, many roods above. I was therefore obliged to cross the orchards and the meadows, climb the fences, and almost invade the court-yards of houses left standing near the banks of the stream, in order to pursue my way along its beloved course.

At length, fatigued with walking and climbing, and half sad to find so little left to recognize, I lay down in the shade of a dilapidated house—once the happy home of a French school-fellow. The bees were humming around me, yet I felt no inclination to brush them away, lest pain should be inflicted upon the descendant of some insect, contemporary with my childhood. The orchard near by was in full bloom. The bobolinks poised themselves high above the trees, and, on quivering wing, poured forth their showers of melting sweetness all around. A cricket chirped beneath a stone at my feet, while a ground sparrow sprang to the roof above, charming the senses with his homely, familiar sonnets. Lulled by the ripple of the river, soothed by the delicious calmness of the atmosphere, and charmed by the music of the birds and the insect tribes, I dropped away into the soft arms of sleep: still imagining myself conscious of the hour, the scene, the sweetness of undisturbed repose.

To my infinite surprise, the building soon began to fill with little quaint figures, in old-time garments, with all the vivacity of life in their looks and their movements. They appeared to treat my presence among them in no unfriendly way. Some merely threw an indifferent glance towards me. Others gazed with more attention, till their curiosity seemed satisfied. Others again, drew nigh, and peered into my face. One said, "He is one of us." Another said, "Oui! oui! he look like his fader." To my satisfaction I soon found that I recognized many of their faces. Although some had changed into little sun-dried fellows, others were almost mummy-like in their antiquity, a few were fresh and fair as ever. I found myself again a boy, and among the simple people of early times. They were mostly French, with here and there an American.

By degrees they formed themselves into groups. Some sat down at games of cards, others drank cider, which they drew from a barrel standing in the corner, unnoticed by me till now; others had hickory nuts to crack. Some ate onions and cold fritters, others picked wild ducks, apparently just killed, or made the silver scales fly from the backs of white-fish; all chatting pleasantly, like so many lively monkeys.

Suddenly the scene was changed by the entrance of a brisk little fellow, wearing a sword at his side, and a cockade in his hat, which, moreover, was adorned by a plume almost a cubit long, composed of red feathers. His costume was not otherwise peculiar, except about the feet. Here he wore a sort of half shoe, half moccasin, termed, in ancient phrase, a shoepac. I was familiar with it, had seen many in my childhood, had worn them myself, but now even their venerable name is extinct.

The new-comer strode directly to the end of the building where I was lying, with eyes wide open in pleasant wonderment, and standing not many paces from me, with his face towards the assembly, he called out—

"Attention, Shoepacs!"

The white-fish, ducks, onions, cards, cider and fritters, disappeared. Every little man jumped to his feet. On all their heads gay plumes were nodding, with here and there a sorry little cock feather. They were diversely armed. One bore a long flint-lock fowling-piece, another an old-fashioned pistol, here a pitchfork, there an umbrella, a few sported broken spears, dangled long, rusty cavalry sabres, and wore helmets with horse hair and scales of brass. All had on their feet shoepacs similar to those described.

But ere I could observe anything further, the little speaker cried out,

"All dose gentlemans present will say here!"

"Here! here!" shouted a score of voices.

"Sacré! by dam! Wait till I call the roll, eh? All dose gentlemans present, when de name is call, will say here; all dose absent will step up and pay the fine!"

The last specimen of what I thought an Irish bull, seemed not at all to affect the risibilities of the warlike host.

The brisk gentleman now commenced calling over his roll.

"Laon Chêne!" A little old man, with thin white hair, stepped forward, and brought his weapon, a duck gun, to an order.

"Henri Gadbois!" Henri advanced, and took position on the left flank of little Monsieur Chêne. Henri was a tough, smeared-face looking lad, armed with a beautiful barn-yard cock, held by a string, and which flew upon Henri's head, flapped his red and golden wings, and gave a loud defiant crow.

"Pierre Gadbois!" No reply. "Pierre Gadbois!"

At the second call a figure seemed to rise from the ground, walk slowly to the summoner, and deposit in his hand an antique coin. It then vanished.

"Francis Laflambois! Antoine Lafleur! Médore

Mélanger! Dominic Riossèle!" These gentlemen, and many others, variously accoutered, stepped forth as their names were called, till a well-ordered array of Shoepacs stood before me in rank and file. The orderly sergeant took his proper post. The captain now appeared. He was a heavily-whiskered, yet tiny man, mounted on a mettled little pony. In an instant the grotesque multitude were marching oddly out of time and order, the be-helmeted warriors frisking on horseback, and clattering their sabres, one moment wheeling and the next moment charging, and anon running races among the trees in tho orchard, while the footmen were striving to catch the step, starting and halting under the shrieks of their orderly sergeant, then dividing, some marching one way, some another, then running hastily together, and finally breaking into a confused melange.

I lay upon my back in silence awhile. But irreverent laughter soon seized me, and I laughed and shouted and rolled on the grass, utterly unable to repress the outbursts of mirth, at the queer little antics cutting around me. In a short time, however, the good gentlemen defiled into the building again; and stood regarding me, all with sad visages. I never witnessed so mournful a sight, such hopeless, woe-begone countenances, such despairing, sorrowful expressions. Why they looked at me with fixed eyes, I could not perceive. I arose from the ground and mingled among them, desiring them, here and there, as I knew one and another, to express to me what it was that sat heavily upon them, and what, if anything, might be done to render them once more the careless, jovial, happy crew I had just seen, and long ago had known them to be. They pointed to the decaying roof of the habitation; they gazed with steadfast eyes on the river, as if they sought their canoes; they turned towards the city below, humming with the business and pastimes of a race that was gradually crowding them from their homes and happy employments; they gave the same sad, wistful look as at the first; then vanishing, not like the pageantries of other dreams, in the twinkling of an eye, but slowly, one by one, with the same sad, wistful look, till all are gone.

I awoke!

Many times afterwards, revisiting the spot, and lulled by the same delicious sounds as before, I slept in the shade of the old ruin; hoping to renew the dream; hoping to gain the secret of wishes so gravely and sorrowfully expressed, yet so little understood. I began to muse over the times, faintly remembered at first, when the simple French people held undisputed and gentle sway along this whole frontier. Standing between the red-man and white-man, mingling with both, disturbing neither, with little to defend, and no desire to aggrandize, their ephemeral existence was as glowing with the pleasure of light-hearted enjoyment, as the insects that sport away their hour of sunshine, and like them passing away unnoticed or soon forgotten.

Fain would we light up the darkness of that oblivion to which they are fast being consigned. But coming late in their day, and seeing them through the medium of childhood, we have not ventured, in these sketches, to attempt more than to throw an occasional flickering ray upon the manners and customs of the simple race. With some of the peculiarities of those who have supplanted them, especially the earlier folk, who caught not a little of their genial light and warmth, our memory is more at home. It may be a pleasure for some, whose pulse is beating high beneath the torrid zone of the present, to have gazed for one short hour upon the cool region of a temperate past—yesterday but still a part of to-day.

THE END.

www.ingramcontent.com/pod-product-compliance
Lightning Source LLC
LaVergne TN
LVHW010148110826
845151LV00002B/461

9781425537593